THE FILM WORK OF

NORMAN McLAREN

Frontispiece:
Multiple-exposure portrait of Norman McLaren by Joseph Szelei. [Courtesy NFB.]

Cover:
The multiple image of McLaren recalls the imagery McLaren used for his film Pas de deux.
The yellow lines suggest the scratched lines of such films as Lines Vertical *and* Lines Horizontal.
The red lines in the main lettering are derived from McLaren's whimsical linear figures which occur in many of his films, most notably in Blinkity Blank.

McLaren image: Joseph Szelei. Design: Terence Dobson.

THE
FILM WORK OF
NORMAN
McLAREN

Terence Dobson

British Library Cataloguing in Publication Data

The Film Work of Norman McLaren
  1. – Terence Dobson

ISBN: 0 86196 656 2

Published by
John Libbey Publishing, Box 276, Eastleigh SO50 5YS, UK
e-mail: libbeyj@asianet.co.th; web site: www.johnlibbey.com

Orders: **Book Representation & Distribution Ltd**. info@bookreps.com

Distributed in North America by **Indiana University Press**, 601 North Morton St, Bloomington,
IN 47404, USA. www.iupress.indiana.edu

Distributed in Australasia by **Elsevier Australia**, 30–52 Smidmore Street,
Marrickville NSW 2204, Australia. www.elsevier.com.au

Distributed in Japan by **United Publishers Services Ltd**,
1-32-5 Higashi-shinagawa, Shinagawa-ku, Tokyo 140-0002, Japan. info@ups.co.jp

Printed in Malaysia by Vivar Printing Sdn Bhd, 48000 Rawang, Selangor

Contents

For Elaine

Preface

I am indebted to the Canadian Government for the
New Zealand Sesquicentennial Canadian Studies
Postgraduate Award. The award enabled me to travel
to Canada in order to carry out essential research in
Ottawa and Montreal. Without this generous award, this
project would not have been feasible. I therefore thank the
Canadian Government for the valuable opportunity and
encouragement it provided. While in Canada I was also able
to attend the Ottawa Animation Festival and participate in
the Society for Animation Studies Conference held at
Carleton University, Ottawa.

A section of chapter one has appeared in *Animation
Journal* while some other parts of this work have been
presented as papers at academic conferences: Association
for Canadian Studies in Australia and New Zealand Con-
ference (ANU, Canberra), Society for Animation Studies
Conferences (UCLA and Carleton University, Ottawa),
Conferences of the Department of English, University of
Canterbury. I am grateful to the people who offered sug-
gestions and support. Further financial support came from
the Association for Canadian Studies in Australia and New
Zealand to enable me to travel to the Canberra Conference.
I am grateful for their assistance.

I also thank those former colleagues and friends of
Norman McLaren. In alphabetical order they are Marthe
Blackburn, Gerald Budner, Tom Daly, Rupert Glover,
Stanley Hawes, Pierre Hébert, René Jodoin, Evelyn Lam-
bart, Colin Low, Don McWilliams, Grant Munro, Eldon
Rathburn, David Verrall and Robert Verrall. They not only
warmly received me and freely gave me their time, but also
offered much useful information. In addition Don McWil-

liams and David Verrall kindly made available to me the 1st Assembly of *Creative Process*. Don McWilliams also, generously gave me copies of numerous interviews conducted with McLaren. Their help is greatly appreciated.

Gary Evans gave me the benefit of his knowledge of the NFB and also entrusted me with his unpublished manuscript which details the NFB's post-war years. I thank him for his generosity. I also thank Louise Cloutier for her information regarding Maurice Blackburn's career.

In Britain, John McLaren gave me a personal insight into his brother's life. I am most grateful.

Various institutions also gave me help. The International Council for Canadian Studies Ottawa (Carol Bujeau and Linda Jones), The Glasgow School of Art (Peter Trowles), The CBC Radio Archives, The Grierson Archives at McGill University, Montreal, The Grierson Archives at the University of Stirling (Sharon Walker), Cinémateque Québequoise (Louise Beaudet and later, Marco de Blois) and in particular the NFB Archives where Bernard Lutz's help was so valuable. I also thank the NFB (Claude Lord and Don McWilliams were most helpful) for their co-operation in finding many of the illustrations in this book.

At the University of Canterbury I thank Dr Reg Berry who, before his return to Canada, provided expert guidance and much encouragement. I am indebted to him. Also at Canterbury, Assoc. Prof. Patrick Evans, undertook painstaking work on my behalf, and I thank him for it.

I have been fortunate in having such a publisher as John Libbey whose expert advice and ongoing support has been invaluable. Mark Turner's internet skills have proven indispensable while I have been Bhutan during the final stages of getting this book to press. I owe them both a considerable debt of gratitude.

Finally, I thank Elaine Dobson, my wife, and Jaya. The latter helped me push my pen and tap the keys. So did the former, who also provided me with the encouragement and support essential in an undertaking such as this.

Terence Dobson
Thimphu, Bhutan
May 2006

Introduction

For half a century, Norman McLaren made films at a prodigious rate – his output averaged more than one film every year. As a filmmaker at the National Film Board of Canada his films received a widespread distribution. They have been screened not only throughout Canada but also throughout much of the rest of the world. His films have drawn an enormous amount of attention, yet McLaren remains a paradoxical figure. As Curtis has noted, on the one hand he has been feted with prizes and honours, writers on film animation have heaped praise on him, singling out the innovative nature of his work for special mention. On the other hand, writers treating avant garde filmmaking – the area in which a filmmaker with innovative strengths would be expected to be found – ignore McLaren and his work almost totally.[1]

Despite Curtis' intriguing observation having been made some time ago, work which focuses exclusively on McLaren and his films remains a rarity. To date only six brief monographs on McLaren have been published. In 1976, Maynard Collins brought out *Norman McLaren*. It primarily consists of a fifteen-page account of McLaren's career and his work, a forty-four page annotated filmography, and a seventeen-page interview. In 1977, the Scottish Arts Council published *Norman McLaren: exhibition and films*. It is comprised mainly of an English translation of a 1975 interview McLaren gave to *Sequences* in which the filmmaker comments on a chronological screening of his films, and a seven-page assessment of McLaren's work by David Curtis. In 1980, Guy Glover's *McLaren* was published by the National Film Board of Canada (NFB). This is

1 David Curtis, "Where does one put Norman McLaren?" *Norman McLaren: exhibitions and films* (Edinburgh: Scottish Arts Council, 1977) 47–53.

a pictorial record of McLaren's work with some informative, yet brief, textual comments. The fourth monograph appeared in 1981. It was written by Alfio Bastiancich and is called *L'Opera di Norman McLaren*. Half of this work is comprised of an appendix consisting of Italian translations from McLaren's technical notes and other writings, a bibliography and a filmography in Italian. The essay in the remaining half of the work is divided into a large number of topics which, while having logical merit, further limits the extent of the various treatments. In 1982 Vallierre T. Richard's *Norman McLaren: Manipulator of Movement* was published. In spite of its considerable length (128 pages) it lacks the detail and analysis one would consequently expect. It also omits important reference material and no original or primary sources, other than McLaren's films themselves, are used. The most recent monograph on McLaren was published by the NFB in 1992. In *Norman McLaren on the Creative Process*, Don McWilliams has compiled and edited some of McLaren's reflections on filmmaking as well as many of McLaren's technical notes pertaining to specific films. While being a font of McLaren's ideas and a guide to a technical understanding of McLaren's films, *Norman McLaren on the Creative Process* does not pretend to cover the social or artistic context in which McLaren worked, while the analyses of McLaren's films that are presented are those of McLaren himself.

Two films have also dealt with McLaren and his work. In 1970 Gavin Millar's *The Eye Hears, The Ear Sees* was released. About half the running time of this film (i.e. thirty of the film's sixty minutes) is comprised of McLaren's films themselves. This is not to criticise their inclusion. Their inclusion is appropriate in a filmic treatment of McLaren. The point is, however, that little time for extensive analysis remains. In 1990 Don McWilliams' *Creative Process* was released. It was made under the auspices of the NFB. There are two versions of *Creative Process*. There is a two-hour version for the cinema (and the 2001 DVD release) and also a forty-five minute version for television. The film format of *Creative Process* has been used well to illustrate McLaren's life and work. The documentary has been divided into sections which explore some of McLaren's interests. However, filmic time constraints and the necessity to space the flow of information in the time available has limited the extent to which *Creative Process* is able to analyse McLaren's work and the associated issues. Thus, no comprehensive and detailed account of McLaren and his film output has appeared to date.

The sources of information in this present work fall into four categories. Firstly, there is the previously published material, the most important elements of which are McLaren's own writings and recorded speech, including the interviews contained in the Collins and Scottish Arts Council monographs; CBC radio interviews; an early interview with Don McWilliams; and statements contained within *The Eye Hears, The Ear Sees* and the various manifestations of *Creative Process* – including *Norman McLaren on the Creative Process*. The second category is comprised of unpublished material gathered by the author. This includes letters to, from and about McLaren; dope sheets prepared by McLaren; technical notes written by McLaren; NFB production notes on McLaren's films; McLaren's answers to questionnaires; references to McLaren in administration files of various organizations; and McLaren's unreleased out-takes and film experiments that he conducted throughout his career. In the third category are the interviews, conducted by the author, of colleagues, friends and family of McLaren. The fourth category embraces McLaren's finished films, paintings and drawings.

This account is divided into three parts, based on chronological divisions in McLaren's life. The first part deals with McLaren's formative years in Scotland and England. The second part deals with his maturation in the USA and Canada. In order to show McLaren's development more clearly, both parts one and two are based on a chronological sequencing. The third part of this account examines specific issues in relation to McLaren and his work and as such is concerned principally with his mature output.

McLaren's films contain incongruities, conflicts and apparent inconsistencies. In exploring these aspects of his work, this book examines the technical processes McLaren used in making his films, the oscillation shown in his films between abstract and representational imagery, and the degree of accord between McLaren's social objectives, his artistic objectives and his filmic achievements. The strands of the exploration often interweave as common causes or explanations arise. As a greater understanding of McLaren's motivation, influences and working methods develops, a surprising measure of consistency on McLaren's part becomes apparent. On the way, the initial paradox is

approached. Through an understanding of the dichotomous tensions in McLaren's works, a clearer comprehension of the paradox of the divergent treatments accorded
to McLaren is also reached.

Part One

Chapter One

An Informative Drawing

N orman McLaren made his first journey to London on 7 February 1935. He was not quite twenty-one years old, his twenty-first birthday being 11 April of that year. Despite his relative youthfulness and his lack of travels outside his native Scotland, the ideas that would come to dominate his artistic outlook had already started to form at this stage.

His visit to London was recognised by McLaren as a significant one since on his return to Scotland he proceeded to record what he did and where he went in a large, c. 100 cm x 180 cm, drawing (see Fig. 2). As this is one of the few detailed records of events in McLaren's early (pre-World War II) life, and is specific in terms of time and place, the drawing is doubly significant. Although the order of events and interests depicted in the drawing do not correspond to the sequence in which the events may have first appeared in McLaren's life, nor necessarily to any order of primacy, exploring and deciphering the drawing piece by piece remains a rewarding and exciting enterprise. Moreover, the nature of the drawing itself (i.e. its structure and use of graphic ideas), is also pertinent.

The *Visit to London* drawing: The Venues

The drawing is of a linear progression and McLaren has used the same starting point for the eye as that used in Western writing – the top left-hand corner. The adoption of such a convention would not only have seemed natural to McLaren but it also would have enabled the viewer immediate access to the drawing. It encourages the viewer to read the drawing, section by section.

Fig. 1 (above). Norman McLaren at about the time of his visit to London. [McLaren Archive/NFB.]

Fig. 2 (facing page). Norman McLaren, Visit to London, drawing, 1935. [Collection Don McWilliams.]

The top left-hand corner then, contains firstly the date (7 February 1935), in bright white chalk, written vertically down the top left-hand edge, echoing the format and luminosity of neon signs attached to city buildings – a foretaste of 1930s London.

The date also suggests that the drawing is a form of diary and an immediate scan to the bottom right-hand corner, where there appears the date of the conclusion of the visit (13 February 1935), confirms this.

Also in the top left-hand corner is a building which has the unmistakable form of the Glasgow School of Art (unmistakable because the turn-of-the-century building was designed by Charles Rennie Mackintosh in an amalgam of Scottish baronial, Art Nouveau and the Arts and

Crafts styles and which, in its austerity, was a forerunner
of the international modernist style). McLaren had been a
student at the Glasgow School of Art since leaving school
at the age of eighteen. As he subsequently said, "I went to
art school because it was my best subject in high school".[2]
According to one account, "McLaren's conscious interest
in the arts was awakened in his early teens when, by chance,
he read a modern poem which broke all the rules he was
being taught at school. Excited by a cartoon in *Punch*
magazine satirizing modern art, McLaren began to abstract
his school drawing and painting projects."[3] McLaren himself is also on record as saying he had been interested in
abstraction since the age of fourteen or fifteen. Indeed,
surviving drawings and paintings from his later High
School years confirm this interest.[4]

　　The image of the Glasgow School of Art blends into
the next image – that of a speeding steam locomotive. The
train is heading towards a map which, with the curve of the
Thames and the triangular green patch of St James' Park,
is recognizable as a map of London. McLaren has indicated
the immense size of London by allowing the streets of the
map to spread to the furthest edges of the drawing. This

2　Norman McLaren as
　quoted in Maynard
　Collins, *Norman
　McLaren* (Ottawa:
　Canadian Film
　Institute, 1976), 74.

3　Donald McWilliams
　and Susan Huycke,
　*Creative Process: Norman
　McLaren*, dir. Donald
　McWilliams, National
　Film Board of Canada,
　1991,
　script 1.

4　Norman McLaren,
　"sch(me)ool" a
　picture-poem (self
　portrait and school
　life) in *The School on the
　Rock,* The Magazine of
　the High School of
　Stirling, No. 8, June
　1931, p. 21, and
　paintings depicted in
　*Creative Process: Norman
　McLaren*, NFB Film,
　television version,
　1991.

Fig. 3. Detail from Norman McLaren, Visit to London, drawing, 1935. [Collection Don McWilliams.]

feature also indicates that all activities depicted in the drawing occur in London.

In his *Visit to London* work, McLaren uses a red line to guide the viewer's eye around the drawing. The red line sweeps into the drawing from the initial date, under the images of the Glasgow School of Art and of the train, and into the map. It then takes the observer to the centre top of the drawing. The large building, around the top of which runs the red guideline, is Broadcasting House, the then-new headquarters of the BBC. McLaren's delight in radio broadcasting began in his childhood. He was born and grew up in Stirling, a small (population approximately 30,000) yet relatively prosperous market town in the Scottish lowlands. His mother's people were farmers. His father owned and ran a decorating business as well as a small art gallery. He had an older brother and sister. The family lived a comfortable, middle-class life in Victoria Place, a street in a wealthy part of town just below the castle on the rock. The high school which McLaren attended was also up on the rock and so it is easy to envisage the circumscribed and therefore sheltered life the young McLaren led. The importance of the radio for the teenage McLaren was not in broadening his knowledge of social issues, but in providing him with his first experience of professional music.[5] Although he was taught to play the violin while a child, his

5   *Creative Process* script 3.

Fig. 4. Detail from
Norman McLaren,
Visit to London,
drawing, 1935.
[Collection Don
McWilliams.]

early exposure to professional orchestras would have been nonexistent but for the radio. He listened to the radio stations of Europe and, of course, the BBC.[6] The function of Broadcasting House can clearly be seen in the *Visit to London* drawing. The radio masts on the building are drawn in detail and the broadcasting signals emanating from them are represented as powerful concentric circles which spread and engulf the surrounding areas. The precise reason for the visit to Broadcasting House is not known. It is possible that McLaren was interested in the technology of radio broadcasting – his later interests in the technology of film would support this conjecture. The strongest attraction, however, would have been the music associated with radio broadcasting. Music was becoming a strong force in his life and would even become, if it was not already, a "... central one in [his] life and work".[7]

After Broadcasting House the red line takes the viewer's eye round a large circle at the top right-hand corner of the drawing. The large blue letters RA overlay the circle. Since McLaren was an art student, the letters, in the context of his visit to London, could only stand for Royal Academy, and indeed the objects depicted within the circle indicate that McLaren visited an exhibition at the Royal Academy's Burlington House. In the RA circle are a strange assortment of objects: armchairs, cutlery, radio, glassware to name just some. The objects reflect McLaren's

6   McLaren as quoted in
    Creative Process script 3.

7   *Creative Process* script 3.

course change at the Glasgow School of Art. As McLaren later said, "I wasn't terribly interested in [art school] and that's partly because I didn't know what I wanted to do".[8] And later he said, "I didn't get great enjoyment from drawing plaster casts, or life models, or any of the things I was taught in art school".[9] So, after completing the two year general course at the art school, McLaren progressed to a three year Diploma Course specialising in interior design.[10] It is likely that his father's professional interests had a bearing on this choice. The earlier decision to attend art school, however, was an independent step. It was a step that his parents respected, although they did not prefer the direction of that earlier first vocational step. The McLaren parental attitudes towards his initial decision to go to art school were revealed in a letter he wrote some years later. In that letter to his parents,[11] McLaren explained that an article that had appeared in *McLeans*[12] had details of a reference to them wrong. In the article's rough draft the reporter had originally written that McLaren went to art school against his parents' wishes. McLaren had then objected to this interpretation. The report that *McLeans* eventually published was a diluted statement and indicated that McLaren went to art school against his parents' better judgment. McLaren explained in his letter to his parents that he had told the reporter that they (his parents) would have preferred him to go into business but had not stood in his way when he wanted to go to art school and had in fact put their faith in his decision. In another letter to his parents at about the same time he expresses his appreciation "... that you let me develop in my own way".[13] Nevertheless, from his third year onwards at the Glasgow School of Art, McLaren was officially studying interior design. This study obligation did not, however, prevent him from continuing to develop "in his own way".

The red guideline of the *Visit to London* leads from the RA circle which is on the right, back towards the centre of the drawing where there is another, but smaller circle. In and around the smaller circle, classical ballerinas are depicted. McLaren was utterly fascinated at seeing, in London, his first ballet. What he particularly admired was "... the creation of the choreography and the changing forms and patterns on the stage".[14] These forms and patterns, albeit of a statuesque quality, are what McLaren has shown in this depiction of his first ballet experience. His love of ballet was as instantaneous as it was enduring – he later said

8 McLaren as quoted in Collins 74.
9 McLaren as quoted in *Creative Process* script 1.
10 The information concerning McLaren's studies at the Glasgow School of Art comes from McLaren's recollections in sources that have been cited, and from letters (23 November 1993 and 15 December 1993) to the author from Peter Trowles, Taffner Curator, Mackintosh Collection, Glasgow School of Art.
11 Norman McLaren, letter to his parents, 30 January 1953, Grierson Archives, University of Stirling, Stirling, Scotland.
12 *McLean's* December 15, 1952.
13 Norman McLaren letter to his parents, 13 May 1950, from Hong Kong. Grierson Archives 31.74.
14 McLaren as quoted in *Creative Process* script 11.

that had he been born in London and gone to the ballet from the age of eight or ten, then he might have wanted to be a ballet dancer and eventually a choreographer.[15] Not only would dancing, and ballet in particular, become a major component of some of his remarkable films, but what he perceived as the essence of dance, that is movement, was also seen as the essence of film. It is appropriate therefore that if the red line on the *Visit to London* drawing is followed from the depiction of the ballet, the next of McLaren's visits is revealed to be to the Fox Film Studio.

In about 1933,[16] during his second year at Art School, McLaren had joined the Glasgow Film Society, where the discovery of "... great works of cinema"[17] had a profound impact. As a young child he had been to the local cinema but the Hollywood-type films he saw did not make an impression on him. The only positive memory of film that McLaren carried from his childhood was of the smell and feel of the cans and film stock which he had discovered in the McLaren attic.[18] "When I was about nineteen years old and going to art school, I was dissatisfied with my painting. It lacked something, and I suddenly, well quite suddenly, yes, realized what it was I was lacking: it was motion. Peculiarly enough it was not through seeing any animated films but through seeing the Russian classic silent films by Pudovkin and Eisenstein. They moved me so much, these films. It revealed to me what film could be."[19] These films made their impact on McLaren through the intimacy of the intercutting, the wide variety of the viewpoint of the subject matter, and cutting from one thing to another.[20] To these features one could also add the travelling camera. The feature that most overwhelmed the young McLaren was the speed and rapidity of movement and change in these films. McLaren also joined a filmmaking club which had been founded at the Glasgow School of Art by three of the younger teachers and some students who were senior to him. It was a spare-time activity, but for McLaren it became all-consuming. Through the filmmaking club McLaren's film production during the rest of his art school years was prolific.

Although McLaren remembers his formal art school studies as years of relative disinterest on his part, he was proficient enough to gain two prizes. In 1932 he won a Winsor and Newton prize and in 1934 he was awarded the James Brough Memorial Prize.[21] Even so, McLaren's recollections of his art school studies were sufficiently

15 McLaren as quoted in *Creative Process* script 11.

16 McLaren as quoted in *Creative Process* script 3, and in *Norman McLaren: exhibition and films* (Edinburgh: Scottish Arts Council, 1977) 6, says it was in his third year at the School of Art (1934–1935) yet if these revelations at the film society preceded his first films – as Guy Glover, McLaren's lifelong companion and friend, also testified that they did – they must have occurred before the first films were made in 1933. Indeed in his recollections included in *The Eye Hears, The Ear Sees*, McLaren himself confirms this dating when he says he was 19 years old (i.e. it was 1933) when he discovered the great works of cinema. See Guy Glover, *McLaren* (Montreal: National Film Board of Canada,1980) 6, and Gavin Millar, *The Eye Hears, The Ear Sees*, NFB/BBC film, 1970.

17 McLaren as quoted in *Creative Process* script 2.

18 McLaren as quoted in Scottish Arts Council, 5.

19 McLaren as quoted in *The Eye Hears, The Ear Sees.*

20 McLaren as quoted in *Creative Process* script 2.

21 Trowles, letter to author, 15 December 1993 1.

coloured for him to state in later years that he had failed his second year of study[22] when in fact the Glasgow School of Art records indicate no such failure and show him progressing normally from year to year through the two-year general course and on through the three-year Diploma Course.[23] Two sources, one of them being Guy Glover, who was close to McLaren on professional and personal terms from the late 1930s onward, state that McLaren failed to graduate from the Art School with a Diploma.[24] Glover and the other souce, Collins, presumably based their accounts on McLaren's recollections; however there is some doubt as to their strict accuracy. If McLaren had failed his Diploma, then this would have been noted on his file card, but no such indication exists.[25] On the other hand, his name does not appear amongst the successful students listed in the School's Annual Report for 1935–36 but apparently such Report lists frequently missed off the names of some graduands. The official evidence, therefore, suggests only that it is probable that McLaren graduated. Whether he graduated or not was of little concern to McLaren and this indifference helps explain his belief that he had failed to graduate. The Diploma meant as little to him as his formal art school studies. His concern about either of these aspects of his art school years was minimal. Film was to be McLaren's future and, increasingly, he knew it.

From the Fox Film Studio the red line in the drawing goes via a tube from Wembley Park station to Trafalgar Square station – an early manifestation of McLaren's sense of fun and love of puns and in this case he makes play of the fact that in London the underground railway is known as 'the tube'. Another visual pun occurs at the next destination. At this Trafalgar Square stop the National Gallery of Art is depicted by and within an elaborate picture frame. The Gallery itself is shown as a never-ending series of vast empty galleries. For McLaren, painting with its tradition of thousands of years, was an exhausted medium – exhausted to the point of death.[26] As well, according to McLaren, it had lost its power to thrill in the way it had in mediaeval and renaissance times. By contrast, even the first films he made in 1933, by painting directly onto the film, created such energy, such a band of effects, that people were not merely interested but excited. Painting was an art in which so many styles had been created and so much done that McLaren felt there was little left to do. Film, on the other hand, was a young medium, only having been

22 McLaren as quoted in Scottish Arts Council 6.

23 Trowles, letter to author, 23 December 1993 1.

24 Glover 8, Collins 2.

25 Trowles, 15 December 1993 1.

26 McLaren as quoted in *Creative Process* script 6 and 21.

Fig. 5. Detail from
Norman McLaren,
Visit to London,
drawing, 1935.
[Collection Don
McWilliams.]

invented twenty to thirty years earlier, and presented a new area for exploration.[27] As McLaren put it, "The new art of the future was movies. And I thought I will make movies."[28]

After the National Gallery the red line on the drawing leads the viewer to the artist's palette on which are depicted, appropriately enough, a paint tube and brushes. Some buildings are also shown. These are in all likelihood the buildings which at that time housed the Royal College of Art, for it is McLaren's visit to the Royal College of Art that this palette ensemble represents. The most noticeable items here, however, are the jug and the tea cup and saucer. Their relevance is ambiguous. Perhaps they represent still-life drawing objects or perhaps cafeteria crockery. Even if they were put in as examples of interior design, the ambiguity of the purpose of their depiction gives the impression that McLaren was only paying lip service to his supposed profession during this visit.

The red guideline continues to the images at the bottom left-hand corner of the drawing. Once again a circle is the most obvious shape, but over it is superimposed a proscenium arch. The words in this theatre tableau spell out the title of the play McLaren evidently saw: *Love on the Dole*. This play was based on the book of the same name by Walter Greenwood. The novel was a best-seller going through five printings or impressions in the eighteen months after it was published in 1933, and then, as a Florin

27 McLaren as quoted in *Creative Process* script 2.

28 McLaren as quoted in *Creative Process* script 21.

Books reissue, a further six reprints in twelve months from March 1935. Subsequently the play was adapted for the screen and in 1941 the film, again called *Love on the Dole*, and directed by John Baxter and starring Deborah Kerr, was released. The dominant image of McLaren's *Love on the Dole* tableau is of the factory chimneys. They not only extend over the proscenium arch but also intrude into the adjoining Royal College of Art palette. Beneath the huge chimneys and massive factory buildings are the roofs of the tiny rows of terraced housing. McLaren's attraction to *Love on the Dole* was primarily that it was a then-rare serious depiction of working-class poverty – and consequent struggle – from a working-class author. Not only were McLaren's artistic sensibilities developed during his teens; in that period he also became aware, for the first time, of the conditions of people in the working classes which, during the Great Depression, were awful. McLaren describes his experience:

> ... remember, when I grew up ... I was born in 1914 ... at the age of 16 or 17, it was the Great Depression. And I had my first experience of the slums. In fact I met someone who was a communist in Stirling, by chance. And he said 'I'd like you to come from your middle class home', it was just a very ordinary middle class house 'just come and see how most of the people live'. And I was utterly shocked. So naturally that's when I started thinking politically what can be done about it. Something was seriously wrong with the economic system. So, like many young people in the Great Depression, our minds went to Russia as a possible experiment along new economic lines.[29]

McLaren joined the Scottish Communist Party. During his art school years McLaren's father "... who was a staunch conservative, pillar of the church and all that, was greatly concerned when he found I had such left wing thoughts and feelings. When I suggested I wanted to go to Russia he said 'Fine. I'll give you enough money for a good tour in Russia, and you'll see how they live, and you'll be cured from thinking that communism is a good thing'."[30] McLaren did go to the USSR a few months after he returned from the London visit – probably in the summer months when there was a film and theatre festival held. What McLaren found to be a liberating artistic environment was not conducive to bringing about the 'cure'.

29 McLaren as quoted in *Creative Process* script 25–26, and *Creative Process* 1st Assembly (film).

30 McLaren as quoted in *Creative Process* script 26, and 1st Assembly (film).

Fig. 6. Norman McLaren's passport photo from about the time of his USSR visit. [McLaren Archive/NFB.]

McLaren remained politically committed to the communist ideology until the late thirties, when he became disil-
lusioned with the Stalinist regime. The 1939 signing of the
Soviet-Nazi non-aggression pact was, for McLaren, an act
of betrayal.[31] Although his allegiance to the Communist
Party was withdrawn, McLaren continued to feel sympathy
for the exploited, and his political inclinations remained
left-wing.

   Moving from the therefore appropriate left-hand
position of the *Love on the Dole* depiction, the red line goes
to another film studio: GB British Film Studios. The
purpose of this next McLaren visit, like that of his visit to
the Fox Studios, was to find out what goes on in a film
studio. He may also have been ascertaining whether such
a studio held suitable job prospects for him. The studio
images in the drawing have been superimposed on another
picture frame – this one bearing the words "Tate Gallery".
Of all the public galleries in London, the Tate Gallery, with
its emphasis on recent and contemporary art, should have
appealed most to the idealistic and progressive young
McLaren. That not a single work of art is depicted within
the Tate Gallery frame suggests, however, that the Tate's
appeal was negligible. Moreover, most of the Tate's tableau

31 *Creative Process* script
27.

Fig. 7. Detail from Norman McLaren, Visit to London, drawing, 1935. [Collection Don McWilliams.]

area has been superimposed by the imagery associated with the film studio. In view of McLaren's opinions regarding the relative importance of painting and the movies, this is apt. McLaren has removed painting and has placed film-making as the contemporary (and future) art form at the Tate. Also apt is the dominant image of this complex – the eye on which the film company's GB logo appears. This image emphasises the visual component of the film medium. The importance to McLaren of the visual imagery in film will be treated later.

From the circular eye, the observer's attention is taken by the red line to the next image which by themic contrast is of a large open mouth in, of course, another circle shape. The large letters above the circle spell out *Elijah*, the title of an oratorio by Mendelssohn. The sound waves emanating from another, smaller, mouth emphasise the vocal nature of the work. The importance of music in McLaren's artistic development has already been mentioned. The appearance of this oratorio provides the opportunity to say that McLaren listened to, loved and used music from across a very broad range: Western and Non-Western music; popular, classical and folk music; and a wide variety of dance music from classical to jazz, to country, to Latin American.

Below the *Elijah* design, the red line weaves its way

through the centre of a yin-yang symbol. In this case, however, the symbol does not have oriental connotations. It was selected by the Swiss founder of Eurhythmics, Emile Jacques-Dalcroze, as a suitable representation of the unifying of the two arts of music and dance. This concept is clearly illustrated by McLaren by placing in the yin a keyboard, and in the yang a dancer. In Eurhythmics, musical rhythm is seen to depend on motor-consciousness for its fullest expression. Dalcroze evolved "... a system of rhythmic movement designed to develop mastery of musical rhythm. This system of musical education uses the body as the interpreter of musical rhythm ... ."[32] In a eurhythmics performance, as the music changes in tempo, duration, dynamics and pitch, so too do the dancer/s respond accordingly. As utterly fascinated as he was with traditional ballet, McLaren was more interested in the non-dramatic form of ballet.[33] The eurhythmic dance performers would have presented dance as pure spectacle, devoid of the narrative overtones of classical ballet. As well, the performance would have employed spontaneity, and consequently would have been less constrained than traditional ballet. These qualities displayed in eurhythmics were soon to play an increasingly important role in McLaren's own filmmaking.

The final two visits illustrated in the *Visit to London* drawing have a lesser connection with McLaren's work than other parts of the drawing. The circle representing his visit to a performance of *Hamlet* contains the obvious elements: skull, crown, spade, cup. It also contains the name John Gielgud. The Shakespearean actor was at that time a new young star. McLaren obviously took this opportunity, on his first visit to London, to see the actor and the play. The last London visit, to a Walt Disney exhibition, was once again work-related, although not as closely as might be supposed. Being an animator, a manipulator of images on film, McLaren sought out the exhibition of this most famous of animators. The labour-intensive production-line methods used by Disney and hinted at in McLaren's depiction by the background grid of drawings were, for artistic and economic reasons, not for McLaren. So while he has expressed admiration for Disney's technical accomplishments and his professionalism, McLaren denied having been influenced by Disney.[34] What McLaren did have in common with the young Disney was a sense of fun. This is revealed by McLaren in his placement of

32 Elsa Findlay, *Rhythm and Movement: Applications of Dalcroze Eurhythmics* (Evanston Illinois: Summy-Birchard,1971) 2.

33 McLaren as quoted in *Creative Process* script 11.

34 McLaren as quoted in Scottish Arts Council 11–12.

Mickey Mouse amongst so many revered, serious institutions and works.

Both the *Hamlet* and Disney images are placed on the back of the train which on the thirteenth of February took McLaren out of London. McLaren took a lot with him from London but one suspects that Disney was left at the station. Although this drawing of his London visit reveals some of McLaren's major artistic directions, the final destination is, symbolically, not portrayed.

The use of graphic ideas and structure in *Visit to London*

Quite apart from the depicted visits and their connotations, there are other aspects of the *Visit to London* drawing which are revealing. These aspects concern McLaren's use of graphic ideas and his structuring of the drawing.

Circle shapes are used repeatedly through the drawings. Many of the tableaux depicting the individual visits, i.e. the RA, the ballet, *Love on the Dole*, *Elijah*, Dalcroze, *Hamlet* and Mickey Mouse, are depicted within a circle shape. In addition, the circle appears within various tableaux (the RA, Fox Film Studio and GB Studio), or around the various tableaux in the form of the London Underground symbol, as well as in the form of the depicted tunnels and tubes of the Underground. The predominance of the circle shape together with the appearance of the London Street map configurations in the spaces between the tableaux gives the drawing some visual cohesiveness, as does the limited and muted colour range that McLaren has used.

In spite of these attempts to give the *Visit to London* drawing cohesion, there are many elements which work against a visually consistent expression. The viewer of the drawing is faced with the task of reconciling the use of a deep, three-dimensional space as exemplified by each of the two trains' disappearance into the distance and the receding rooms of the National Gallery, with the diagrammatic two-dimensional space of the London map segments and the flat, disc-like circles (that no tableau containing a circle appears as an oval suggests the circles all lie parallel to the picture plane). Also to be reconciled are the semi-transparent objects, e.g. in the *Elijah*, Royal Academy and Royal College segments, and the solid objects, e.g. in the *Hamlet*, Fox Film Studio and National Gallery segments.

Another dichotomy of representation exists. Some representations such as the Glasgow School of Art, Broadcasting House and the tube (underground railway) station, are naturalistic, whereas others such as Dalcroze with its yin-yang, *Elijah* with the mouths, and the GB Film Studio with its eye and rolls of film, are less naturalistic symbols. In some cases the naturalistic and symbolic are mixed in the same tableau as in the National Gallery segment where the Gallery's naturalistically-depicted interior is placed within a symbolic frame. The task of reconciling these various dichotomous treatments is made more difficult by the apparent lack of a reason for the adoption of a particular approach, other than (the obvious one) that McLaren used what seemed to him the most obvious, and therefore the most direct, means of representation in each case. The drawing's lack of visual consistency, however, does not prevent this early work of McLaren's from offering even further evidence of his early development.

Many of the circles in the drawing serve also as clock-faces – which, incidentally, further emphasises their previously discussed flatness. Each of these clock-faces is associated with a particular visit, and only some of the numbers are depicted on each dial. For example, in the large RA circle/clock-face only the numbers 3, 4, 5 and 6 appear. The implication is that McLaren was at the Royal Academy between three and six o'clock. Most of the tableaux contain a similar indication of the time spent at the locations and, as in the RA depiction, some of the clocks are extremely prominent in that they comprise the shape within which the tableau is contained, i.e. the Ballet, *Love on the Dole*, *Elijah* and *Hamlet* tableaux.

The drawing contains an even more prominent and more consistent indication of time, and that is the guiding red line which takes the viewer sequentially through McLaren's week-long London visit. With this time-line, McLaren provides the viewer with the means of reading his drawing in the correct order. This treatment of time in a drawing, while very pertinent in the case of McLaren the embryonic filmmaker, does have its limitations in static, graphic works like drawing and painting. Most viewers are capable of relating various parts in a drawing or painting in a number of ways: left with right, top with bottom, bottom-left with top-right, the centre with the edge, and so on. The contemplation time that a viewer of a drawing or painting has, allows a thorough exploration of the parts and their various relationships. There is irony in that it is McLaren's preoccupation with time that initially constrains the viewer's use of viewing time. McLaren's purpose, however, is not to restrict the viewer's opportunity to deliberate over the drawing. The earlier observations of the drawing are an indication of the wealth of detail McLaren has placed within it and which may be discovered by the more acute and patient viewer. There is an expectation that the viewer should take time in absorbing the intricacies and nuances of the drawing. However, McLaren is concerned also with making the original sequence of events obvious, and uses the line to provide a visual structure to the drawing as well as providing the primary pathway for the viewer to follow through the drawing.

The notion of presenting ideas sequentially in a drawing or painting was hardly a new one. Nor was it the first time McLaren had used it. In his senior years at Stirling High School, McLaren had created a painting which is structured using a time-line. The drawing depicts the history of the modern western era and may be termed McLaren's *History* painting.

In this early painting the time-line is a conventional,

Fig. 8. McLaren as he appeared in a class photo at Stirling High School. [McLaren Archive/NFB.]

horizontal one. Time is depicted as advancing with the viewer's scan from left to right across the painting. In fact the advancing years are specifically labelled on the time-line at the base of the painting, while the corresponding events are depicted directly above their respective dates. Such an arrangement, while being easy to read – a pertinent function in this case – does have its limitations. Unless the work's proportions are to be stretched scroll-like, the number of sequential events which can be depicted is small. In his large drawing of *Visit to London* McLaren has attempted to overcome this limitation by allowing the time-line to sweep first to the right across the top of the drawing, then mid-way down back across to the left, and finally, in the lower half, left to right again. The time-line is therefore in the form of a (reversed) big 'S'. This structure more than triples the time-line's length. The numerous events – fifteen in all – depicted in the drawing are ordered according to the time at which they occurred during McLaren's London visit, e.g. the positioning of the National Gallery visit between the Fox Film Studio and RCA visits indicates that McLaren visited the RCA, then the National Gallery and then the Fox Film Studio in that order. The 'S' shaped time-line also allows the juxtaposition of non-sequential events. The GB Film Studio visit, for example, occurred four visits after the visit to the Fox Film Studio but their respective depictions have been placed in such a way on a bend in the 'S' time-line that they lie almost next to each other, the one above the other (see Fig. 5). In order to see and relate thematic connections, the viewer is encouraged to explore the drawing more thoroughly than through simple scans of sequences along the time-line.

Such a non-linear relating of the elements in *Visit to London* was a necessary compromise of a rigidly sequential reading. It was an unavoidable consequence of adopting the longer 'S'-shaped time-line. Nevertheless the time-line, with its beginning and ending dates prominently emphasising its function, remains the single most important element in both structuring and understanding the *Visit to London* drawing. The time-line in this seminal work demonstrates McLaren's pre-occupation and fascination with chronological sequencing in the visual art medium. This emphasis on a temporal aspect should be seen in conjunction with McLaren's other artistic interests of the period. These interests are depicted in the *Visit to London* drawing and have already been mentioned, viz: music,

dance, theatre and film. These are each temporal arts, and therefore organize their elements essentially in a sequential manner. It may be asked whether these other arts of music, dance and drama were in some way causal, or consequential, to McLaren's interest in and approach to film. McLaren's first film was made in 1933.[35] In his subsequent recollections, which for this topic constitute the bulk of the evidence upon which the researcher relies, McLaren does not mention theatre or drama as being childhood interests. However, his interest in music certainly predates his first film. It has already been pointed out that when he was a teenager McLaren became absorbed in radio broadcasts of music. He also formally studied the violin for several years from when he was nine years old.[36] Although this gave him a grounding in written and performance music, the lessons did not fire him with enthusiasm for music. The visual arts became the predominant media of the young McLaren's artistic expression. McLaren has acknowledged that art was his best subject at high school.[37] Drawings of McLaren's that were published in the school magazine echo the notion that he was already an accomplished draftsperson – as does the earlier-discussed painting of *History*. These works, however, are manifestations of a more general aesthetic development of the adolescent McLaren. Years later, he recalled the period and revealed the dawning of a 'wide' aesthetic sensibility in quasi-religious terms evocative of a profound revelation:

> Our house, it had a big square garden. This is a square lawn and a path around it, and flower beds, one of

35 Glover 6.

36 *Creative Process*, 1st Assembly (film).

37 McLaren as quoted in Collins 74.

my mother's sunniest flower beds she gave over to roses. Her greatest interest was in gardening. Well, [at the age of 13 or 14,] at adolescence, a big change came over me. I remember the day and the experience when it first hit me. It was a lovely, brilliant, sunny morning – going out into the back garden of the house. And suddenly, everything seemed magical – the drops of dew on the grass, [and the rockery, the flowers,] – and the shapes of the flowers. [Everything was thrilling.] But that morning it just overwhelmed me, and I think I went indoors and tried to write a poem expressing this.[38]

When he came across works of art, either by chance or by design, the adolescent McLaren was not only ready to absorb, but also to respond.

In his early teens he read a poem by e.e.cummings. This excited him because his perception was that "... it broke all the rules [of poetry] he was being taught at school".[39] Thus, when he saw a *Punch* magazine cartoon making fun of modern art, instead of seeing it in satirical terms, McLaren saw its visual diversions from the accepted manner of drawing as a wonderful illustration of expressive means that were new to him. He used the cartoon as an inspiration to abstract his own drawing and painting. Again reference to his *History* painting is helpful. In the painting, shapes are simplified; the sizes of images are symbolic of a progressive importance through time rather than spatially representational; line – as opposed to form – takes predominance; and the images merge into and re-emerge from each other. With the exception of the size element, similar treatments are characteristic of McLaren's *Visit to London*. In this later drawing, sizes of images vary considerably as they are placed in successive positions along the 'S' shaped time-line. The largest component of the drawing is the RA tableau. It could be construed that McLaren depicted this visit with the largest image because it was the most important of his London visits, and similarly the visits to the ballet and the Dalcroze School of Eurhythmics were the least important because their representative images are the smallest in the drawing. Such an interpretation, however, does not take into account other drawing treatments which counterbalance the relative importance placed on images through their size. For instance, in the large RA image, the RA letters themselves and the objects within the RA circle

38 McLaren as quoted in *Creative Process* script 8, and McLaren in *Creative Process*, 1st Assembly (film).

39 *Creative Process* script 1.

are depicted, in the main, by thin lines. This engendered lack of visual substance is accentuated by overlaps in which the lines of the overlapped objects remain visible. This, together with a 'floating' placement of many of the objects within the RA circle, gives this tableau an ethereal and subdued quality. On the other hand, the objects depicted in the two smaller tableaux, of the ballet and the Dalcroze visits, have several qualities which increase the visual impact of the small tableaux to at least that of the largest, the RA. The shapes in the ballet disc are solid, and in the Dalcroze disc a large dark shape strongly contrasts with a very light shape. As well, the component shapes in these smaller tableaux fill their respective circles and fit them exactly. There are also few subsidiary shapes in each of these smaller tableaux. Indeed, each of these tableaux has only two or three major subdivisions. Such strengths given to the smaller tableaux of the *Visit to London* drawing have the overall effect of making each tableau, on the whole, equal in visual impact and interest with the others. The blandness and even quality of the drawing are increased by McLaren's use of a very subdued and limited range of colour. The boldest exception to the drawing's generally muted colour is the red time-line. The painting's structure is thereby enhanced with this emphasis and, as well, the theme of time itself is stressed. In view of McLaren's subsequent career in film, the pre-eminence of the time-line is appropriate.

The drawing *Visit to London* is important, then, for three broad reasons. Firstly, it is as an early example of McLaren's pre-occupation with exploring the notion of time in a visual medium that gives *Visit to London* significance. Secondly, the drawing shows that McLaren's graphic skills even at that stage of his career enabled him, in spite of some stylistic inconsistencies which were a result of an over-exuberant exploration of the medium's stylistic possibilities, to communicate directly and easily. The third reason for the the drawing's importance is that it serves as a document of McLaren's interests in early 1935. Most of the interests displayed in the drawing were to become central and enduring facets of McLaren's work.

Chapter Two

The Early Films

McLaren and Klein

E ven before going to art school, that is while he was still at school and during his adolescent period of aesthetic and intellectual awakening, McLaren read a book which was to have a profound effect on him. The book was *Colour-Music*, written by Adrian Bernard Klein.[40] At this stage in his life McLaren quite naturally absorbed the accepted and pre-eminent Western view of history as progress towards an improved state. McLaren's school painting of *History*, which has been previously mentioned because of its horizontal time-line, clearly illustrates this concept of social progress. In spite of the occasional hiccough, like the Great War, buildings get bigger and cleaner, as do ships and planes, the assumption being that people become, if not bigger, at least healthier and cleaner, and also by inference happier since suffering is removed. Even at the age of 18 McLaren felt that art could help fill that social function: He wrote a story about life in 2066 and "... the function of art in McLaren's brave new world was to make life gloom-proof".[41] Political consequences of his belief in social progress were also adopted by McLaren but, going hand in hand with them were artistic implications in seeing society in a state of progress. One of these implications was that art itself, being a cultural manifestation, was also in a state of progress. From the vantage of Scotland in the late twenties the view of modern history confirmed this notion. Waves of new art movements followed each other, advancing steadily up the beach: Impressionism was followed by Post Impressionism which in turn was followed by Expressionism and then by Symbolism. Then came Cubism to be followed in turn by

40 A.B. Klein, *Colour-Music* (London: Crosby, Lockwood and Son, 1926). By 1937 a 3rd and enlarged edition was published under the title *Coloured Light: An Art Medium* (London: Technical Press, 1937).

41 Donald McWilliams and Susan Huycke, *Creative Process: Norman McLaren*, dir. Donald McWilliams, National Film Board of Canada, 1991, script 7.

42 Not one significant exhibition of Dada work reached Britain before the Second World War. See the list of Futurist and Dadaist Exhibitions which forms an appendix in José Pierre, *Futurism and Dadaism* (Geneva: Heron, 1969) 140–144.

43 All McLaren's colleagues contacted by the author are united and emphatic in endorsing McLaren's integrity.

44 McLaren speaking in Don McWilliams interview, *Creative Process*, 1st Assembly (film), dir. Donald McWilliams, 1989.

45 Klein for example, displays a similar attitude towards the "... army of middlemen distributors, who are often liars, cheats, knaves, and thieves; by the nature of their office imposing on the speculative bourgeoisie their specious jargon of 'coming men', 'monumental geniuses', 'national art' and what not." Klein 32. Such sceptical attitudes have been common amongst the artistic community, the majority of whom could, rightly or wrongly, feel that their work was undervalued or even ignored in the commerce of art.

Abstraction (or Non-Objective painting) and then Futurism. Although this is a simplified schema – there were many overlaps and some waves persisted longer in some parts of the beach than in others – it does represent a generally accurate perception of a sequence. The most recent of the art movements in the 1920s was that of Dada which arose during the Great War and flowed through the following decade. The philosophy of the Dada movement was anti-art. Its anti-art ethos was the expression of the belief that the economic and social system devalued and distorted art's contribution to society as a whole.

By the time of his art school years, McLaren was becoming disenchanted with the value of painting as a means of expression. In view of this stance regarding the futility of working in the field of painting, it would be logical to conclude that McLaren's attitude stemmed directly from the Dadaists. In spite of the logic, this would be an erroneous conclusion. Firstly, the spread of artistic ideas in the earlier part of the century was not nearly as fast or as pervasive as it was to become later. This is particularly so in the case of Britain's awareness of, and receptivity to, new ideas in painting. Furthermore, just as Britain was a provincial outpost of Europe, so Scotland was a provincial outpost of Britain. In the Scotland of the 1920s, Dadaism, if it existed at all, would have been a very dilute mixture.[42] Consequently, its hold on any young artist of that time and place would have been at best tentative, particularly if that artist, renowned for his honesty,[43] as McLaren was, had never mentioned Dadaism in connection with his disenchantment with painting. McLaren mentioned no specific art movement, not Dadaism or any other, in this context. Secondly, and conclusively, the Dada philosophy, although hitting mainly painting, was a scattergun blast aimed at all forms of art. McLaren, however, did not find all forms of art futile – just painting. It is acknowledged that one reason for McLaren's aversion to painting had the same social basis as those of the Dadaists, viz, "... the intrusion of the art dealer and the snobbery connected with a lot of paintings and painters".[44] However, such a general scepticism was hardly unique to the Dadaists.[45] As intimated earlier, McLaren's negative attitude to painting stemmed from two further views; firstly, his conviction that the medium lacked any creative potential, and secondly, his view that painting had lost its power to surprise and excite. With the ensuing social and technical changes in the following decades, McLaren believed that the rightness of his attitude on the second point was confirmed. In 1986, less than a year before his death, he said: "I think fewer people take an interest in [painting] and with the advent of TV even more so. ... with the advent of still photography first and then movie photography we don't experience the same thrill as a mediaeval churchgoer would have when going into church and seeing a stained glass window or a painting of a biblical scene."[46] In the same 1986 interview, he recalled his attitude on the first point when he said: "... in painting [with hundreds of years of tradition], thousands of years, in fact [if you look at the paintings of Rome, ... so many things have been tried out ... by this school and that school] that I felt that painting was a dead medium or a dying medium ...which to me is partly true. Still I believe that."[47]

In this matter, McLaren is in accord with Klein who, in the opening sentence of his chapter dealing with painting, stated "Painting is no longer a vital art".[48] But whereas McLaren saw painting as an exhausted medium, Klein gives an account of successive movements in Modern art which, while being generally negative, does have a positive strand. In his assessment, though, Klein displays an unfortunate inability to judge paintings. For example, in the appreciation of the work of three artists whose contributions are seminal in the modern era, Klein is somewhat less than perceptive. Van Gogh is discussed as one whose uncontrolled emotionalism clouded his intellect and resulted in quaint histrionics and disorderly colour,[49] Gauguin "... was a poetic illustrator"[50] and Kandinsky was "... unquestionably only a decorator, his methods being too haphazard to yield anything but a superficial prettiness".[51] Even so, Klein's analysis of the theoretical underpinning of the various movements is more perceptive. For him the ideas of Cezanne, the Cubists and the Synchromists were cumulative "Cezanne's tablecloths and apples were not conceived in the spirit of representation, but as affording the excuse for organizing groups of forms interesting as proportions, as relationships, as balancings, *not as apples*".[52] Thus Cezanne was perceived as a precursor to the abstractionists, as were the Cubists, who were "... unconsciously preparing the way for a pure art of vision comparable to music."[53] The Cubists were lauded as initiating "... the first serious attempt to use arbitrary forms",[54] as an extreme attempt to carry form by emphasis, exaggeration and simultaneity. The Cubists' adoption of the device of simultane-

46 McLaren speaking in Don McWilliams interview, *Creative Process*, 1st Assembly (film), and McLaren as quoted in *Creative Process* script 21.

47 McLaren speaking in Don McWilliams interview, *Creative Process*, television version (film), and McLaren as quoted in *Creative Process,* script 21. The passages within square brackets have been edited out of the transcript version.

48 Klein 31.

49 Klein 34.

50 Klein 34.

51 Klein 36.

52 Klein 33-34.

53 Klein 35.

54 Klein 34.

ity, by which was meant "... the combined presentation of a number of aspects of the same object from many different angles",[55] was also perceived by Klein to help them move away from the traditional modes of depiction. For the Synchromists, Klein reserved a special place. He presented a long quote from the main advocate of Synchromism, Willard Huntington-Wright.[56] It begins "So long as painting deals with objective nature, it is an impure art, for recognizability precludes the highest aesthetic emotion. All painting ... moves us aesthetically only in so far as it possesses a force over and beyond its mimetic aspect," and continues, "Therefore a picture, in order to represent its intensest emotive power, must be an abstract presentation, expressed entirely in the medium of painting; and that medium is colour".[57] Klein reiterated and endorsed these – as he saw them – optimistic views. Further and more provocative ideas were offered by Klein to his readers in the Huntington-Wright quote:

> There are no longer any experiments to be made in methods ... Ancient painting sounded the depths of composition. Modern painting has sounded the depths of colour. Research is at an end. It now remains only for artists to create. The means have been perfected; the laws of organization have been laid down. No more 'innovatory movements' are possible. ... New forms may be found. But it is no longer possible to add anything to the means at hand.[58]

Klein allowed the Synchromists to present their ideas in his book in their own words. He was not critical of their ideas nor did he offer any qualifications. He also said that his own painting, while being better than that of Kandinsky, was not as good as that of the Synchromists.[59] One could reasonably conclude that he endorsed the Synchromist ideas he presented. Nevertheless, in spite of the lauded emergence of the Cubists through Cezanne and of abstract painting, through the Synchromists, Klein went on to summarize the century of painting he had just reviewed as a decline. He lists many causes and features of the apparent decline but one aspect is of primary importance: "... [art has] ceased to play a part of any importance in the life of our time".[60] He elaborates:

> The people neither hunger for, nor do they require art; particularly the art of painting; nine hundred and ninety-nine out of every thousand being fully satis-

55 Klein 35.
56 Willard Huntington-Wright was not related to Stanton Macdonald-Wright who was one of the leading Synchromist painters.
57 W. Huntington-Wright, as quoted by Klein 35.
58 W. Huntington-Wright, as quoted by Klein 35.
59 Klein 36.
60 Klein 31.

fied with photography and cinematography, for these are, of course, their criterion of the excellence of painting. Were every picture gallery in the world burnt to the ground tomorrow, not a tear would be shed by the vast majority of the people, nor for that matter by the modern artist;* but the end of the world can as well be imagined as the closing up of the cinema houses.[61]

This not only serves to explain the demise of painting but also it elevates the temporal art form of the film. He further states that painting was limited by its static conditions. Although the Futurists were recognized by Klein as seeking to liberate the medium of painting by depicting sequences of events on their canvases, he judged that their work failed entirely in this respect.[62] Nevertheless, it follows that he saw the element of time as a positive attribute in the visual arts. With this element married to visual abstraction, a new, invigorating art form was possible. This art form would be a visual parallel to what Klein termed the ideal art of music. Klein proposed to develop this new art form as one of performance. He had considered and rejected another performance art form, that of dance, as a possible vehicle of "Colour-Music" – dance was seen as too limited because, against a large and static background, the relatively small human figure provided only a limited range of movement and, as well, the resulting movement would necessarily form only a small portion of the total visual field.[63] Klein therefore devoted himself to furthering the cause of the "Colour-Music" performance instrument. A number of these instruments had been developed by the 1920s – they had evolved through a development period of several hundred years since Father Louis Castel first envisaged the basis of such an instrument in the early eighteenth century. The 1920s instruments were light projectors which could modify the colour and sometimes the form of their projections, such modifications being controlled by an organ-like keyboard.[64] With the advocacy of the colour organ, Klein's book works towards a preconceived end. It is an attempt to justify in theoretical terms his, and others, "Colour-Music" instruments. [65] It is ironic that the cinema, which he saw as occupying the lofty position once held by painting, was seen only as a possible venue for his envisaged abstract light shows. A further irony is that it was film that was to be the art form which has come closest to realizing a visual form of music.

61 Klein 31. *"That is by the really 'modern artist', who never visits a picture gallery, and detests 'old masters'."

62 Klein 35.

63 Klein 37.

64 McLaren's absorption and adaption of ideas he found in Klein's book is indicated by a drawing executed while he was in the Interior Design Course at the Art School. McLaren concocted (in drawn form only) an instrument that would affect not just the senses of sight and hearing, but also those of taste and smell. The drawing of the multi-sensory cocktail bar is not dissimilar in its appearance to an illustration of a colour organ designed by an Australian, Alexander Burnett Hector, which is included in Klein's book on page 202.

65 The Klein Keyboard colour projector is illustrated in Klein facing p. 208.

McLaren's attitude to painting, while being similar to Klein's, was based less on dogma which was working towards a preconceived end, but more on pragmatism. McLaren saw the successive art movements as increasingly restrictive. With each new painterly approach revealed in the successive movements, McLaren would have felt less able to make a significant contribution himself. Much later, towards the end of the thirties, McLaren did discover a movement that he found liberating and with which he found an empathy, but by that stage he was already firmly committed to film. McLaren's encounter with Surrealism will be discussed later.

McLaren's attitude to painting may be contrasted to his attitude to film. When asked about tradition in film, McLaren replied, "Ah, that's the one reason why I chose film. Because there are very few traditions in filmmaking. And so it seemed to me here is a medium that's full of possibilities. It's just beginning to be explored."[66]

To dwell on the reasons McLaren did not take up painting is to stress the negative. While he found painting less attractive, it is more appropriate to turn to the reasons for his attraction to film as a medium of expression. It will be recalled that, as well as the contents of Klein's book, there were many other influences on the young McLaren. His passionate interest in the arts included not only the visual arts but also the temporal arts of music and dance. With the vantage of hindsight one can see a predisposition to film. It will also be recalled that McLaren felt his painting lacked something and it was on seeing films by Pudovkin and Eisenstein at the Glasgow Film Society that he realized what it was that was lacking – motion.

The first film

Although McLaren found himself sympathetic to and in-spired by the implications of the new montage techniques displayed in the live action films of the Russian directors, the first film he had a hand in making was more directly tied to another inspirational source. Among the films screened by the Glasgow Film Society was yet another which was to be a pivotal influence on McLaren's film work. McLaren's receptivity to this particular film was engendered not only by the general aesthetic awakening which he experienced at adolescence. Something more specific was involved, although it, too, was connected to

66 McLaren as quoted in *Creative Process* script 18.

Fig. 10. Norman
McLaren, Scottish
Rhapsody *pastel
drawing, c.1933.
[McLaren
Archive/NFB.]*

his overall aesthetic sensitivity. Mention has already been made of McLaren's fondness for listening to music – a fondness which grew from the radio broadcasts he had heard at home in Stirling. The adolescent McLaren listened intently, and when he listened to the music he could imagine (or see in his mind's eye), a moving visual equivalence to the music. Of such experiences McLaren has said, "I see movement, rather than specific images".[67] Not unnaturally, he tried to render these visual equivalences. He did a series of abstract, coloured, pastel drawings which were clearly inspired by music – they even carry the names of their corresponding music: e.g. *Hot Dance Music, Scottish Rhapsody, L'après midi d'un faune, Military March, Based on Improvised Music, Hot Cocktail, Oriental Music by Turkish Orchestra, Carioca, and Zigaine interpretation of Hungarian Music.*[68] The film which so excited McLaren was an abstract film, made just two or so years earlier (in 1930–31). Although the film was black and white it had an accompanying music track. The music track was Brahms' *Hungarian Dance No. 5* and the white shapes in the film cavort and dance in strict synchronization to the music.[69] McLaren later reported the revelation he experienced in seeing this Oskar Fischinger film, *Study No. 7*, for the first time: "I said 'That's it, film's the medium to express my feelings about music'."[70] With hindsight, McLaren's decision to use film seems an obvious if not inevitable step since it was based on such a logical sequence of ideas:

1. Music is an aural, temporal art form
2. McLaren had attempted to render music in visual terms

67 McLaren as quoted in Maynard Collins, *Norman McLaren* (Ottawa: Canadian Film Institute, 1976) 77.

68 *Creative Process* script 4. The film version strongly implies that the pastels were executed prior to McLaren's film work. The similar styles of pastels certainly suggest they were all drawn at the same period and titles like *Hot Cocktail* suggest the thirties, and others, like *Scottish Rhapsody*, suggest Scotland. There is little doubt that even if these particular works slightly post-dated McLaren's first film, he would have executed very similar abstract pieces prior to that film.

69 For an analysis of the relationship between the visual and musical structures of Fischinger's *Study No. 7* see Terence Dobson, *Towards Abstract Film*, unpublished M. Phil. thesis, Griffith University Qld, 1984: 100–109.

70 McLaren as quoted in *Creative Process* script 4.

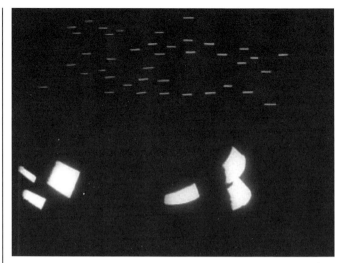

3. Painting is static and, despite McLaren's attempts in *Visit to London* to make it otherwise, is essentially a non-temporal art form.

4. Film is a visual temporal art form and therefore suitable for visually expressing the temporal ideas associated with music.

McLaren had tried another method of rendering visual imagery incorporating the temporal element. This method shows the influence of Klein's approach, since it was a performance manipulation of coloured light. McLaren recalled the order of events which led him to the film medium:

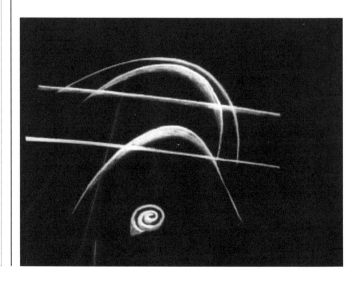

[The first influence during my film career was] Oskar Fischinger with his *Hungarian Dance No. 5* [*Study No. 7*] because this film gave me the courage of my convictions. I wanted to make abstract films – not necessarily abstract films – but to compose abstract images based on music, and at that time I did not know how to go about it. At home, I constructed coloured lights and moved them by hand over paper. But when I saw Oskar Fischinger's [*Study No.7*], I told myself that the solution was to make abstract films.[71]

Another recollection of this experience is a little more evocative. "[One of the] films which excited me the most [was] Oskar Fischinger's *Hungarian Dance No. 5* [*Study No.7*], an abstract film which realized in its fusion of visuals and music what I had only dreamed of at the time."[72] Thus liberated and invigorated, McLaren sought to express his own ideas through film. He and fellow art student Stewart McAlistair, who joined McLaren on this project, met with some considerable difficulties. They had no movie camera. They did not even have any unexposed movie film. There was only one piece of movie equipment available to them.

Fig. 13. Oskar Fischinger around 1934. [Fischinger Archives.]

71 McLaren as quoted in "Interview", *Norman McLaren: exhibition and films* (Edinburgh: Scottish Arts Council, 1977) 6.

72 McLaren as quoted in Guy Glover, *McLaren* (Montreal: National Film Board of Canada, 1980) 6.

McLaren's recollections of the subsequent sequence of events is precise: "There was at the art school where I happened to be, in Glasgow, Scotland, an old 35 mm projector, so I begged an old print of a commercial film, soaked it in the family bathtub for about two weeks – so no-one could have a bath for two weeks [McLaren chuckles] – to get off the emulsion, to make it clear."[73] The next step in the process had already been envisaged since the film had been prepared for it, and the resulting method of creating movie images was one that was enforced by the lack of a movie camera. The method was to draw or paint the required image directly onto the frames of the clear film. At first McLaren and McAlistair tried to animate an image by drawing in each single frame. The time-consuming effort of repeating and carefully modifying a 35mm sized image frame by frame in order to get an illusion of controlled movement when projecting the film, proved to be too monotonous for the two students. The next step was as radical as the idea of painting directly onto film. "So we took stretches of film. We would apply it [the dyes] on film regardless of the frame, painting stripes, red this way, and the other side of the film; ... painting wriggly patterns, dotted patterns, all sorts of patterns,"[74] McLaren described the resulting imagery: "When projected of course, everything was at a terribly frantic motion on the screen but we found that when we used very fast popular music of the day, the tempo of the music was so fast and what was in front of the eye was so fast, that there [was] more than a 50 per cent feeling of synchronization."[75] McLaren has been forthright in his evaluation of his first film effort. "[It] wasn't a work of art. It was like an endless band of effects. It had no climax or conclusion."[76] The filmmaker later was to be embarrassed by the matter of the filmic structure and discipline of his early works, and one can therefore appreciate his ready admission in this case. The film no longer exists but given the nature of the film's assembly together with the fact that it was a first effort, McLaren's assessment of it is credible.

Even so, McLaren has not given sufficient weight to the more than 50 per cent feeling of synchronization with the music with which the film was subsequently screened. The perception of even a partial, i.e. 50 per cent, synchronicity would have entailed the structure of the accompanying music's having lent itself to the film's visual component. The perception of the whole film would there-

73 McLaren speaking in Gavin Millar, *The Eye Hears,The Ear Sees*, NFB/BBC Film, 1970.

74 McLaren speaking in *Creative Process*, 1st Assembly (film).

75 McLaren speaking in *Creative Process*, 1st Assembly (film).

76 McLaren speaking in *Creative Process*, 1st Assembly (film).

fore have been of a work which possessed a degree of structure. The synchronicity so readily perceived in his film, in spite of a lack of the close synchronization of the music/visual relationship that was possessed by Fischinger's *Study No 7*, was to become a consideration in many of McLaren's later films. The film's borrowed structure was most important because it provided McLaren with a profound lesson. The fact that it provided coherence to the film enabled the work's most outstanding feature – its frenetic, colourful, abstract imagery – to be more fully indulged. McLaren described the context of the film's screenings:

> At the end of each year in art school, the painters had an exhibit of their best work. You'd visit it and saw a very dull affair. But when we got these students and their friends into the theatre we had in the art school, and had a movie which was entirely abstract – . Of course the music was 50 per cent of the kick in it too, but we found the reaction very stimulating. It made us feel that if you can do something so simply with a movie as to excite people, surely if you were more careful with movie you've got a field of excitement lying there to be explored ... .[77]

McLaren was excited;[78] and so were the audiences. In their acclaim the audience must have been very demanding for more screenings. It was mentioned before that the film no longer exists. This is because the original (of which no copy was made), was simply worn out by the repeated projections.[79]

Seven Till Five and a different approach to film

McLaren's next film project was also undertaken in 1933. This time however, he decided to do a live-action film trying out some of the montage effects he had recently seen in the films of the Russians Pudovkin and Eisenstein. He had seen these films at the screenings of the Glasgow Film Society. Enthused with filmmaking, McLaren had also joined the recently-formed Glasgow School of Art Kiné Society. He felt very much a junior member of the group, which, it will be recalled, comprised three young teachers and some students more advanced in their art studies than he then was.[80] This situation worked somewhat to McLaren's advantage when it came to deciding on the

77 McLaren speaking in *Creative Process*, 1st Assembly (film).

78 McLaren speaking in the *The Eye Hears*.

79 Glover 6.

80 McLaren as quoted in "Interview", Scottish Arts Council 6.

Society's initial filmmaking project. Other Society members, perhaps conscious of their more senior status, submitted film plans that were overly ambitious, costly and consequently unfeasible. McLaren, on the other hand, perhaps feeling junior and certainly showing a pragmatic sense of proportion, submitted a project which was very simple: a film on a day at art school.[81] The film was to be titled *Seven Till Five*, indicating the hours of the art school day.

The film project was a superb idea on the part of McLaren. Firstly, the idea was accepted by the Kiné Society. McLaren, as the director, had the other members' assistance at his disposal. Judging from the filmic consequences, this assistance was readily forthcoming. Secondly, McLaren's film project had an inbuilt structure: the structure was provided by the sequence of the topic itself. The film would begin with the start of the art school day, would include the events and activities of the day and would conclude with the finish of the art school day. It was a simple, sequential, temporal narrative. In this respect, it was similar to his subsequent drawing (1935) *Visit to London*. It will be remembered that the red time-line provided the drawing's structure. As well, just as in the *Visit to London* drawing, clocks figure prominently, this time to demarcate the art school activities and to show the progress of both the day and, of course, the film. McLaren saw the clock as the basis for the film's rhythm. He also endorsed its thematic importance when he referred to the clocks as the film's *leit-motiv*.[82] The clocks, incidentally, were an even stronger feature because they are those that Charles Rennie Mackintosh designed in his distinctive and simplified style used for his Glasgow School of Art building. The shots of the clocks and their associated ringing bells give a vivid, visual suggestion of sound. Technical and financial restraints meant that the ten-minute film was silent, but McLaren did have gramophone music for the film.[83] No doubt after the experience of the important function of music in his directly painted film, music was also considered a necessary part of *Seven Till Five*. This is supported by McLaren's acknowledgement that gramophone music was selected and used for the film. A more exact evaluation of the contribution of the music component of *Seven Till Five*, however, is hampered by not knowing precisely what the music was, together with an absence of any description of its character or effect. Fortunately, unlike McLaren's

81 McLaren as quoted in "Interview", Scottish Arts Council 6.

82 McLaren speaking in "Interview", Scottish Arts Council 6.

83 McLaren speaking in "Interview", Scottish Arts Council 6.

Fig. 14. Seven till Five *The ringing bell.* [NFB.]

first film, *Seven Till Five* was not totally dependent on music for its structure, which, as has been noted, was an intrinsic part of the subject itself.

The third reason which made the day in the life of the art school proposal such a good one for McLaren was that the project was a modest one. This was not only a major factor in gaining the project's acceptance by the Kiné Society, it also meant that the means of making the film had to be cheap. The camera that was used was of economic necessity the simplest one possible. It could be started and stopped but there were no facilities on it for making dissolves, mattes, wipes, superimpositions or single frame shooting. The change from one shot to another could best be achieved by a simple cut. This circumstance gave McLaren the opportunity to explore the cutting techniques he had so admired and had found such a revelation in the films of Pudovkin and Eisenstein. Moreover, it gave McLaren this opportunity without the encumbrance or distraction of those other methods of changing from one shot to another.

Seven Till Five shows evidence that McLaren had observed Eisenstein's films closely. For example, the film contains a sequence showing a tea-break in which single

84 David Bradwell and
    Kristin Thompson,
    *Film Art: An
    Introduction,* 3rd ed.
    (N.Y.:McGraw-Hill,
    1990) 238.

85 J. Dudley Andrew
    summarizes: "For
    Eisenstein, both the
    method (dialectical
    juxtaposition of
    thematically
    interpenetrated [yet
    visually colliding]
    representations) and
    the final image which
    that method [and
    ultimately the
    spectator] creates, will,
    in the proper film, join
    the creators (both
    artist and spectator) to
    the true processes and
    themes of life. This, he
    was certain, would
    advance that state of
    life most consistent
    with the real processes
    of nature and history,
    the dialectical
    movement toward the
    Marxist millennium."
    in J. Dudley Andrew,
    *The Major Film
    Theories: An Introduction*
    (Oxford: O.U.P.,
    1976) 74.

86 Further, it should be
    remembered that the
    most disseminated of
    the Russians' theories,
    those of Eisenstein,
    were in a state of
    evolution through the
    1940s. See Andrew
    42–75.

87 McLaren as quoted in
    Creative Process script 2.

88 McLaren in
    "Interview".Scottish
    Arts Council 6

89 McLaren in
    "Interview",Scottish
    Arts Council 6

90 McLaren as quoted in
    Creative Process script 2.

profiles of students alternate; a left profile on a white background followed by a right profile on a black background and so on. Such related yet visually opposing shots accord with Eisenstein's idea that film viewers must be visually shocked by such visual contradictions in sequential cutting so that they thereby participate in a dialectical process of synthesizing what they had seen.[84] For Eisenstein such an approach had Marxist justifications.[85] The intricacies of Eisenstein's political theories were not considerations for McLaren. The translated, detailed theories of the Russians were not at that stage available to him.[86] He had only just discovered their films. His political leanings, however, would have made him sympathetic, not only politically but artistically, to those films from the Soviet Union. For McLaren the Russians' impact was directly through their films, and this impact was an artistic revelation of the movement and technique of the Russian use of montage. "I saw the works of Pudovkin and Eisenstein. I know they did have a terrific impact. The intimacy of the intercutting, the wide variety of viewpoint of the subject matter, cutting from one thing to another ..."[87]

Seven Till Five, duly completed, was entered in the Second Scottish Amateur Film Festival, held in Glasgow in October 1934 (which coincided with the beginning of the next academic year at the Art School). The film was awarded the Festival's first prize.[88] Important as this was to the young filmmaker, more significant still was McLaren's subsequent meeting with a stranger. After the Festival the unknown person, presumably impressed with McLaren's *Seven Till Five,* approached the filmmaker and lent him a very good camera with which to make his next film.[89] "On the [next] film I got a camera which could do fade-ins, fade-outs, double exposures, split frame, and it could do a single frame at a time."[90] The stranger, however, had handed McLaren a double-edged sword.

Camera Makes Whoopee and two other films

The film McLaren made with his newly acquired Ciné-Kodak Special camera was *Camera Makes Whoopee,* a title which reflects both the exuberance he felt with his new possession and the fact that the film was intended as a celebration of the camera and its gadgetry. McLaren took as his theme the Glasgow School of Art Christmas Ball for which he had originally designed the decor. Even so, he found that the decor was inadequate for the film and that he needed much additional material.[91] For this he co-opted Helen Biggar, a sculptor who was also studying at the Glasgow School of Art. Biggar suggested using balloons, an Indian mask and some of the objects that were used in double-exposure sequences. The film was meticulously planned and executed – even to the extent of in-camera editing: "We shot the scenes once each. We planned to do things so well that we would only need to put them together afterwards."[92] Considering the number and complexity of the techniques he was exploring for the first time, this was quite an undertaking; however the group's enthusiasm was kindled and maintained largely by McLaren.[93] Fellow students performed in the film and one of the School's younger tutors, Willie McLean, not only gave invaluable technical help but also made his room at the college available to students, even though "... he could never quite comprehend what it was Norman and Helen were trying to do".[94]

By dividing *Camera Makes Whoopee* into two sections – firstly the preparations for the Ball and secondly the Ball itself – McLaren established a thematic structure for the film. The structure thus decided, the filmmaker then sought to further develop his film. "...right from the beginning, I used to think of the camera as my instrument – just as the violin was my musical instrument. Your camera is your instrument and you have to use it. Of course being a beginner I wanted to use it fully – use every knob that was on it ... ."[95] In *Camera Makes Whoopee* the results of McLaren's various technical explorations can be seen. Some are memorably bizarre, such as the scene which shows huge upright screws superimposed over the smaller image of dancing couples. The impression is of dancers moving through a forest of massively proportioned screws. McLaren subsequently stated that this instance of overprinting was necessitated because "...we had no 'background' for the dancers. We could not film the ballroom floor, so we filmed screws."[96] At the end of the film McLaren used the camera's facility to shoot one frame at a time. Being able to shoot one frame and then move, add to, or subtract from his image before taking the next shot and so on, gave McLaren the opportunity to animate his subjects. In the final section of the film McLaren animates a movie camera. The camera is seen to move of its own volition and it puts itself to bed. Using the camera as an object – even if only in a small part of the film – was

91 Anna Shepherd, "Helen Biggar and Norman McLaren", *New Edinburgh Review* (1978) 25.

92 McLaren as quoted in 'Interview', Scottish Arts Council 9.

93 Shepherd 25.

94 Shepherd 25.

95 McLaren as quoted in Collins, 66.

96 McLaren as quoted in "Interview", Scottish Arts Council 8–9.

McLaren's whimsical comment that the end of the film
was the time that the camera is put away. In this part of
Camera Makes Whoopee, the camera is empowered with
movement and is self-directing. This is McLaren's acknowledgement of the central role in the filmmaking that
was played by the camera and its technical possibilities. One
of the Russian film pioneers, Dziga Vertov, had five or six
years earlier made a film in which the camera is central to
the theme. However, at the time of making *Camera Makes
Whoopee* McLaren had not seen Vertov's *Man With a Movie
Camera.*[97] Moreover, the two films differ in the treatment
of the camera. McLaren treats it as a live being on the screen.
Vertov is more interested in exploring with the camera's
eye; his subject is what and how the camera sees, and he
uses points-of-view shots so that the viewer is conscious
of seeing through the camera-lens.

Another technique used by McLaren in *Camera Makes
Whoopee* also has similarities with another important film.
McLaren again used the single-frame device of the Ciné-
Kodak Special to animate some calligraphic marks painted
in pastel. The lines have a mesmeric effect as they are made
to grow and shrink. The fact these animated lines are
superimposed over dancers does not disguise their similarity with parts of Oskar Fischinger's last major completed
film, *Motion Painting No. 1.*[98] Fischinger's film was made
over a dozen years after McLaren's film, so McLaren could
not have borrowed the animation-of-painting-technique
from Fischinger, and as screenings of McLaren's film were
extremely limited geographically, it is improbable that
Fischinger was aware of this particular technical achieve-

97 McLaren as quoted in
"Interview", Scottish
Arts Council 8.

98 For analysis and
description of *Motion
Painting No.1.* see
William Moritz, "The
films of Oskar
Fischinger", *Film
Culture 58–60* (1974)
37–187 and Dobson
125–132.

ment of McLaren. Fischinger's exploration of the animated-painting technique was a response to the pressures of time and money he was then experiencing.[99] The technique can also be seen as a development of the metamorphosing paper cut-outs or charcoal drawings of his earlier *Studies* series of films, one of which, *Study No. 7*, has already been noted as an acknowledged influence on McLaren's work. McLaren's use of the animated-painting technique ocurred subsequent to his seeing *Study No. 7*. Whether or not Fischinger's film was an inspiration to McLaren specifically in developing the animated-painting technique is difficult to establish. It would be fair to say, however, that someone who had completed an art school, two-year, general course in painting, as McLaren had, and who was exploring the animation techniques possible with a new camera, as McLaren was, would sooner or later use painting itself as the source to be animated. Further, the animated painting technique is an extremely simple process; one paints, shoots a frame, paints a little more, shoots, paints, shoots, etc. and it is a process that is not far removed from the traditional method of animation where one draws, shoots, draws, shoots, etc.. The major difference is that, whereas in traditional animation a *series* of related drawings is used, in animated painting the artist modifies a single painting.[100] McLaren's background, together with his familiarity with the traditional animation methods, establish a strong basis for saying that the young filmmaker, in his fascination and determination to explore and exploit all the techniques that the Ciné-Kodak Special offered him, initiated the animated-painting technique independently of other filmmakers who may or may not have also independently developed the same technique either before or after McLaren. A similar context surrounds McLaren's earlier development of direct drawing onto the film stock itself in which he also ignored the frame divisions. In 1935, Len Lye, the New Zealand-born filmmaker and sculptor, made a film called *Colour Box* which also employed the direct method. This film was made for the British General Post Office Film Unit and was produced by the head of the Unit, John Grierson. In an interview conducted in 1970,[101] McLaren stated that Lye was the first to employ the direct animation technique, although he also added that he was unaware of Lye's film when he first used direct animation in his own first film. In other words, McLaren indicated that he came to the method independently, just

99 Moritz 71.

100 In *Motion Painting No.1*. Fischinger's paint became so thick that he placed a transparent sheet of plexiglass over the painting so that he could continue painting on apparently the same painting – he eventually used a total of six plexiglass sheets in making the film. Moritz 71.

101 McLaren speaking in *The Eye Hears.*

as Lye did. The account given previously, in which McLaren relates the bath-tub immersion of the film, the original and unsuccessful attempt to draw directly but within the boundaries of the frame, and the subsequent abandoning of such a restriction to paint and the decision to draw on the film, ignoring the frame divisions, gives further credence to McLaren's assertions. The young McLaren enthused with ideas concerning the filmmaking process. His technical tour de force, *Camera Makes Whoopee*, is abundant evidence of this fact.

At the same time as making *Camera Makes Whoopee*, McLaren worked on two shorter and simpler films. One was *Polychrome Fantasy* (two minutes), which lists in the credits W.N. McLaren,[102] W.H. Finlayson and T.D.Allan as the filmmakers. As this film also came under the auspices of the School Kiné Society, it would be logical to conclude that they were also from the School. It is likely that *Polychrome Fantasy* was used by McLaren as a test or trial in the preparation for *Camera Makes Whoopee*. The short film's primary technique was the use of the mask. A brief description of the film and the technique was offered by Glover: "Material of crystal formation was shot through a low-power microscope, using polarized light with the lower part of the picture masked off. The film was then rewound in the camera and the scene of the dancers was shot."[103] To which should be added that the top of the picture was masked off so that the small images of the dancers occupied only the lower third of the picture area. The live thematic elements of the film are visually incongruous: one being a live action shot of dancers, the other being a display of vague shapes which fluctuate and change colours. The incongruity is not helped by the two images separating into two distinct areas of the picture frame. Whatever artistic shortcomings this early work may have had, the film does demonstrate McLaren's sustaining interest in the art of dance and that of moving abstract images. It is also an early manifestation of what was to become a growing preoccupation to somehow marry these elements into a filmic unity. The film also demonstrates McLaren's technical accomplishment in the cine-masking process.

The second short film McLaren worked on in this period was called *Colour Cocktail* and like all his other films from his art school days it was silent. Like his first film, *Colour Cocktail*'s only version (no copies were ever made) was worn out by repeated projection. Descriptions of the

102 McLaren's first given name was William (his father's name), but even formal acknowledgements of it, such as in this film, get rarer until it no longer appears after about 1936 – except that is when, in some private letters and other communications to friends, he sarcastically uses William to cast himself as a pompous figure. For example, see the card to Maurice Blackburn reproduced in *ASIFA Canada* 5.1 (April, 1987) 81.

103 Glover 7.

film are brief, but agree that the film employed a number of techniques which included live action and slow motion.[104] Despite using live action, the film is described as abstract.[105] One could conjecture that McLaren abstracted the live action shots by the use of silhouette or by the superimposition of different images – such techniques had been used, for example, by Hans Richter in his *Filmstudie* of 1927. Whether or not the term 'abstract' could justly be applied to all of *Colour Cocktail* is not now known, but the film did by all accounts contain at least one sequence which was abstract. This sequence used the interplay of lights on coloured paper.[106] This section would be fascinating to see, since it was a recreation of the experiment with lights and paper McLaren had unsuccessfully tried out much earlier at home in Stirling. It will be remembered that he was attempting to recreate what he saw when listening to music (see above p. 35). This filmic attempt in *Colour Cocktail* must have been considered by McLaren to be relatively unsuccessful, since, although the music-visual art relationship remained central to much of his subsequent work, this technique of expounding it was never used again by him. In *Colour Cocktail*, McLaren explored the music-visual art relationship not only by expressing musical ideas in a visual form. Although the film was a silent one, a gramophone recording was selected and was played with the film during its screenings. "The accompanying musical recording synchronized so well that it was taken for a sound film."[107] Despite this recurrence of a successful marriage of a pre-recorded, and previously unrelated, music source with moving abstract visual imagery of film, McLaren was not overwhelmed by *Colour Cocktail*. It was as if it were almost a trivial plaything compared with his purposeful technical explorations of *Camera Makes Whoopee*.

The Third Glasgow Amateur Film Festival and an odd triumph for *Camera Makes Whoopee*

The Third Glasgow Amateur Film Festival was scheduled for January 1936. The adjudicator was to be the already-renowned John Grierson. By the mid-1930s, Grierson was in the forefront of the cinema world. His 1929 film *Drifters* was a pioneering cinematic statement which depicted working class people as themselves and documented their work. Grierson had learned from the films of the Russians, Eisenstein and Pudovkin, and employed their montage of

104 Collins 23, Glover 7.

105 Collins 23.

106 Collins 23.

107 Collins 23.

percussive juxtapositions in developing his new genre: the film documentary. For Grierson, though, the film was more than a device for recording events and people; it was most importantly an agent of social reform – an agent of untapped and therefore unknown power. After the astounding success of *Drifters* (it was screened in company with *Battleship Potemkin* at the London premier of the Soviet film and its impact was considerable), Grierson became an immensely forceful advocate of the use of film to inform and persuade.[108] He wrote newspaper articles. He extolled the need for improved systems of production for the British film.[109] He set up production units and he promoted his ideas for greater Government involvement, through film screenings for Government ministers and public servants, in what he saw as the socially powerful film medium. By 1935 he was also head of the General Post Office Film Unit. In Britain of 1935 the GPO was a government organization which not only operated the mail system and post offices but also the phone system, a savings bank and even the meteorological office. The GPO's main function was communication, and it is apt that such an organization should not only set up its own means of communication, the GPO Film Unit, to inform the public of the GPO's function and means, but also that John Grierson – the leading advocate of the film medium – should be the Film Unit's head.

Young Norman McLaren decided to enter the Film Festival for which Grierson had been appointed adjudicator. He entered two films. The first was his technical tour de force, *Camera Makes Whoopee*. The other film he submitted was the five-minute film, *Colour Cocktail*. McLaren's description of the festival and the aftermath conveys the trauma he experienced:

> When Grierson came to the final evening of the festival and gave his assessment of the films, he started with my fancy film and gave it hell. He said, "Technically it's very competent, but artistically it's nothing but a jumble and a mess. It's got no sense of form or organization, it's got no development, and it's totally zero as far as being a work of art." I was counting on this occasion, so I thought well, there it goes, I had hoped to work in films for the rest of my life and that's it, I've had it. Then he came to my little film and gave it first prize – the little abstract film. He said, "That is a work of art". Later on that evening he said,

108 James Beveridge, *John Grierson: Film Master* (NY: Macmillan, 1978) 43.

109 John Grierson, "The Future for British Films", *London Spectator*, May 14, 1932, reprinted in Beveridge 55–56.

"Come round to my hotel and have a drink". I did. I was very impressed with the man, and I was rather awed and frightened by him too. I'd never seen such a lively person, full of vehement opinions – and then sitting over a drink, he said, "You know you have a very dirty mind, Norman. Yes, that film of yours about the art school ball was full of Freudian and sexual symbolism." I said, "I didn't know that. What scenes?" "Well", he said, "you've got the dancers moving among superimposed impressions of balloons and screw nails", and mentioned other scenes. And I'd done it in all innocence ... .[110]

Several features and conclusions may be drawn from this McLaren anecdote. Firstly, an image of John Grierson emerges which more than hints at the forthright and electrifying Grierson personality which inspired not only by confrontational argument, but mostly by the force of his personality. The second point to be drawn from the anecdote is the nature of the Grierson-McLaren relationship. Not surprisingly, and as he acknowledged, McLaren found himself awed by Grierson. This awe was accompanied by respect. For his part, Grierson gradually assumed a remote yet fatherly attitude to McLaren. Given Grierson's personality, he no doubt assumed a similar posture towards most of his staff, and so Grierson could laugh about his parental attitudes when, looking back in 1970, he said in describing McLaren, "He comes from my home village in Scotland" and jokingly added, "I once promised his mother I would look after him".[111]

A third point to emerge from McLaren's story is the fact that the film on which he had pinned so many hopes, *Camera Makes Whoopee*, not only failed to win any prizes but was singled out by Grierson for some potentially devastating criticism. McLaren took Grierson's comments to heart. On numerous occasions, quite apart from the one quoted above, McLaren has recounted the lessons learned, the faults Grierson saw in *Camera Makes Whoopee*.[112] McLaren came to the conclusion that what he called an intellectual structure (a theme) was an insufficient means of ensuring a unifying filmic expression, not just for *Camera Makes Whoopee* but for any filmic statement. McLaren discerned the need for a visual structure as well.[113] What McLaren meant by visual structure is best gleaned by comparing his later films with *Camera Makes Whoopee*. His

110 Norman McLaren as quoted in Beveridge 80–81.

111 John Grierson as quoted in Beveridge 80–81.

112 See, for example, McLaren in Collins 66, *Creative Process* script 3 and "Interview" Scottish Arts Council 8.

113 McLaren as quoted in "Interview", Scottish Arts Council 8.

post-student films possess a visual coherence, which is to say that in such later films one part relates to another part in terms of appearance, movement and/or metamorphosis. The detail of McLaren's subsequent films will be examined later but it should be borne in mind that the philosophical underpinnings of their structure may be traced to Grierson's reaction to *Camera Makes Whoopee*. In his last film interview (1986), McLaren encapsulated, in simple and direct terms, the aesthetic consequences such considerations of visual structure meant for him when he said: "A work of art has to have cohesiveness and consistency but not so much cohesiveness and consistency as to become boring and not so much non-cohesiveness as to fall apart. It [the work of art] has to be organically linked and yet it must have surprises in it ... surprises that are relevant to the whole work."[114] Simple as this statement is, it also carries suggestions of McLaren's social purpose in filmmaking. That is, McLaren has an audience in mind when he uses terms like 'boring' and 'surprises'. The development of McLaren's social concerns will be taken up again shortly. The present reason for raising the 1986 expression of McLaren's attitude towards structure in a work of art is that it emphatically demonstrates how thoroughly McLaren learned his early lesson from Grierson.

Camera Makes Whoopee then, at first gave the young McLaren cause for great optimism, in that the film was the vehicle for his technical adventures with the gadgetry of the Ciné-Kodak Special camera, but the film then came to be the object of such demoralizing criticism that McLaren believed his professional film career had ended before it had started. The special camera won through the earlier competition, provided him with hope and confidence of accomplishment but then the very profusion of gadgetry on the camera encouraged a profusion of adventures in technology which in turn resulted in what Grierson saw, and McLaren subsequently saw, as a jumble:[115] an impressive object of criticism. The Ciné-Kodak Special 'prize' provided a cloud-castle which turned into a cloud storm. The storm, however, was brief. The experience of the adjudication, harrowing as it must have been, was one that was to benefit McLaren. That he subsequently learned a filmic lesson was to be clearly demonstrated in his later films. Just as important was another outcome of Grierson's attendance at the Scottish Amateur Film Festival.

The above account by McLaren of the Festival's

114 McLaren speaking in
Creative Process
(television version).

115 McLaren as quoted in
Collins 66.

results revealed that Grierson awarded a prize to what McLaren thought of as one of his make-weight entries to the Festival, *Colour Cocktail*. The obvious implication is that of McLaren's entries, Grierson was impressed only by the little abstract film. Grierson's criticism of *Camera Makes Whoopee* would support this view. It could also be the case, however, that Grierson was also impressed by the technical virtuosity displayed in *Camera Makes Whoopee* but, for reasons connected with genuine concerns about the film's weakness and/or with his own desire to be confrontational and controversial, chose publicly to dismiss the film. This scenario would be consistent with Grierson's perceptive abilities and his provocative personality. It is also the more likely alternative, since Grierson certainly did not overlook McLaren's imaginative potential. *Colour Cocktail* and *Polychrome Fantasy* displayed these characteristics of McLaren's work, and, for all its faults, so did *Camera Makes Whoopee*. Whatever the case, it is evident that the flaws that Grierson saw in *Camera Makes Whoopee* were not sufficiently great to rule McLaren out as a potential filmmaker. Grierson offered McLaren a job. "Anyway, the best thing – and it was much better than the prize I had received – was that he said, 'When you're finished your training at the Art School come down to the GPO in London. You have a job waiting for you, and you can get your training as a professional filmmaker.' So I accepted right away."[116] The prospect of such a job must have been both reassuring and giddyingly exciting. Reassuring because, firstly, it would have had the effect of quelling the possible parental fears for the immediate and professional security of their youngest child. This in turn would have enabled McLaren to envisage the move to London with that part of his filial duties fulfilled. Secondly, the job offer was a vote of confidence in his ability, from an eminent source. The offer was exciting because it gave him the almost impossibly rare chance to not only pursue his vocation of filmmaking, but also to learn in an environment of, and presumably from, a collection of some of Britain's leading artists, directors and writers.

McLaren's last student film

First, McLaren had to finish his final months of his studies at the Glasgow School of Art. For McLaren, though, this meant more film work. In these final film projects as an amateur, McLaren went off on another tack. These projects

116 McLaren as quoted in Beveridge 81.

were not abstract films, nor ones centred on exploring technique. They were expressions of McLaren's increasing pre-occupation with social issues. The political contents of these two projects – an aborted film on Glasgow's housing problems provisionally titled *Homes v. Health*, and the anti-war, anti-capitalist statement *Hell UnLtd* – are of course important and will in due course be examined, but at this point the formal artistic qualities of McLaren's last amateur film tasks will be scrutinized.

The *Homes v. Health* project was fully scripted, but it never reached the stage of shooting, as the Glasgow Corporation refused permission for filming in Mearnskirk Hospital.[117] Comments on the project's aesthetic features would therefore be almost totally conjectural and consequently of little use.

Fortunately, *Hell UnLtd* was completed and remains to provide evidence of McLaren's filmmaking attitudes and achievements just prior to his move to the GPO Film Unit. The film was another collaboration with Helen Biggar – sculptor and political activist – but it was McLaren's conception. Even though the two pooled ideas and shared the work, his plan was largely adhered to.[118] The film was, and still is, a blatant call to political action. And, despite Grierson's earlier criticsm of *Camera Makes Whoopee's* lack of visual cohesion, *Hell UnLtd* displays a crude mixture of styles as well as techniques. It contains, for example, live action and animation, newsreel shots and still drawings, three dimensional models and two dimensional diagrams, and static, posed tableaux and dramatic shots of a burning fire victim. In their enthusiasm for their cause, McLaren and Biggar allowed themselves to depict the various segments of the film in manners which, although expedient for the particular segment concerned, bear inconsistent visual connectedness with preceding or succeeding segments. For example, in one part of the film the following sequence occurs:

- rapid cutting of a series of messages lettered on cards alternating with live-action crowd scenes
- cut to a world map, the countries of which are successively overlaid with the word 'strike'
- cut to a card on which the message is revealed as "No Government can act with things at a standstill" followed by two quick cuts; "Act Now" and "Act Now" (angled)

117 Shepherd 25.

118 Shepherd 25.

- cut to a tableau with model figures protecting their piles of coins from the outstretched hand of the armament merchant
- cut to a live-action shot of the armament merchant collapsing
- cut to his body
- cut to symbolic model of a falling mercury gauge of western countries.

While it is true that some of the images in the above sequence are developments of images which occur earlier in the film, their combination within this section remains crude and disjointed.

The mixture of visual means is not the only impediment in this film. The film is silent, and so use is made of shots of lettered cards to communicate its verbal message. There are times in the film when written message after written message appears, thereby reducing the film's visual impact and slowing its momentum (time has to be allowed to read such messages as "No Government can act with things at a standstill"). As well, in order to make them more understandable, many of the model tableaux carry numerous labels. An example from the above sequence concerns the western nations' piles of coins for armament expenditure: the overall coin collection is labelled 'expenditure' and each pile of coins is named for a particular country. Again, such heavy reliance on the presentation of the written word interrupts the flow of the film. (The models which carry such a burden of explanatory labelling on the whole are static.) Such a reliance on presenting ideas in a written form has not in *Hell UnLtd* resulted in the most effective or exciting way of delivering visual ideas in film. A comparison with McLaren's own work of his later years, *Neighbours*, illustrates that anti-war ideas can be powerfully and compellingly conveyed without resorting to spoken or written words (the only words in *Neighbours*, apart from those in the titles and credits, are the headlines on the newspapers that the neighbours are reading; 'peace certain if no war' and 'war certain if no peace'. Here the message is succint and easy to read quickly. Most importantly it creates not only a verbal but also a visual mirror which is consistent with the thematic symmetry of the two neighbours). The pacifist theme of *Neighbours*, however, is delivered primarily through the action of the two neighbours. As such, movement becomes an essential aspect in present-

ing the film's theme. By contrast, the models in *Hell UnLtd* which carry such a burden of explanatory labelling on the whole lack intrinsic movement. The models are essentially little stage sets and are static – even the camera work associated with them is a static long shot (long in time as well as distance). Movement within the set or shot is limited to one element, for example: a pile of coins falling over.

An even more stilted segment of *Hell UnLtd* is of a tableau which contains the armament merchant. The well-dressed merchant is holding a scroll, which is labelled 'profits'. In his other hand he holds strings the other ends of which are attached to the various European capitals mapped out at his feet. The camera in a slow pan down this motionless figure in its motionless setting also reveals that the armament merchant is standing on a cloth cap. The symbolism of the merchant's alleged power over countries and the workers is obvious. The problem with the tableau, however, is that it is static and its lack of movement is emphasized by the camera's slow pan. The impression is of staginess. The episode lacks the power to move – in both senses of the word.

The film is not without its achievements. One part of the film depicts the imminent victims of war. A screaming, frantic woman, a victim of bombing played by Helen Biggar, is engulfed by fire. Her stark, gesticulating image is superimposed by a gas-masked, death-like, military figure. There is then a cut to a close-up of meat being fed into a whirring mincer. The camera pans down to the minced meat oozing from the machine's exits. Next is a cut to a close-up of mincemeat as food on a plate. The food is being manoeuvred by a fork. The image is then cut to a fork lifting minced food from a plate. The camera pans up with the fork to reveal the person who is consuming his meal with relish – it is the armament merchant (see Figs. 17–23). Various facets of this sequence contribute to its coherence:

1. The even rhythm of the cutting.

2. The use of cutting to similar imagery, in order to make a connection from one shot to the next, for example, from the mincemeat of the grinder to the mincemeat on the plate.

3. The movements within each shot and of the camera itself also lend cohesion and logic: from the wild movements of the burning woman within the stable frame the movement next is down with the camera pan following the dropping mincemeat; the following image is once again stable with the only movement being that of the fork within the frame; the next shot comprises the logical and balancing upward pan of the camera following the fork; the camera then comes to rest on the smirking face of the arms dealer.

These various elements combine to make a coherent piece of cinematic action, the horror of which compares with the sliced-eye sequence of Luis Buñuel's *Un chien andalou* (1929).

The student achievements

Most of McLaren's achievements at this stage of his career were embryonic rather than accomplished. Nonetheless they were of crucial importance. Many of the interests which were to become fundamental factors in his subsequent film work had already been developed. Not only film but also music, painting and dance, allied with a sincere concern for his fellow being, had become central to his life before he left Scotland for London. There were two very tangible achievements, however. One was the development of the hand-made (cameraless), film independently of, although almost simultaneously with, Len Lye's similar work. Although the early examples of his directly painted films no longer exist, McLaren's achievement can be measured. On the one hand, the success and achievement was

Fig. 17. Hell UnLtd
Sequence: i.
*Victim (played by Helen
Biggar) afire.*
[NFB.]

Fig. 18. Hell UnLtd
Sequence: ii.
The meat mincer.
[NFB.]

Fig. 19. Hell UnLtd
Sequence: iii.
*The meat falls to the
plate.*
[NFB.]

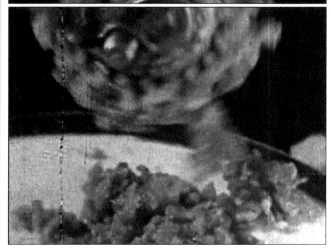

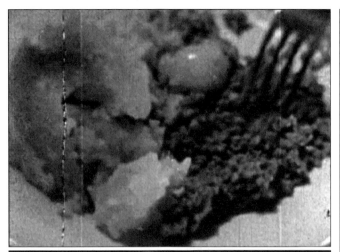

Fig. 20. Hell UnLtd
Sequence: iv.
The fork in the meat.
[NFB.]

Fig. 21. Hell UnLtd
Sequence: v.
The camera begins its
pan up with the fork.
[NFB.]

Fig. 22. Hell UnLtd
Sequence: vi.
The meat is eaten.
[NFB.]

Fig. 23. Hell UnLtd
Sequence: vii.
The evil, eating face of
the capitalist arms-dealer.
[NFB.]

119 See McLaren as
    quoted in "Interview"
    Scottish Arts Council
    11.

120 McLaren as quoted in
    Creative Process script 3.
    The context in the
    script suggests that
    these words were
    spoken by Grierson
    when adjudicating
    Camera Makes Whoopee,
    but McLaren, as
    quoted in "Interview"
    Scottish Arts Council
    11, makes it clear that
    Grierson said these
    words to McLaren on
    the latter's arrival at
    the GPO Film Unit.

recognized by McLaren himself – as well as Grierson – and directly-painted films were to become an important part of his later output. On the other hand, the achievement exemplifies the fundamental nature of McLaren's approach to film technology, an approach which consistently occurs in his later film work. The second tangible achievement at this juncture in McLaren's career was the GPO Film Unit job offer from Grierson. It was to take up this offer that McLaren was to move to London in October 1936. Grierson also offered the young filmmaker some advice, in the form of stinging criticism, concerning McLaren's enthusiastic over-application of gadgetry in *Camera Makes Whoopee*. McLaren's next film, *Hell UnLtd*, demonstrates that although McLaren may have absorbed Grierson's advice on a conceptual level, he had not been able to apply it in *Hell UnLtd*. This last film as an amateur displays energy, idealism and the occasional flash of a cohesive cinematic expression, but McLaren had been so preoccupied with the mission of the film that he had largely ignored the film's structure.[119]

McLaren subsequently became only too aware of the shortcomings of his early film work, so much so that Grierson's words on the young filmmaker's arrival in London became etched into his memory: "Grierson said, 'You've got lots of imagination, trying all kinds of new things, but totally undisciplined, unharnessed. You don't know how to make a film and we're going to knock some discipline into you ... .' These were his very words: knock some discipline into you."[120]

Chapter Three

McLaren at the GPO Film Unit

John Grierson's process of 'knocking discipline' into the newly arrived Norman McLaren got off to a puzzling start. McLaren came down from Scotland in October 1936 to take up his filmmaking vocation with what was, under Grierson's leadership, not only a pioneering filmmaking organization but also a collection of remarkable talents in areas ranging from the newly-established documentary film idiom to experimental film and the allied arts of music and literature. In early November McLaren was summoned to Grierson's office. The head of the GPO Film Unit suggested that the new recruit take some leave of absence. Ivor Montagu was going to Spain and needed a cameraman to help record the Civil War there. One can imagine the waves of incredulity followed by enthusiasm and even elation felt by McLaren as he listened to Grierson. The young filmmaker Ivor Montagu, who like Grierson was on the council of the London Film Society,[121] wanted to make a film about the effect on the Republican side of the siege of Madrid. The shooting of the film was to take about three weeks.

Why was Grierson dispatching the young McLaren off overseas after so short a time at the Unit? Who did Grierson envisage would benefit? What was the benefit and how would that benefit be realized? Did he see the GPO Film Unit benefiting? Himself? Montagu? The Republican causes? McLaren? Was the project likely to knock discipline into McLaren? Was there no suitable work for McLaren at the GPO Film Unit at that time?

[121] Montagu was in fact one of the Society's founders. See Adrian Brunel, *Nice Work: The Story of Thirty Years in British Film Production* (London: Forbes Robertson, 1949) 112–113.

Fig. 24. Norman McLaren at the GPO Film Unit. [McLaren Archive/NFB.]

The last question is the easiest to answer. Documentary filmmaking's many tasks in pre-production (researching, script writing), production (shooting, sound engineering, lighting, location work), post-production (cutting, editing, sound mixing) as well as in titling, offered a wide scope for employing a junior person as an apprentice or learning assistant. Indeed, on his return from Spain McLaren was used – and thereby educated – in such a manner. McLaren could certainly have been similarly employed at the GPO Film Unit at the time of his going to Spain.

The other questions may be answered jointly. Grierson was astute. The request for help in Spain gave him the means to meet several obligations in one fell swoop. Firstly, of course, by giving him the assistance of McLaren (on leave), Grierson was giving Montagu his unofficial help in obtaining rare footage of the Republican side in the Spanish Civil War. Grierson's action to help Montagu would not

Fig. 25. John Grierson
in the 1930s.
[Grierson Archive.]

necessarily have sprung from political considerations. The
conflict in Spain could also be seen in moral terms; however, the most important factor for Grierson was that the
Spanish war was a conflict which was being sanitized in its
presentations to the rest of the world. It would be unjust
to assume that Grierson, in meeting Montagu's request,
was working from purely selfish motives. He would have
been aware, though, that the training and experience
McLaren was likely to gain would be of eventual benefit to
McLaren's long term employer – the GPO Film Unit
(moreover, it was training they were not paying for); and,
providing Grierson was correct in his judgement of
McLaren's potential and commitment, to the film medium
generally. For all these benefits to be realized it would be
necessary for McLaren to actually learn these filmic lessons
in Spain.

Grierson had the odds stacked in his favour.
McLaren's learning capacity was accentuated by several

factors. Firstly, the brevity of the experience had the effect of intensifying it as did the increased sense of urgency imparted by the environment of civil warfare with its danger, scenes of destruction and displays of uninhibited emotion.[122] Secondly, Montagu's film project was to be an attempt to present the war from the side of the Republicans, that is to say the anti-Fascist side. Prominent in the anti-Fascist forces were the communists. Bearing in mind McLaren's political leanings and his still-current membership of the Scottish Communist Party, his sympathies were certainly with the anti-Fascists. He was therefore strongly motivated to present the Republican perspective of the conflict. Thirdly, McLaren's rôle in Spain was that of an assistant. This meant he could concentrate on learning, since he was free of carrying the responsibilities for the overall project.

The content of McLaren's learning would not have been restricted to the skills of operating a movie camera efficiently. Because it was only a two-person team, director and cameraman, both deliberations and decisions were channelled through McLaren, who consequently learnt the number and variety of options facing a director – for example, the theme of the movie/sequence/shot, the selection of the subject of the movie/sequence/shot, the selection of the position of the shot, the closeness and angle of the shot as well as the lighting. McLaren had to be continually aware of these options and to learn to make judgments on their various merits in the context in which the work was being constructed. The Montagu project had another more specific corollary which was in accord with Grierson's avowed objective of knocking some discipline into the young McLaren. The speed of events in the war arena would ensure that Montagu, and therefore McLaren, would not have time to use camera gadgetry and exploit camera tricks of the sort seen in *Camera Makes Whoopee*. Indeed, the use of obvious tricks would have ruined audience perception of the resulting film as a veracious document of war. To put it bluntly, film tricks would have been counterproductive to the object of the exercise. Thus, the film's objectives – as well as the difficult and dangerous war-time filming conditions faced – dictated that filming would have to concentrate on straightforward cinematography. A further factor contributing to that same end was the fact that no film could be processed until the return from Spain. In this context, camera gadgetry and in-camera

122 McLaren's letter to his parents, 2 December 1936, graphically describes the horror he saw.

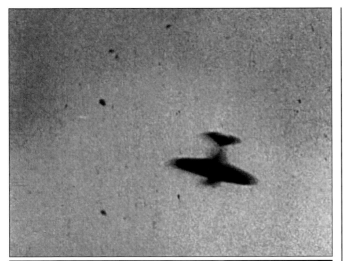

Fig. 26. Defence of Madrid. *A plane on the attack.* [BFI.]

Fig. 27. Defence of Madrid. *A coffin with a child's body in it.* [BFI.]

experimentation were a danger to the enterprise. That there would usually be only one chance to film a particular incident also entailed that simplicity and directness were hallmarks of the film. In summary, there was little cause for Grierson to doubt that the imagination that he thought McLaren had in abundance would be channelled into straight camera work: i.e. McLaren would be required to look not for the trickiest shot but for the ethos of the project.

Although the film that was shot in Spain was cut and edited entirely by Montagu, thereby making it decisively a Montagu film, it supplied sufficient evidence that McLaren did the job required of him. Nothing flamboyant is attempted in the camerawork. The shots are direct and simple takes. They do not detract from the content. They are an acknowledgement of the eloquence and power in the imagery of warfare. The film *Defence of Madrid* and the subsequent career of Norman McLaren are testimony to the wisdom of Grierson's judgement in sending the young filmmaker with Montagu to Spain. It should not be construed, however, that those lessons concerning restraint and appropriateness of technique were immediately and totally absorbed by McLaren. On his return from Spain, McLaren resumed his GPO Film Unit duties of assisting other filmmakers in such functions as editing. The training was to continue. His first film for the Unit was to be over a year away. Here is revealed yet another aspect of Grierson's ploy in sending McLaren to Spain. The Montagu project may have been fortuitous in its timing as far as Grierson was concerned, but he was able to use it to advantage. Realizing that McLaren could not be given a GPO film at that raw stage of his career, Grierson contrived to give McLaren a significant involvement (as cinematographer) in a project he knew would be an exciting and inspiring mission for the young filmmaker. Moreover, as Montagu was working on a topical subject and to a tight schedule, Grierson knew a completed film was likely to emerge quickly – and it did. McLaren was thereby given a sense of achievement very early in his professional career.

The GPO Film Unit and John Grierson

The GPO Film Unit in which McLaren worked was an institution that had been and was being moulded by Grierson. It was the offspring of the Empire Marketing Board – a government organization which had been established in 1926 on the wishes of the Imperial Conference (the conference of the Dominion heads of government). The Board's objective was to promote the notion of a non-tariff preference for Empire goods in the UK market. The promotion was to be pursued through research and advertising.[123] The prudent, yet progressive Secretary of the Board, Sir Stephen Tallents, initially concentrated on the media of posters, newspapers, exhibitions and the school classroom wall. To begin with, film did not play a large part. However, as the Board's grant increased so Tallents' thoughts turned to the medium of film. It was at this juncture that Grierson had the good fortune to present himself to Tallents. Grierson's studies and travels to the

123 Gary Evans, *John Grierson and The National Film Board: The Politics of Wartime Propaganda* (Toronto: University of Toronto Press, 1984) 27.

USA had opened his eyes to the potential the mass media possessed to create an informed citizenry and thereby improve not only the individual citizen but also society as a whole. Tallents was impressed with Grierson and his view of the man is worth repeating:

> Grierson was a man who had been steeped, but never dyed, in the colours of orthodox education: 'a man with a propagandist flair and love of films, a twenti-eth-century radical, shrewd, forceful, no poet but a social prophet, an oxy-acetylene firebrand with the showmanship of Barnum and Bailey and the sincerity of Moody and Sankey'. The fiscally wise young man could also accept a totally inadequate budget to make an inadequate film which would produce a larger but still inadequate budget to make a more ambitious film. This was the stuff of which responsible public servants were made.[124]

Tallents employed Grierson as a film officer in late 1928 and almost immediately questions were asked in Parliament about the appointment of a film officer who had no practical experience of films. Although the questions were side-stepped, it was not long before Grierson set about gaining some practical experience through making his own film. In that film, *Drifters*, Grierson portrayed the fishermen of a boat in the North Sea herring fleet. No actors were used. At one stage both camera and cameramen were lashed to the wheelhouse. The result was a film which depicted the harshness of the work and the humanity of the fishermen with an unprecedented directness and honesty. *Drifters* was first screened in 1929 at the long-delayed (for censorship reasons) British premiere of *The Battleship Potemkin*. Although Grierson had studied *Potemkin* and in *Drifters* had adopted its techniques in picture composition and editing, the two films were seen to be in contrast. The Russian film was an exuberant expression of the spirit of the Soviet Revolution utilizing the large scale and peppered with poignant, if not heavy, symbolism. By 1929, even though this was a British premiere of *Potemkin*, this subject and approach seemed a little passé and somewhat irrelevant to the UK context. The placement of *Drifters* on the same programme intensified and clarified such feelings. Grierson's new film focussed on the ordinary. *Drifters* was the first and therefore a pioneering example of a British-based documentary movement. Grierson remarked, a decade

124 Tallents as quoted and paraphrased from Sir Stephen Tallents, unpublished chapter from Tallents' autobiography which was never completed. This chapter appeared in *Journal of the University Film Association* 20. 1 (1968) 16–19. – in Evans 29.

after the documentary movement was premiered by *Drifters*, that the movement resulted from "... a desire to make a drama from the ordinary to set against the prevailing drama of the extraordinary".[125] Grierson's innovative approach to his filmmaking in *Drifters* not only struck a sympathetic chord; it also gave rise to a new optimism for British film amongst filmmakers, critics and, as the film became more widely known, the public.

A little known yet revealing fact associated with *Drifters* concerns Grierson's initial selection of the subject matter for his filmmaking debut:

> The unpretentious subject of herrings was the tactical choice for the film that was to become *Drifters*, mainly because the financial secretary to the Treasury, Arthur Michael Samuel, had a mania for the subject and the Treasury was the biggest obstacle to overcome. Samuel had written a book, *The Herring: Its Effect on the History of Britain*, and it did not take much salesmanship to convince him to support a film on the herring industry. The Treasury allotted Grierson £2,500 to make his film.[126]

This episode reveals that Grierson knew which people had power and how that power could effect his ambitions; and, just as importantly, that Grierson knew how to achieve his ends with and through such people. He managed this through flattery (as in the above case), through the logic of argument, the force of his character and through any combination of these. In the ensuing years, first at the Empire Marketing Board, then notably at the GPO Film Unit and the National Film Board of Canada, Grierson was to put such powerful attributes to affective use.

In the meantime, in the aftermath of the success of *Drifters*, the Empire Marketing Board had established a Film Unit to which Grierson recruited young people whom he assessed as potential filmmakers and whom he proceeded to train and weld into an enthusiastic and energetic team. The recruits came from various backgrounds – academic, artistic, overseas and home grown. Most of the recruits had a common passion for film. The recruitment of Basil Wright – who was to make such films as *Song of Ceylon* (1934) and *Night Mail* (with Harry Watt, 1935) – was along very similar lines to Grierson's later recruitment of McLaren:

125 John Grierson as quoted in Evans 32.

126 Evans 31.

I was at Cambridge, you know. I took a degree in classics and economics. It had always been my intention to be the world's greatest poet, playwright, novelist. But while I was there I was suddenly exposed to the cinema. I decided that this was a new art. So I devoted myself to this idea, I got my family all combined together to buy me cinematographic apparatus for my twenty-first birthday, and I started to make experimental films. Grierson went to a festival of amateur films and saw one of mine; he then wrote offering me a job. It was as simple as that. He was then at the Empire Marketing Board; this was November 1929. It was just after the premier of *Drifters*. And *Drifters* became to me the type of film I really wanted to make. I was hunting about for Grierson to get an introduction to him when he suddenly wrote to me saying, "Will you come and have a chat with me?" And he gave me a job. Two pounds a week.[127]

The methods Grierson used to find and recruit McLaren and Wright are evidence that Grierson kept a sharp eye on the work shown at amateur film festivals. In that way Grierson found those people likely to be keenly interested in making films – why else had they gone to so much trouble to make a financially unrewarding film? By being at the festivals, Grierson was also able to assess the merits of the films made. Grierson did not always recruit in such a methodical way. Harry Watt, for example, tells of being out of work and, having secured an interview with his fellow-Scot on the grounds of being a distant relative, was in the process of boring Grierson with "the dreary sequence of lousy jobs I had been doing".[128] Suddenly Watt mentioned that he had been in a crew of five that sailed a schooner to Newfoundland. Grierson's interest was awakened and Watt recounted the whole schooner story. Watt's explanation of his subsequent offer of a job was that Grierson shared with him a passion for the sea. On the face of it, Watt's recruitment suggests that Grierson was sometimes prepared to take a gamble in staff selection. Even so, Grierson realized the risks were small. He knew the type of person he wanted at a particular time. In Watt's case, for example, he was able to assess such personal qualities as energy, intelligence, integrity and initiative, and his judgement of Watt's potential turned out to be accurate. Of course the names of the Grierson recruits who went on to

[127] Basil Wright as quoted in James Beveridge, *John Grierson: Film Master* (NY: Macmillan,1978) 63.

[128] Harry Watt as quoted in Beveridge 83.

Fig. 28. Basil Wright in
the 1930s.
[BFI]

do great things are often quoted in studies of Grierson.[129] However, since the number of people who dropped out of the Grierson's Film Units is not known, his success ratio cannot be exactly calculated. Be that as it may, it cannot be denied that he had a large number of successes.

To summarize, Grierson did adopt a number of strategies in order to obtain recruits of the highest possible calibre. Firstly, he scoured amateur film festivals for new, young filmmakers; secondly, he relied on his ability to quickly assess the potential recruits; thirdly, the option of dismissing or not re-employing a recruit who did not come up to potential was always available; and fourthly, the growing reputation of Grierson's Units attracted applicants who wished to be involved in films – in other words, increasingly applicants were self-selective.

By mid-1933 over thirty filmmakers were employed

at the Empire Marketing Board's Film Unit.[130] The Great Depression was, however, forcing cut-backs in government expenditure. In addition, there had been little progress in establishing an Empire free-trade bloc. The government, therefore, decided to disband the Empire Marketing Board on 30 September, 1933. Tallents was invited to transfer to the GPO. This invitation was accepted with the proviso that the Empire Marketing Board Film Unit and the Film Library transfer with him. The Empire Marketing Board Film Unit together with the Film Library thus moved intact to the GPO. The personnel remained the same, doing essentially the same job: "There wasn't any change in the purpose of the documentary group. We had to wear a different hat, but we were still going on with the same *use* of the film – you know, for sociological purposes. All that happened to us was that instead of selling the Empire, we were now selling the Post Office."[131]

While the commercial obligations were, as Wright puts it, to sell the Post Office, the much more powerful, unwritten objective was based on social improvement. Moreover, the particular concept of social improvement was largely Grierson's. Basil Wright recounted the situation:

> Grierson used to get very impatient with us, I mean my generation, Arthur Elton, Edgar Anstey and myself and various others around at the time, because we were interested in film art, and he said, "Okay, you're interested in film art. I'll do a bargain with you. You must get interested in social betterment." He never used the word revolution. I'm exaggerating a little here because all of us were left-wing in any case: but what he had to do was to get our minds off the glorious new technique of the Russian cinema and onto the fact that first of all we were civil servants and were responsible for spending public money, and secondly, that any new development in film aesthetic must be disciplined by the demands of the subject at hand; therefore the subject that one was dealing with must control the technique, or the experimental technique. We all came from different areas, from different points of view, and we were all interested in the creative possibilities of cinema. Grierson's great genius was to get this group of people to concentrate not just on the idea of social reform or social revolution, but on social reform through capitalism.[132]

130 Evans 33.

131 Basil Wright as quoted in Beveridge 69.

132 Basil Wright as quoted in G.Roy Levin, *Documentary Explorations: 15 Interviews with Film-Makers* (NY: Anchor, 1971) 37.

For Grierson, the term 'social betterment' carried educational overtones and was based on a liberal ideal of democracy, the goal of which was the improvement and participation of each individual, which in turn was achieved not just by the action of the individual but also through politics and the actions of the state. "[The Liberal] idea was to free men, politics, and the state from the antiquated practices of patronage and to pay homage verbally and in practice to moral improvement, moral effort, and rationality. The Liberal hope, expressed rationally, was that society as a whole might be improved. Moral improvement began with each individual."[133] Given these ideals and his background in examining the embryonic mass media of the USA, Grierson's view of his own place in the grand scheme is not surprising: "Grierson wanted to organize a movement to preach, spread, and maintain the democratic faith by inspiring the citizenry".[134] Moreover, "... the task was to be undertaken by speaking intimately and quietly about real things and real people, which in the end would prove more spectacular than the spectacle itself".[135]

Seeing Grierson's aims in these terms, it is difficult to understand why he was perceived as a closet socialist and therefore a threat to the establishment. Several factors, some of which have been broached, help explain why such a view of Grierson was held. Firstly, Grierson was a persuader and inspirer of people. In the course of these activities he used such techniques as exaggeration, confrontation and provocation. Statements made in such circumstances could be misconstrued if the context was not taken fully into account. Secondly, in the course of building and maintaining his Film Unit, Grierson made enemies.[136] Whether or not they believed Grierson was a socialist or even a communist, such people attempted to constrain Grierson's efforts. Thirdly, Grierson was guilty by association. Many of the men and women employed by Grierson were openly left-wing. It is an irony that many of them remember having to be cajoled from making films of aesthetic interest only into making films of social awareness. Many of Grierson's connections were also in the progressive mould. For instance, in March 1934 he made an appointment to go to Dartington Hall in Devon where an experiment in rural industry living was associated with a progressive school, the curriculum of which placed a heavy emphasis on the arts. The school was also one of the earliest to include filmmaking (under the direction of

133 Evans 40.
134 Evans 36.
135 Evans 36.
136 See Evans 46–47.

William Hunter) in its curriculum. No doubt it was in this connection that Grierson was invited to Dartington.[137] Fourthly, many of the films produced by Grierson's Units humanized the presentation of that largest sector of British society – the working class. Before Grierson's intervention, the filmic portrayal of the people of the working class was limited to minor stock comedy rôles. Grierson's elevation of the working class was therefore easily misunderstood; in class-ridden Britain, class warfare was the feature of socialism most readily identified by those in other echelons who feared loss of power and wealth, and the breakdown of social order.

A fifth reason for Grierson's identification with socialism was his unorthodox use of establishment institutions, both government and commercial, in producing films. Although Grierson ostensibly produced films to celebrate the aims and achievements of the sponsoring institution (EMB, GPO, Shell, Gas, etc.), such messages were often superficial. A theme central to many of the films was the work performed, romanticized as it often was, in the accomplishment of the relevant institution's various functions. To take an obvious example, *Night Mail* (Basil Wright, Harry Watt and Alberto Cavalcanti, 1935) celebrates the work necessary in getting the mail out. Grierson had to do a lot of talking to persuade the government officials or the commercial executives that such films did explain the workings or aims of their organizations and, more importantly, put their organizations in a good light. Thus Grierson often used his sponsors to convey social messages. It should be borne in mind, however, that the social context of these films was visually informative, rarely negative and never revolutionary. It is easier to see this in hindsight. At the time, the films were often astonishing revelations and the contemporary viewer could reasonably wonder what was to come in the next film.

It is therefore ironic that Grierson's use of government and non-government organizations in making films has been seen by critics from the left as evidence that not only was he no revolutionary but, worse, he was a pacifier – his films gave the (allegedly) false impression that social changes were taking place – and, worse still, he was an agent of the government and non-government establishment and furthered their interests.[138] The Empire Marketing Board's celebratory *Song of Ceylon* (Basil Wright, 1935) is criticized for totally ignoring the questions of economic exploitation

137 John Grierson. letter to L.K. Elmhirst, 12 February 1934. Dartington Hall Archives, Dartington, Eng.

138 Joyce Nelson, *The Colonized Eye: Rethinking the Grierson Legend* (Toronto: Between the Lines, 1988) 38–41.

of the colonies and colonial labour. As well, an attempt is
made to taint Grierson by association with multi-national
oil companies (Shell-Mex BP) that in turn had an executive
with Nazi sympathies.[139] These charges are extreme and
the so-called Nazi link is a smear. The *Song of Ceylon*
celebrates the island's culture – a rare enough event in those
Eurocentric days. It is not an examination of labour issues.

Grierson's general aim was democratic fulfilment
which he tried to foster from within the system. Some
caution was therefore necessary in the selection of film
subject matter. Nevertheless, there were repeated filmic
attempts to raise the consciousness of the public to social
issues. In fact, Grierson and his filmmakers were walking
a potential tight-rope. The political circumstances in which
Grierson's Units of the 1930s worked is graphically illustrated by one of those young directors, Harry Watt:

> We were always financed by the Establishment and
> the Establishment basically regretted that they'd
> started this thing. To start with we were left-wing to
> a man. Not many of us were communists, but we
> were all socialists and I'm sure we had dossiers be-
> cause we demonstrated and worked for the Spanish
> war. Grierson overtly never did. Now what he did
> behind the scenes – I knew nothing about his political
> beliefs. But we were on a razor's edge. ... It would
> have been utterly impossible, we'd have committed
> suicide, to have come out and made completely left-
> wing statements. As you know, in the EMB days, a
> detective was put in as a trainee editor, a man from
> the Special Branch. And we all knew who he was and
> we made his life such hell by going behind the cutting
> room door and saying, 'All right for tonight, Joe? Got
> the bomb? The job's on.' He twigged of course
> immediately that he'd been spotted. ... But there were
> always people until the late thirties who were wanting
> to shut us down and cut us off. We weren't permanent
> civil servants or anything like that. Our life was really
> precarious. ...[140]

The Grierson presence

The atmosphere within Grierson's Film Units, of enthusiasm and commitment to the idea of film and its possibilities, was due mainly to Grierson himself. He had, of course,
recruited people who were, on the whole, already strongly

139 Nelson 40.

140 Harry Watt as quoted
in Evans 47. Originally
quoted in Elizabeth
Sussex, "The Golden
Years of Grierson",
Sight and Sound 41.3
(Fall 1972): 149–153.

committed to the film medium. Nevertheless, Grierson continually strengthened, extended and channelled this commitment among his protégés. His presence was dominant. As a producer, he extracted maximum efforts from his filmmakers. Basil Wright described Grierson's prowess in this regard: "... his genius as a producer is to me quite extraordinary. I owe him practically everything I have in life, as a filmmaker, because of his ability to understand someone else's potentialities and drag them out of him without imposing his own ideas at all."[141] Wright gave a practical account of Grierson's powers of judgement and of his power to demand more.

> [Grierson was perceptive] in seeing rushes and [would say] "It's not good enough. Go back and do it again." He'd say, "You know perfectly well you could have shot that better". He didn't say how I should have shot it. He said, "Just look, you only have to look at that sequence – how's it going to cut? It's no good. Go back tomorrow and do it again." He'd do that on the telephone when you were five hundred miles away [on location]. And he was very tough. He was quite frightening. But it happened, and he was always right.[142]

The last comment stands as a measure of Grierson's perception and of the enduring respect he engendered among his young staff. Grierson's presence, however, extended through formal discussions and meetings to more informal gatherings. Grierson's Friday nights "... were the cultural institution of their time".[143] The words of the participants most vividly evoke the nature of these gatherings. Jacoby, an American at the GPO Film Unit, recalled that

> ... when you went to work for Grierson, Grierson really didn't have to give you the party line day and night. You heard him talk, you knew what it was all about, you osmosed the spirit of the place. These Friday nights that I mentioned had a lot to do with that. Because the crowd for that was always big. Everybody came to that. Directors, writers, cameramen, secretaries – everybody was welcome. And those nights went on long after the meetings. When the meetings broke up we went to the pubs as long as they were open, and then on to somebody's house to finish the evening.[144]

141 Wright as quoted in Levin 38.

142 Wright as quoted in Levin 38–39.

143 Jacoby as quoted in Beveridge 91.

144 Jacoby as quoted in Beveridge 93.

Basil Wright is also eloquent on the matter:

... in those pubs were Robert Flaherty, and Grierson, and Cavalcanti and anybody who happened to be in London concerned with films, talking like mad. And we little boys, the ones who were learning to make our little films, we were there. If you weren't on location, you were there in the evening, arguing and arguing, talking and talking, and Grierson was marvellous there too, for he would put on a different attitude. Still be quite tough, but then he would talk much more freely and without the sense of discipline which he had to keep and always kept in the more formal matters, you know, seeing rushes, or looking at rough cuts ... .[145]

Wright also spoke of the absorption of the atmosphere and consequently the prevalent attitudes of the Grierson Film Units by those working within them, particularly the younger members.

Of course there were others such as trainee cameramen, editors, young people coming up who subsequently became famous and so on, but who were all still being influenced by this attitude, this atmosphere, this ambience, in which we all lived.[146]

McLaren's work for the GPO Film Unit

One of the young people to absorb the Grierson spirit, the ambience, was, of course, Norman McLaren. His left-wing credentials were brightly polished, even more so after his leave to go to Spain to act as Montagu's cameraman for the pro-Republican *Defence of Madrid*. McLaren experienced no difficulty in fitting in with the ethos and aspirations prevalent at the GPO Film Unit. Although his views were then more radical than those current at the Unit – he was, after all, still a member of the Communist Party at that time – he found himself sharing the views of his colleagues concerning the nature of the problems faced by society. His earlier, aborted film focussing on the squalor of British slums is even paralleled by a landmark GPO Film Unit production *Housing Problems* (Arthur Elton and Edgar Anstey, 1935).

At the GPO Film Unit, however, McLaren was content to concentrate on learning his discipline. This was just as well, for the films he was entrusted to make were not

145 Wright as quoted in Levin 38.

146 Wright as quoted in Levin 40.

intended to be grand social statements. Indeed, on his
return from Spain, McLaren was dispatched to the cutting-
room as an assistant editor to Evelyn Spice (later Cherry)
– a Canadian filmmaker who later would make films at the
National Film Board of Canada. McLaren says he spent
about four months working as Spice's assistant.[147] It was
about the spring of 1937, therefore, when McLaren was
told by Alberto Cavalcanti that a film about the London
telephone directory was wanted and that McLaren was
thought to be the person to make it. Cavalcanti was one of
the senior men at the Unit. He was a rarity in that he had
an established film career (in France) before he joined the
Unit. He was also a specialist in film sound. Calvacanti was
appointed as McLaren's producer, which presented the
young Scot with the rare and therefore all the more valuable
opportunity to learn from someone with extensive practical
filmmaking experience.

McLaren was keen to make the most of his chance,
so when Calvacanti told him to take a few weeks to research
the topic and come up with a draft script, the young
filmmaker was diligent in the extreme. "I spent most of my
time in the British Museum studying the history of the
London telephone directory. Anyway, I produced a draft
script about the history, with a lot of little pencilled drawings of this scene and the next scene and the next scene."[148]
As McLaren said elsewhere, "It was full of little sketches,
pictures and detailed instructions – you pan from here to
here and so on".[149] McLaren continued, "It was very elaborate and very detailed with sketches, which is a thing I'd
never done in my own filmmaking. I'd seldom made
sketches as an amateur, I'd just gone ahead and shot".[150]

McLaren was in for quite a shock, judging from
separate and distinct accounts in different contexts. In these
accounts McLaren was verbalizing from the single mental
image – e.g. in one account he used the term "paralyse your
imagination" while in the other the phrase was "freeze your
imagination".[151] The image, therefore, was deeply seared
in McLaren's mind. The event which created that image
was memorable in a traumatic sense.

So Cavalcanti took a look at it, immediately tore it
up, flung it in the wastepaper basket, and said, "That's
not the way to make a film, you shouldn't make
sketches ever, because if you have a preconceived idea
of what the shot is going to look like you freeze your
imagination when you come to shoot. Actual living

147 McLaren as quoted in
Beveridge 81.

148 McLaren as quoted in
Beveridge 81.

149 McLaren as quoted in
Maynard Collins,
Norman McLaren
(Ottawa: Canadian
Film Institute, 1976)
66.

150 McLaren as quoted in
Beveridge 81.

151 McLaren used the
"freeze your
imagination" phrase
amid recounting his
Grierson connections
and experiences
(Beveridge, 81)
and the "paralyse your
imagination" was used
in connection with
his own filmic
development
(Collins, 66).

Fig. 29. Norman McLaren at the GPO Film Unit editing Book Bargain. *[NFB.]*

material in front of you will be much richer than your imagination, and you can make your decision when you are in front of the material with a camera or a viewfinder." Then he said, "Go down into the factory that makes the London telephone directory, and see what you can do there". Well, I went down and spent two days there, came back, and said, "I can make a film of that without a script, just a few notes". So I did this.[152]

Cavalcanti's teaching methods were spectacular and extreme. They were also sincere. More importantly for McLaren the lesson was a valuable one which suited his approach to film, and one that, according to the above reminiscence, he had already established prior to his GPO work. McLaren thus resumed his open-ended planning approach for pragmatic reasons. Shortly, he was also to find an intellectual justification for such an approach. In the meantime, he continued to learn the skills involved in mastering his discipline, and to experiment.

Cavalcanti's teaching methods were spectacular and extreme. They were also sincere. More importantly for McLaren the lesson was a valuable one which suited his approach to film, and one that, according to the above

[152] McLaren as quoted in Beveridge 81.

Fig. 30. Alberto
Cavalcanti around the
time Norman McLaren
worked with him.
[BFI.]

reminiscence, he had already established prior to his GPO work. McLaren thus resumed his open-ended planning approach for pragmatic reasons. Shortly, he was also to find an intellectual justification for such an approach. In the meantime, he continued to learn the skills involved in mastering his discipline, and to experiment.

McLaren's experimental work of these years is not apparent in the first three films he made for the GPO Film Unit. The first film *Book Bargain* was released in 1938 and is in all respects a straightforward treatment of the production of the London telephone directory. The film's main claim to attention is the incident described above. Although McLaren's meticulous preparation was torn up and thrown out, the rejection did have another positive feature. By confirming McLaren's previously usual open-ended approach, Calvacanti was in effect giving the young man's confidence a boost. Considering McLaren's circumscribed output during his first few years at the GPO Film Unit, this was a desirable effect. From the point of view of an idealistic young man with innovative filmic ideas and who

153 Norman McLaren,
*Animated Sound on
Film*, (Montreal:
National Film Board
of Canada, 1950): rpt.
in Robert Russett and
Cecile Starr,
*Experimental Animation:
Origins of a New Art*
rev. ed. (NY: Da Capo,
1976) 167. A fuller
version "Notes on
Animated Sound",
appears in Roger
Manvell and John
Huntley, eds.,*The
Technique of Film Music*
(London: Focal P,
1957 [rev. ed. 1975]),
where the source is
named as *Hollywood
Quarterly* 8.3 (1953).
McLaren's annotated
version: "Animated
Sound in Film",
appears in *New
Developments in Still and
Motion Picture
Production Techniques*
vol. 1, No. 6 (Ottawa:
Division of Technical
Operations, National
Film Board of Canada,
December 1953) 1–6.
An earlier brief
account "Animated
Sound on Film", was
issued by the New
York Office of the
National Film Board
(22 December 1948),
to accompany
*Workshop Experiments in
Animated Sound* in
which McLaren
considered his initial
sound tests. Although
the author of that
paper was not
acknowledged it is
likely to have been
McLaren. He would
certainly have been the
source for the
information. The
structure of the paper
is similar to the later
lengthy account.

was keen to see the world's economic and social structure change, his first professional film was a failure. *Book Bargain* contained nothing that supplied any reason for social or economic reform, other than a tenuous association with keeping up-to-date, for the film did show what a marvel technology was. The subject of the film had been imposed on McLaren. There was little he could do about that. He could, however, attempt to incorporate some filmic innovation into *Book Bargain*.

The innovation McLaren proposed to his producer, Calvacanti, reveals that even at this early stage of his career his film experiments encompassed extraordinary aspects of the medium. In this case, McLaren had been working on the sound-track of the film stock. A film's sound-track consists of a series of shapes which as they pass through a movie projector are converted, by means of a photo-electric cell, into electric signals which in turn are converted into sounds. Normally, the live sounds that are to be used in the film are recorded. They are then converted to electrical signals which in turn are converted to the visual shapes that appear on the sound-track. In Russia and in Germany, work had been done in circumventing this process in which the visual configurations on the sound-track were obtained through recording live sounds. The visual nature of the sound-track had inspired the logical step of creating the sound-track not by recording but by drawing or painting shapes and then photographing these shapes onto the sound-track. The shapes were carefully formed and systematized so that the resulting sounds could be predicted. A.M. Avzaamov, the inventor of one of the systems, intended to free his music "... from the restrictions of the twelve-tone tempered scale", and to create "... new tonal systems assimilating many of the scales of the traditional folk music of the Eastern and Southern Republics [of the USSR] ...".[153] Usually however, those that photographed their images onto the sound-track used their resulting sounds to construct versions of traditional music. N. Voinov made versions of Rachmaninoff's *Prelude in C Sharp Minor* and Schubert's *Moment Musical*. Rudolph Pfenninger made a version of Handel's *Largo*.

The aim of the Russians, Voinov, his successors E.A. Scholpo and G.M. Rimski-Korsakov, and of Pfenninger in Germany, was to create pure and controlled notes enabling them to recreate traditional forms of music. Although the work in Germany and Russia was done independently and in ignorance of the work being done in the other nation, the filmmakers in each country worked towards similar goals and devised similar systems. Pfenninger produced a card system. On each card was a drawing which, when photographed onto the sound-track, created a single pitch. His library of cards gave him a range of sounds graded in semitones. Voinov also had a system of cards graded in semitones. The range exceeded seven octaves of the twelve-tone, equally tempered chromatic scale. Scholpo and Rim-ski-Korsakov used oscilloscope-derived images to build up their system of sounds. However, the Voinov system proved to be a practical one to use and as such it was a forerunner of work McLaren himself was to pursue some years hence; that is, after World War II.

Other experiments aimed at finding alternative means of providing the visual imagery for the sound-track fall into a different category. Avzaamov in the USSR and in Germany – again independently – the Fischinger brothers, Oskar and Hans, were working on projects with a shifted emphasis. Avzaamov's work and the interesting experiments of the Fischingers gave some primacy to the visual origins of the sound-track. Rather than seeking shapes which produced preconceived sounds, these experiments used instead a preconceived visual pattern of simple geometric shapes. These shapes produced sounds with new tone qualities.[154] In their experiments, the Fischingers went on to create further visual shapes that had the object of exploring further sound possibilities; that is, finding unusual or amusical sounds.[155] Lazlo Moholy-Nagy used an even more unexpected source for the sound-tracks he constructed in the late 1920s. He used not only geometric signs but also letters of the alphabet, fingerprints and human profiles.[156] The sounds produced would have been strongly aleatoric. Moholy-Nagy went on to use the same imagery for the visual component of his film; this startling notion will be closely examined in the chapter concerning McLaren's film which uses that approach; *Synchromy*.[157] Although each of those European sound pioneers had also succeeded in circumventing one of film's technical processes – that of recording – Maholy-Nagy's work on the film sound-track differs in one significant respect. Those other systems involved photographing the visual constructions onto the sound-track whereas in his experiments Moholy-Nagy drew, painted or printed the images (of letters, geometric signs, drawn profiles and fingerprints) directly onto

154 McLaren, "Animated Sound on Film" in Russett and Starr167.

155 Robert Russett, "Experiments in Animated Sound", Russett and Starr 164.

156 L. Moholy-Nagy, "Problems of the Modern Film (1928–30)", *Moholy-Nagy*, ed. Richard Kostalanetz (London: Allen Lane, 1971) 136–137.

157 Russett 163.

the sound-track. In 1933 he made a film which applied his experiments. It was called, appropriately considering his imagery, *The Sound ABC*.

The technique of hand-drawn sound not only by-passes a process. More importantly, it also generates greater freedom to explore and develop sounds never before heard since the visual configurations are not necessarily prede-termined. As well, hand-drawn sounds have greater irregu-larities, and therefore distinctive sounds, than images derived from either recording or visual geometry. Jack Ellitt, an Australian musician working in London, had been coincidentally working in 1933, the year McLaren made his first film, along Pfenninger's lines when he switched his approach and began drawing sound directly on the celluloid without the use of a camera.[158] In 1937 Norman McLaren also began experimenting with producing film sound by drawing directly on the sound-track. At this point, the usual questions associated with 'who did what first?' arise. Did Ellitt know of Moholy-Nagy's writings? Did Ellitt draw sound directly on film before seeing Moholy-Nagy's film? Did McLaren know of Moholy-Nagy's work? Did McLaren know of Ellitt's work? Fortunately, the ques-tions most pertinent to this study can be answered through an examination of relative dates and by considering McLaren's various recollections.

The photographed-on animated sound system had a wide currency due to Pfenninger's work. The German had in the early 1930s made a film which clearly demonstrated his method of making animated sound. McLaren saw this film early on. "When I was a student in Glasgow, the film society showed the latest experimental films from Europe. Amongst them was a film called *Tonal Handwriting* [*Tönende Handschrift*] made by a German engineer from Munich – Rudolf Phenninger [sic]. He had evolved a system [of photographing cards onto the sound-track to obtain musi-cal sounds]."[159] It was to be at least a decade, however, before McLaren followed up with work of his own on this particular system of animated sound. In 1937 it was the technique of drawn-on animated sound that figured in McLaren's endeavours.

One would have expected that in initiating his drawn-on animated sound experiments McLaren derived ideas from Moholy-Nagy, whose thoughts about animated sound had circulated in Europe[160] and who had moved to London in 1935, staying for two years and associating

158 McLaren, "Animated Sound on Film" in Russett and Starr 168.

159 McLaren in "Interview", Collins 73–74.

160 McLaren "Animated Sound in Film", (annotated, 1953) 1.

himself with, among other cultural circles, Grierson's GPO Film Unit.[161] Equally, Ellitt could be expected to be a font for McLaren's ideas since the Australian was working alongside Len Lye helping to make the Lye films under the auspices of the GPO Film Unit. A third expected source for the drawn-on sound technique could have been McLaren's own work in drawing on the picture area of the film stock. It could have been this same concept that inspired its re-application to the sound-track area of the film stock. In fact, none of these three plausible accounts are accurate.

The discovery of drawn-on animated sound is another instance of independent and almost simultaneous realization of a new technique that had occurred, for example, when Len Lye and Norman McLaren each spontaneously and in ignorance of the other's work, drew and painted directly onto the picture area of film. Jack Ellitt is acknowledged, by McLaren, to have in "... 1933 pioneered in drawing sound directly on the celluloid without the use of camera".[162] Thus McLaren discounts himself as having given Ellitt the idea. Although Ellitt's work predates McLaren's and was conducted within the ambit of the GPO Film Unit, McLaren's recollections indicate that he was unaware of it. Two facts help explain McLaren's then ignorance of Ellitt's pioneering work. First, Ellitt's work as music editor on Len Lye's films at the Film Unit did not result in films with animated sound. Even those Lye films that used predominantly or entirely hand-drawn visual images – *Colour Box* (1935), *Kaleidoscope* (1935), and *Rainbow Dance* (1936) – did not incorporate hand-drawn sound. Thus Ellitt's work on animated sound was not as widespread or prominent as the Lye association suggests. Second, as McLaren himself said "... I did not in fact work in close proximity to Len Lye when at the GPO Film Unit".[163] By extension, neither did McLaren work in close proximity to Ellitt who was in Lye's circle. Harking back to Moholy-Nagy's stay in London and association with the GPO Film Unit, a similar disconnection with McLaren can be made. In London, Moholy-Nagy moved in the Herbert Read, Ben Nicholson, Henry Moore group. Lye was also associated with this group. The implication is that Moholy-Nagy's association at the Film Unit was with Lye and his group. On closer examination, therefore, McLaren's account of his separate development of the drawn-on animated sound technique is credible.

161 Richard Kostelanetz ed., *Mohloy-Nagy* (London: Allen Lane, 1970) xvii.

162 McLaren, "Animated Sound on Film" (annotated, 1953) 2.

163 McLaren as quoted in Cecile Starr, "Norman McLaren and the National Film Board of Canada", Russett and Starr 117.

In his account, McLaren modestly describes the events that led to his drawn-on sound experiments:

> Before the war, at the GPO Film Unit, I was running some blank film on the sound head of the moviola. I had a knife and just sort of tapped it [the film], played it back and it made a scratchy noise ... I played it and realized that you could get different kinds of sounds, very primitive and limited, but still ... I started playing around with this.[164]

An exclusive emphasis on an order of primacy is undesirable. Identifying the originator of an idea or technique helps identify a person of originality, who makes a great contribution to his or her field of endeavour. This test of primacy, however, is not the only means of identifying such people, although since it has a clear-cut standard of measurement, it is the most usual. As there is a less-than-perfect correlation between being on the one hand an originator and on the other being a worthwhile user or exploiter of the new idea or technique, it is advisable to examine how a development was used and by whom.

Evaluating Ellitt's work in experimenting with hand-drawn sound is made difficult by a lack of availability of those experiments. It has already been noted that none of the Lye films on which Ellitt worked as a music editor feature hand-drawn sounds. McLaren's own drawn-sound work from this period has not survived, although his recollections of the context of the experiments and his subsequent work give some idea of the nature of the sound experiments he conducted. The first experiments concentrated on rhythm:

> My first conception was that a sound track is full, you've got to fill it up. Then I realized when you left a space, you got a much better effect, you got a musical sound. So I did a sound track for the film *Book Bargain* because it was full of scenes of panning along machinery, close-ups of machines, and complicated machinery. An arm would come up, something would go "bump ... bup ... bup ..." and pan along to some other kind of operation. I worked out rhythms for those machines and it fitted very nicely. I sort of actually mixed. I did a series of loops then mixed one loop to the other with the panning shots. Then [eventually] I got the complete sound track for the film.[165]

164 McLaren as quoted in "Interview" in Collins 73.

165 McLaren as quoted in "Interview", Collins 73.

Unfortunately, conclusive evidence in the form of the sounds themselves is no longer available, but from the above it is clear that the sounds were rhythmic, probably with little variation in pitch or timbre. The sounds were associated with machinery and it has been suggested that they had a harsh quality.[166]

> ... Cavalcanti my producer, said "We can't use it. It competes too much, because we have to have a commentary on the film." And I said, "How about playing it low?" But he felt it would still compete.[167]

McLaren was in no position to argue. His was the position of an apprentice. Moreover Cavalcanti, his producer, was an expert on film sound – a fact which must have been initially encouraging for McLaren when he began his sound experiments for the film. The released form of *Book Bargain* shows no hint of McLaren's experimentation. It is a competent explanation of the book production process.

McLaren's next film, *News for the Navy* (1937–38), displays the same characteristics. Like his previous film, this film is an explanatory one, and uses narration. McLaren was continuing to learn the film craft. Discipline was being knocked into him.

This particular pill was somewhat sweetened by a project that McLaren worked on at the same time. The film concerned was a composite of several directors' contributions. McLaren had a two-minute segment and in that section provided the visual highlight of the film, *Mony a Pickle* (1937–38). The film extols the benefits of saving with the Post Office Savings Bank. A young couple begin to envisage what they could do with £1,000. At this juncture McLaren's fancy and fantasy take over. Using just one of the many techniques he had used earlier in *Camera Makes Whoopee*, furniture and other household objects are animated. As McLaren acknowledges, the principle of stop frame animation goes back to the early French movies of the Méliès epoch.[168] Méliès, and others since him, made people and objects disappear and reappear by stopping the camera in mid-shot and removing or replacing the said people or objects before resuming the shot. As in *Camera Makes Whoopee*, McLaren takes this process further. The objects not only disappear and appear suddenly (pop-offs and pop-ons) and slowly (mix-ins, mix-outs) but also move, apparently of their own volition. The objects were

166 Collins 25.

167 McLaren as quoted in "Interview", Collins 73.

168 Norman McLaren, *Some Notes on Stop-Motion Live-Action Technique as used in the visuals of "Neighbours" (1952) and "Two Bagatelles" (1952)* (Ottawa: National Film Board of Canada, 1952) 1.

moved little by little between a succession of single-frame shots so that when the resulting film is projected the illusion of the object's independent movement occurs. Piece by piece the young couple's room is transformed as old furniture and other items first disappear and are then replaced as new items appear which in turn magically move into new positions.

The exploration of just one technique, that of stop-frame animation, and its application to a limited set of objects, according to the theme of the film, contributes to the coherence and strength of McLaren's segment of the film. Although this fact was far from lost on McLaren, another major influence on his thought and work was occurring at around this time.

Surrealism

In 1937 McLaren became aware of surrealism. The process of his enlightenment is another case which belies the artistic context within which he found himself in London and the GPO Film Unit.

London's initiation into surrealism occurred when the International Surrealist Exhibition was held at the New Burlington Galleries between 11 June and 4 July 1936. The leading surrealists exhibited as did their till-then-isolated British counterparts. The exhibition was a remarkable one and the cause of notoriety beyond artistic circles.

> On the evening of the private view the guests were joined by a 'woman with a head of flowers', whose head was entirely hidden in a bouquet of roses. Salvador Dali turned up to lecture wearing a diving suit and holding two white greyhounds on a leash.[169]

The exhibition and the events associated with it may have brought surrealism to the surface of public consciousness, but, judging from his complete lack of comment on the matter, McLaren was, at the time at least, unaware of these incidents and of the Exhibition. When it is considered that two members of the GPO Film Unit exhibited works at the London International Surrealist Exhibition, McLaren's unawareness becomes, at first glance, even more puzzling. The two Film Unit members were actively involved within the British surrealist circle which consisted of such luminaries as Paul Nash, Herbert Read, Henry Moore and Roland Penrose – and with these people and sixteen others, were the co-signatories to the International

169 Surane Alexandrian, *Surrealist Art*, trans. Gordon Clough (London: Thames & Hudson, 1970) 138.

Surrealist Bulletin issued in Hampstead, London on 7 July 1936 after the close of the exhibition.[170]

These two GPO filmmakers however, were each somewhat distant from McLaren. One of them was Len Lye and the other was Humphrey Jennings. McLaren's own acknowledgement of his distance from Lye has already been noted, and Jennings was a professional as well as artistic associate of Lye – in fact Jennings' filmmaking career, which was in live-action cinema, began at the GPO Film Unit at this time when he collaborated with Lye on the latter's *Birth of the Robot*.

One reason for McLaren's unexpected ignorance of surrealism is associated with geography. At the time of the London exhibition, that is in the summer of 1936, McLaren was still an art student based in Glasgow. He was working furiously on his own film projects of *Homes v. Health* and *Hell UnLtd*. The previous year he had gone on an artistic reconnaissance to the USSR. In 1936, his final year at art school and Glasgow, his energy was more directly focussed on those activities of his vocation – filmmaking. Even when he did arrive, in the October of 1936, for work at the GPO Film Unit in London, he was dispatched almost immediately to the Spanish Civil War to be a cameraman for Montagu's pro-Republican film. This synopsis of McLaren's activities makes it clear that for much of 1936 he was geographically remote from London. Further, it also demonstrates that, in 1936, McLaren's activities, filmic and otherwise, revolved around his political convictions, which in turn centred upon reforming the social and economic systems of the day. Such activities as those enacted by Dali were not in themselves conducive to affect a young man keen on social reform.

What brought McLaren to surrealism was an English translation of the writings of André Breton, published in 1936 by Faber and Faber: *What Is Surrealism?* Those seeking an answer to the question which comprises the title would be attracted to the similarly named article within the book. A person predisposed to communist ideals would at once be captured, if not inspired, by Breton's language of revolution and his call for a radical transformation of the world. The first paragraph reads:

Comrades:

The activity of our surrealist comrades in Belgium is closely allied with our own activity, and I am happy

170 André Breton, *What is Surrealism?: Selected Writings*, ed., Franklin Rosemont (London: Pluto Press, 1978) 336. Among Len Lye's close-knit circle of friends Humphrey Jennings, Henry Moore and Ruthven Todd were signatories at Hampstead. Wystan Curnow and Roger Horrocks, *Figures of Motion: Len Lye/Selected Writings* (Auckland: Auckland Univ. P., 1984) xiii.

to be in their company this evening. Magritte, Mesens, Nougé, Scutenaire and Souris are among those whose revolutionary will – outside of all their consideration of their agreement or disagreement with us on particular points – has been for us in Paris a constant reason for thinking that the surrealist project, beyond the limitations of space and time, can contribute to the efficacious reunification of all those *who do not despair of the transformation of the world and who wish this transformation to be as radical as possible.*[171]

The first part of the article goes on to give a stirring social history of late nineteenth and early twentieth century Europe. Breton warns of the peril of what he calls the disease of fascism, which, as McLaren was only too aware after his first-hand experiences in Spain, had "... advanced greatly over Europe recently".[172] Particularly poignant for someone such as McLaren, who had come to communism after witnessing the plight of miners and their families back home in Stirling, is the passage in which Breton confronts the poverty and powerlessness of the miners.

On the same page was another photograph – this one of the unemployed of your country [Belgium] standing in front of a hovel in the Parisian 'poor zone' – with the caption *Poverty is not a crime.* 'How delightful!' I said to myself, glancing from one picture to the other. Thus the bourgeois public in France is able to console itself with the knowledge that the miners of your country were not necessarily criminals just because they got themselves killed for 35 francs a day. And doubtless the miners, our comrades, will be happy to learn that the committee of the Belgian Coal association intends to postpone till the day after tomorrow the application of the wage cut set for 20 May. In capitalist society, hypocrisy and cynicism have now lost all sense of proportion and are becoming more outrageous every day.[173]

As if this were not enough of an appeal, Breton merges the interests of capital with those of fascism when he asks "Is not the evident role of fascism to re-establish for the time being the tottering supremacy of finance capital?"[174] It is not difficult to imagine the maker of *Hell UnLtd*, with its depiction of a domination of political events by capitalist armaments companies, the cameraman who had seen the

171 Breton 112.
172 Breton 114.
173 Breton 114.
174 Breton 115.

effects of fascist guns and bombs in Spain, answering an emphatic "Yes!" to Breton's question.

Having gained the sympathy of left-wing readers Breton moved on to discuss surrealism itself. The link between the politics being espoused and surrealism was neatly encapsulated by Breton: "... today, more than ever, the *liberation of the mind*, the express aim of surrealism, demands as a primary condition, in the opinion of the surrealists, the *liberation of man*", which would be achieved by the proletarian revolution.[175] Breton ignored the possibility that systems other than the one he espoused could liberate. He also ignored the possibility that liberating the mind did not necessarily entail freeing (however that may be defined) humanity first. Many of Breton's fellow surrealists disagreed with his political stance and left his group.

Be that as it may, McLaren read Breton's book, found much with which he agreed, and extracted from it those features of surrealism that accorded with his view. One view of Breton's that is at odds with McLaren's concerns music. McLaren, it has been noted, loved music. Breton, however, found musical imagery too imprecise and confusing:

> Auditive images, in fact, are inferior to visual images not only in clearness but also in strictness, and with all due respect to a few melomaniacs, they hardly seem intended to strengthen in any way the idea of human greatness. So may night continue to fall upon the orchestra, and may I who am still searching for something in this world, may I be left with open or closed eyes, in broad daylight, to my silent contemplation.[176]

It would seem Breton did not have musical experiences like the synaesthetic ones of McLaren. Even if he had, their abstract, i.e. non-objective, nature would have entailed that he would have found these images similarly imprecise. Breton saw the real and subconscious realms in terms of the real world. Surrealist painters, on the whole, did not paint totally non-objective paintings. And as an art form, musical composition was noticeable by its absence from surrealism's fold.

The surrealists' antipathy towards total abstraction is in accord with McLaren's persistent reluctance to completely forgo representational imagery even in his otherwise frameless, directly painted films such as *Fiddle-de-dee*

175 Breton 115.

176 André Breton, "Surrealism in Painting", in *Theories of Modern Art: A Source Book by Artists and Critics*, ed.Herschel B. Chipp (Berkeley: University of California, 1971) 403. English trans. David Gasgoine in André Breton *What is Surrealism?* (London: Faber, 1936) 9–24.

(1947) where a butterfly-like object can be seen moving across the dancing abstract forms, or *Begone Dull Care* (1949), where single frame images of, for example, towers or trees may be discerned. As well, even the totally abstract imagery of films like *Dots* (1940) and *Loops* (1940) moves in an anthropomorphic manner as do the numbers in *Rythmetic* (1956). McLaren also suggested that perceived gravitational forces accounted for the different effects of the otherwise similar abstract films of *Lines Horizontal* (1961) and *Lines Vertical* (1960). McLaren, however, did not see this 'subversion' or 'compromising dilution' by inserting concrete images into his otherwise abstract imagery as anything more than an embellishment and/or aid to viewers who could not understand totally abstract imagery.[177] The anthropomorphic movements of abstract imagery as well as the perceived effects of gravity on abstract imagery are explained not by any dogmatically-held surrealist convictions but by McLaren's kinesthetic empathy with his films. This in turn is partly a consequence of his love of dance. McLaren's use of surrealist ideas, therefore, is demonstrably selective. Not only did McLaren use abstract visual imagery in his films, but the abstract art of music played a major conceptual role in his filmic career.

In view of the importance of surrealism to McLaren, the question arises: What did McLaren adopt from surrealists' philosophy and practice?

Back in his art school days McLaren was impressed by the montage in the films by the Russians Pudovkin and Eisenstein. The impact "... was due to juxtaposition by cutting – and viewpoint and angle – but essentially cutting. Cutting from one thing to another is rather similar to the mental process of human beings. Your mind is able to jump, instantly, from sitting here to something say fifteen years ago in your life, or what happened ten minutes ago. It's instantaneous."[178] McLaren's statement reveals his impression of the working of the mind. It also reveals that understanding and using the mind's working process can form the basis of an exciting and important means of expression. Sentences in Breton's definition of surrealism contained in the *What is Surrealism* book read by McLaren are pertinent to these observations and concerns of McLaren.

The dictation of thought in the absence of all control exercised by reasons and outside all aesthetic or moral preoccupations ... Surrealism rests in the belief in the

177 McLaren as quoted in "Interview", Scottish Arts Council 26.

178 McLaren as quoted in *Creative Process*, script 2.

superior reality of certain forms of association neglected heretofore; in the omnipotence of the dream
and in the disinterested play of thought.[179]

At this point McLaren found common ground. Since
returning from Spain, where he had witnessed horrible
scenes from the war, McLaren was disturbed by nightmares. The surrealists and their ideas not only enabled the
drawing of a parallel between dreams with that internal
logic of illogicality and works of art such as those produced
by the Russians, they also provided a theoretical framework
which justified such works as manifestations of the super-
reality. This did not escape McLaren. Looking back on the
techniques of the Russian filmmakers it is evident that the
logic of the dream had been legitimized for him: "It's
instantaneous. A sudden juxtaposition of two things very
different from each other, as in a dream. Its spirit is able to
jump around with an extreme rapidity in spite of the laws
of logic."[180] The filmic evidence of McLaren's adoption of
a surrealist flow of ideas is expressed in abundance in his
next film. Before this film is discussed, however, there
remain other aspects of his affinity with surrealism to be
examined.

The next aspect is in fact so closely related to surrealism and McLaren's notions of the workings of the mind
that the topic has already been broached. It has been noted
that the surrealist view of dreams and fantasy as important
aspects of an individual's total reality struck a sympathetic
chord in McLaren. Such ideas not only legitimized his
filmic exploration of the realm of fantasy but provided him
with the awareness that he would not be working in an
artistic vacuum. He was free to combine numerous and
various permutations of logic and illogicality characteristic
of fantasy and dream. Within some structure, or logical
framework, there may be several illogicalities, environ-
mental (or spatial) illogicalities or illogically placed objects
or figures. Any or all of these elements may be switched
from 'logical' to 'illogical', including the structure.
McLaren's first foray into such an area is to be discussed
shortly; however a further point needs to be made. Although McLaren experienced nightmares after returning
from Spain and suffered personal anguish over various
social issues – and particularly war – his films from 1937
onwards tend to ignore this darker side. They are, on the
whole, about dreams rather than nightmares. Such broad

179 Breton *What is
Surrealism?* 122.

180 McLaren as quoted in
Donald McWilliams
and Susan Huycke,
*Creative Process: Norman
McLaren,* dir Donald
McWilliams, National
Film Board of Canada,
1991, script 2.

statements are of necessity qualified. The topic is not a simple one and is deserving of a more detailed examination, which is offered in chapter eight.

As a further consequence of his exposure to the ideas of surrealism and therefore also of Freud, McLaren took a particular stance concerning talking or writing about his work. For surrealists the subconscious was the repository of the imagination, or at least the source of unfettered expression.[181] Imagination was released by forgoing overt or conscious control of expression. Breton called his method automatism. In the eyes of an adherent to surrealist ideas, a danger existed in talking or theorizing about the making of a past or present work of art, or about the meanings contained in it, or about the plans for future works, because such intellectualizing would bring these thoughts to the surface, into conscious reality. Thus the artistic process itself would be threatened with the possibility of creative death. Surrealism provided McLaren with the justification to refrain from detailed theorizing about his work as a whole and detailed analysis of much of his output.

Many visual artists have adhered to the philosophy that the work of art should be the sufficient and full means of communication and that literary elaborations on the work were not only unnecessary but also unlikely to be revealing of the work due to the intrinsic difference of the media. This attitude is encapsulated in the following: If what has been expressed visually could also be expressed in words, why bother with the visual expression? Oskar Fischinger, one of McLaren's mentors, was reluctant to put his filmic ideas and statements into words, and even wrote an article called "My Statements are in My Work".[182] McLaren was concerned about the possibility of words foreclosing or limiting both the meaning in and the experience of his films. Thus, on the rare occasion of a detailed explanation of a work, significantly not a film, McLaren finishes the piece-by-piece analysis with a statement that immediately shifts the account from the definitive category to the category which contains many alternative explanations: "I don't know. These are just random interpretations of the things I doodle."[183] By using the words 'random' and 'doodle' McLaren also belittles both his interpretation and his work (and thereby doubly belittles the interpretation). Through his later work at the National Film Board of Canada, McLaren received many requests about his films.

181 Breton "What is Surrealism?" 137.

182 Oskar Fischinger "My Statements are in My Work", *Art in Cinema: a synopsis on the avant-garde film* ed. Frank Stauffacher (1947, rpt. NY: Arno P, 1968) 38–40.

183 McLaren as quoted in *Creative Process,* script 20.

Whether these requests were for analytical explanations or for technical help, his response was invariably generous, but within strict parameters. McLaren as much as possible interpreted the questions as requests for technical information, and by the time he retired in 1984 he had built up a formidable collection of technical notes on each of his films, pertinent copies of which could be dispatched in response to those frequent entreaties.

Surrealism was to have a further implication for McLaren's working methods. His own words reveal his thinking: "So, the subconscious plays a very important role. It perhaps has the whole thing pretty well formed from start to finish. It's a matter of the consciousness not knowing that form but creating it and getting uncomfortable, nervous and neurotic even if it's going wrong."[184] The lack of a conscious plan for an entire project entailed concentrating on the immediate. In describing working on an animated film, moving from frame to frame, McLaren said:

> I wasn't aware of the general line of what was going to happen ten, twenty seconds from now. I was always aware of how things were developing: this is going to happen in the next five seconds. But a minute from now in the film, what's going to be happening I just don't know.[185]

McLaren had previously preferred working by continually improvising as a project progressed. Cavalcanti's teaching confirmed the value and, as well, the appropriateness of the method for live action documentary work. The artistic process of improvisation and spontaneity expounded by surrealism accorded perfectly with McLaren's previously established inclinations.

> Surrealism meant cutting down the conscious control of what was happening. Now I had tended to be an improviser in earlier films, so this fitted in with the idea of surrealism. You let it come out of your own subconscious – what the image is going to do next. Knowing about surrealism and having seen just one or two surrealist paintings released me to make films like *Love on the Wing* where the image keeps metamorphosing.[186]

Love on the Wing

Having found that important practices and attitudes of surrealism were either already used by him, or were

184 McLaren as quoted in *Creative Process*, script 7.

185 McLaren as quoted in *Creative Process*, script 7.

186 McLaren as quoted in *Creative Process*, script 4–5.

sympathetic to his current theories and working processes, McLaren made a film which not only used such surrealist elements but which established much of the imagery, movement and whimsy with which McLaren's *oeuvre* has subsequently been identified, to the extent that this film *Love on the Wing* has been called the first McLaren film. McLaren agreed with this assessment.[187]

By 1938 McLaren was feeling frustrated by making live action documentaries in spite of the interlude of playful pixillation of household effects he was allowed in *Mony a Pickle*. McLaren himself suggested making a publicity film, using fantasy, for the new air-mail service.[188] Thus the film, its subject and treatment, was a product of McLaren's own ideas. In this sense alone then, unlike McLaren's earlier GPO Film Unit contributions, this was a McLaren film.

It is unclear which occurred to McLaren first: the notion of using postal letters and changing them into characters and even into different things, or the idea of animating hand-drawn images directly on the film through which fantastic transformations could occur. Obviously the subject suits the technique, and the technique suits the subject.

Love on the Wing is the earliest extant film in which McLaren drew, throughout the length of the film, directly on the film stock – a technique he would use again and again, without any fundamental change, through the years. Its simplicity and directness were after all two of its main attributes. Back in 1933, all of five years earlier, McLaren and Stewart McAlistair in their ultimately frameless application of paint to film, had initially tried to paint or draw an image which was maintained, albeit with minute modifications, from one frame to the next. They gave up because it took so long to do. For *Love on the Wing* McLaren revived the technique. This time, however, he made some adjustments. Firstly, the drawn images were simplified: they were restricted entirely to linear configurations, all unnecessary detail was ignored, leaving only basic imagery; he used only one colour (black) India ink to draw with an ordinary pen on clear film. Secondly, the slight misregistrations, from frame to frame, inherent in such direct animation work, were accepted by McLaren. The resulting effect, known as 'boiling', was over-powered, and therefore seemingly to the viewer reduced, by the speed and sweep of the images' general movements. As well, the extremely fast pace of the

187 McLaren in "Interview" Scottish Arts Council 12.

188 McLaren in "Interview" Scottish Arts Council 12.

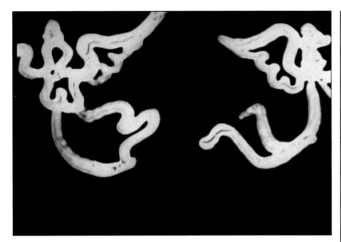

Fig. 31. Love on the Wing. *The male and female figures, appropriately for a film promoting air-mail, have wings.* [NFB].

film reduced the perceivable effects of the trembling image so that what boiling that remains is perfectly acceptable and is interpreted as another contribution to the film's energy. Thus, by by accepting an "imperfect" registration from frame to frame and by simplifying the image, McLaren was able to work fairly fluently. Also of considerable help in speeding the drawing process was the improvisatory method of working McLaren had utilized with increasing confidence.

The theme of *Love on the Wing* is change and the nature of that change is metamorphosis. There were two sources from which McLaren's use of the process sprang. One was the work of Emile Cohl. McLaren had only encountered the work of this turn-of-the-century French pioneer animator in the previous year – 1937.[189] Cohl's work, although not drawn directly on film, was simple and linear. He also manipulated the lines of the images to transform them into other images. In these two important aspects the connections with McLaren's *Love on the Wing* could not be more direct. Characteristically, McLaren's debt to Cohl, particularly in respect of the simplicity of his imagery, was dutifully acknowledged.[190] The second influence on the making of *Love on the Wing* was, of course, surrealism.

I was also influenced to some extent by surrealism, which I had just discovered ... . The film was largely improvisation ... . I started with two letters and then I changed them into two characters, because surrealism had liberated my thinking. With surrealism you can after all change anything into anything.[191]

189 McLaren in *Creative Process*, script 5.

190 McLaren in "Interview", Scottish Arts Council 12.

191 McLaren in "Interview", Scottish Arts Council 12.

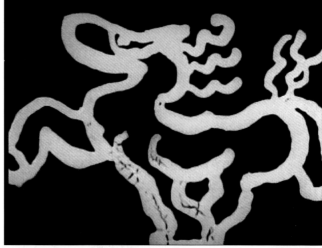

Fig. 32. Love on the Wing. *Simple linear drawing, this one also of a horse, is typical of the film.* [NFB.]

Fig. 33. Love on the Wing. *Another powerful horse image.* [NFB.]

The images in *Love on the Wing* metamorphose with extreme rapidity. Hardly has the viewer recognized the transformed image before it metamorphoses into something else, and so on. The flow of imagery becomes a play of associations: column; eye; pipe; letter; male stick figure; figure loses hat; snail; bone; flying bone with wing; phallic-shape; scissors; scissors cut column into two parts which become flowers, meanwhile scissors grow a phallic part which becomes a man; flowers become a woman.

The male and female imagery is fairly obvious, except for the use of a column as a female substitute. McLaren explains, "Remember the scene of the woman who turns [into] a column. I had seen columns in surrealist painting

Fig. 34. Love on the Wing. *Film-stock showing parts of the dismembering horse sequence.* [NFB.]

and I used this image without thinking. But the other images had a more determined function."[192]

A memorable sequence of the film depicts a horse, which has metamorphosed from the male line of transfor-

192 McLaren as quoted in "Interview", Scottish Arts Council 12.

mations, chasing a letter which had previously attacked the couple with some vigour. In the hectic chase the horse loses, item by item, his legs, tail, body, neck and even his face, leaving the eyes and other features without a context (see Fig. 34). Fortunately from another transformation an axe emerges and attacks the letter, which presumably was a symbol for bad news.

The white lines of these extraordinary images (the negative image of McLaren's original black lines had been used), are placed over a background of clouds and other forms suggestive of space. The backgrounds were photographed from a multiplane construction. The layers were moved past the camera at various speeds – those layers closest to the camera being moved the fastest and more distant layers progressively slower until the furthest layer, the background, is moved only slowly. Multiplane travelling background devices were at that time being developed and used by such commercial studios as those of Disney and Fleischer.[193] McLaren used his device to increase the suggestion of space and of movement (the white linear image, while retaining its overall position in the frame, is seen against a moving background). The perception is that the background is stationary with the foreground image in motion; in other words the essence of a live-action tracking shot is mimicked.

The illusionistic space of *Love on the Wing* places the extraordinary metamorphoses of the foreground image in a plausible space, the dimensions and movements of which, as in the multiplane backgrounds, conform to reality. This conforming to reality makes the metamorphoses even more extraordinary. It also gives the film a dream-like quality, which is hardly surprising considering McLaren's prevailing interest at the time.

Unfortunately present prints of *Love on the Wing* are of poor quality and the background images are difficult to see. The reason for the poor quality is that the original material for the film, including the master negative from which prints were struck was destroyed during the war in an air raid on London. Current prints were struck from a negative that was made from a 16mm print which fortunately was found later. That prints and negatives were not more widely dispersed in the first place was a consequence of a decision by the British Postmaster General. When he saw McLaren's film, the Postmaster General thought it was unsuitable for release. Several features of the film

193 Mark Langer, "The Disney-Fleischer dilemmas product differentiation and technological innovation", *Screen* 33.4 (Winter 1992)343–359.

displeased him. McLaren's understanding was that the government minister found the film too erotic and too Freudian.[194] That the film contains erotic sequences is undeniable as is its surrealist (Freudian) flow of images. As well, the film has its violent moments. Nevertheless, on the whole the film is exuberant and fun. McLaren has not recorded his feelings about the banning of his film, but his reaction can be gauged by the fact that in subsequent years he maintained an awareness of his potential audience and modified his films according to his perception of his audience. John Grierson had left the GPO Film Unit in 1937 and started the Film Centre in London along similar lines to the GPO Film Unit. The genial Cavalcanti had taken over from Grierson. One wonders if Grierson, with his strong personality and power to persuade, would have allowed McLaren's film to be banned.

Coincidentally, McLaren's next film, *The Obedient Flame* was made for the Film Centre while he was on loan from the GPO Film Unit. By this time, though, 1939, Grierson had moved on again. McLaren duly made his film, which uses conventional photography and some animation to show the advantages of cooking with gas. After the exuberance of *Love on the Wing*, the gas film is decidedly pedantic.

By 1939 McLaren had other preoccupations. A British war with Nazi Germany was looking increasingly likely and increasingly ominous. Then Hitler and Stalin signed a nonaggression pact between their respective countries. McLaren, with his communist ideals, felt betrayed.[195] He withdrew his support of communism. His experiences in the Spanish Civil War had caused him to become a pacifist. As such, he did not want to become involved in what was an increasingly likely conflict in Europe. He decided to emigrate to the United States of America. He and a young Canadian, Guy Glover, who he had met at a London ballet in 1937 and who was to play an important behind-the-scenes role in McLaren's future life, embarked for the USA only days before the Second World War broke out. Also on the other side of the Atlantic was John Grierson.

194 *Creative Process* (1st Assembly film).

195 *Creative Process,* 1st Assembly (film).

Part Two

Chapter Four

New York Interlude

Early difficulties

McLaren arrived in New York in late October 1939. He had with him some letters of introduction, a portfolio of drawings, 3,000 feet of film (prints of his own films) and $120. On disembarking from the ship he immediately encountered problems. Customs assessed his films as dutiable to the sum of $25. Conscious of the need to conserve his money, McLaren left his films in bond.[196] He retained his letters of introduction which were from such eminent contacts as Paul Rotha, a senior filmmaker colleague of McLaren at the GPO Film Unit who had recently been in the USA (i.e. from 1937 to 1938). The newly-landed immigrant immediately began to seek out the people to whom the introductions were written:

> My first move was to the American Film Centre. Donald Slesinger introduced me to Mary Losey who helpfully drew up a list of people I should see; she also suggested that A.F.C. could oblige me by bringing in duty-free my films, which, though then becoming A.F.C. property, would on my consulting A.F.C. still be available for showing to any interested party. This seemed to me a satisfactory arrangement, and they went ahead with it.[197]

McLaren followed up some of his contacts and, like the Slesinger one above, many resulted in further introductions and more names of people – but no firm offers of work.

In the above-quoted letter, he also talks of going to the Museum of Modern Art and being offered projection

196 Norman McLaren, letter to John Grierson, 6 December 1939 1. Grierson Archives, University of Stirling, Stirling, GAA 4:23:51.

197 McLaren letter to Grierson, 6 December 1939 1.

facilities for the screening of films. The Museum visit, during which this arrangement was struck, was a very early contact, only his third in fact, and so on subsequent interviews with his contacts – who were increasing in number – McLaren invited them to see his films just as soon as he could arrange a show at the Museum. This plan, however, did not work well:

> It was not until some weeks later, unfortunately, that A.F.C. got my films out of bond, so there was a considerable delay between these and other interviews and the show, a factor which may have contributed to the failure of the show – for failure it was. Despite written and phoned invitations to about three dozen people, only a handful turned up, even though it was arranged at a convenient hour. Other factors contributing to this result may have been the slight active cooperation on the parts of the Museum of Modern Art and A.F.C. Whether this was due to my being an outsider, or to my not having been tactful (or pushing) enough, I don't know.[198]

Having endured this frustration and disappointment, McLaren encountered further obstacles when he asked the AFC to consent to sending his films for viewing at the University of Minnesota. He was informed that under the terms of entry to the USA, the films could not possibly be sent out of New York. McLaren's exasperation at this bind,

198 McLaren letter to Grierson, 6 December 1939 2.

and desperation at his increasingly-precarious economic plight, is evident. He wrote to Minnesota explaining the situation and saying he was hoping to circumvent the difficulties. His letter to Grierson continues:

> Unfortunately, I have had to think twice (and am still doing so) about paying the $25.00 duty, taking control of the films myself, and sending them thereupon to Kissack [at the University of Minnesota] in the hope of fertilizing his interest – as this expenditure would diminish my means of subsistence in N.Y. by two weeks, in which time as valuable an alternative might present itself here.[199]

Plainly, with his efforts to secure further money from Britain being frustrated by British currency regulations, the original $120 was getting very low. He had been in New York six weeks. If $25 represented two weeks' existence, he would by then have used $75. He therefore had just $45 left – less than one month's existence. No wonder he finished his letter to Grierson with "Any advice and suggestions from you will be more than gladly received". Under the circumstances this was a request showing considerable restraint but then, as has been seen, the rest of the contents of the letter made McLaren's situation quite clear. Within a week he was writing to Grierson again – this time with much better news.

The stages required in finding his initial breakthrough were many. They give an idea of the extent of the difficulties McLaren found in getting work. Letters of introduction had taken him to John Marshall who had put him in touch with two further people, one of whom was Felix Greene, the BBC representative in New York. Greene introduced McLaren to a CBS television executive and also to Thomas Hutchinson of NBC Television. It was McLaren's approach to Hutchinson that produced work. It was a "... very small job to do for their Xmas program: a mobile 'Xmas Card' – 200 feet of hand-drawn symbolic 'jitter doodle' on 35 mm".[200] McLaren drew like mad for ten days.[201] The film which resulted has subsequently been given the title *NBC Greeting*. It is a directly drawn film (obviously), black and white (since TV was monochrome in those days it was pointless considering colour), thirty seconds long and is figurative – along the lines of *Love on the Wing*. It was designed as a Christmas greeting. Its festive contents, however, were sufficiently ambiguous for it to be

[199] McLaren letter to Grierson 6 December 1939 2–3.

[200] McLaren letter to Grierson 12 December 1939 1, Grierson Archives, Stirling, GAA 4:23:54.

[201] McLaren letter to Grierson 12 December 1939 1.

*Fig. 36. Hilla von
Rebay at about the time
McLaren knew her.
[NFB Archive.]*

202 McLaren as quoted in
Maynard Collins,
Norman McLaren
(Ottawa: Canadian
Film Institute, 1976),
67.

203 Guy Glover, *McLaren*
(Montreal: National
Film Board of Canada,
1980) 10.

204 McLaren letter to
Grierson on 12
December 1939 1.

used also as a New Year's greeting[202] and as a Valentine's greeting.[203] The NBC thereby extracted maximum use from the film. Unfortunately, even though his film was being broadcast during the various holiday times during the next few months, McLaren was again out of (paid) work. The ten days of intense activity was the only work for which he had been paid in six months or so in New York.

Dots, *Loops* and the Guggenheim

McLaren had hoped that his short film for the NBC would lead to further work of a similar type for the broadcaster.[204] But it did not and, in spite of continuing his search, which became increasingly wide-ranging in terms of film genre, he continued to find very little. Even so, McLaren continued to make his own films but they were necessarily on a private basis and they did not relieve his then increasingly sorry economic state. In this vein McLaren had, by October 1940, made *Stars and Stripes*, a hand-drawn, predominately abstract frolic to a Sousa march and, again using abstract imagery, *Allegro* (which was originally two films *Allegro*

*Fig. 37. Norman McLaren at work, on a subsequent film, drawing sound
directly onto the film-stock.
[McLaren Archive/NFB.]*

Spiritoso and *Allegro Moderato*) in which both the picture and
sound tracks were hand-drawn.[205] He did hear, however,
that a New York artist called Mary-Ellen Bute was making
a semi-abstract film with the intention of illustrating Saint-
Saens' *Danse macabre*. McLaren was invited to do the
animating. He did not care much for the way the music
had been illustrated. The figures of ghosts had been devised
to dance in a figurative illustration to the tone poem. The
concept of this illustrative work was therefore quite different from McLaren's filmic attempts to create a visual
abstract expression of music. McLaren was able to suggest
a simplification of the figures to be used and agreed to
animate the film for Bute – which was done using the
cel-animation technique with some sections in the
directly-drawn animation technique. McLaren's artistic
input into *Spook Sport* was not therefore great, and he
expressed a lack of satisfaction with the film.[206] He did
receive $200 for his work. This remuneration was impor-
tant to him for his economic plight continued to be in
crisis.[207]

It is little wonder that when in about October 1940[208]
McLaren eventually did find something, something that
would not only earn him money but which was within his
original speciality of film experimentation, his recollection
is of a grand occasion. Two McLaren accounts, which are
here interlocked, provide a vivid picture:

205 The chronology, as
well as the number
and type of films made
by McLaren during his
New York period has
been confused by
McLaren's own
recollections (which
are at odds with
contemporary letters
written by McLaren
himself) and also by
entries published in
André Martin *Norman
McLaren* (Annecy:
Journées
internationales du
cinéma d'animation
Montréal:
Cinémathèque
Canadienne, 1965).
This interesting tribute
to McLaren
unfortunately contains
some inaccuracies in
chronology and film
titling which have
been subsequently
replicated by Collins
and by the Scottish
Arts Council in their
otherwise informative
accounts of McLaren's
career. That
McLaren's 1940 letters
are fairly detailed and
were written very soon
after, or at the same
time as, the making of
the above films make
these letters more
reliable sources of
information than
unsourced
publications or even
McLaren's own
recollections of some
decades later. The
information regarding
McLaren's early New
York films comes from
a letter he wrote on 14
October 1940. The
letter is contained in:
Joan M. Lukach, *Hilla
Rebay: In Search of the
Spirit in Art* (NY:
George Braziller,
1983) 218.

206 Collins 68.

207 Collins 30, 68.

208 Lukach 216–217.

209 McLaren in Collins 67.

210 McLaren as quoted in "Interview", *Norman McLaren* (Edinburgh: Scottish Arts Council, 1977) 13.

211 McLaren as quoted in Collins 67.

212 McLaren as quoted in "Interview," Scottish Arts Council 13.

213 McLaren as quoted in Collins 67.

214 William Moritz, "The Films of Oskar Fischinger," *Film Culture* 58-60 (1974) 65.

215 McLaren as quoted in Collins 67. In another account given in "Interview" Scottish Arts Council 13, McLaren states that he did not have any films with him, but the context of the statement makes it clear that he meant that he did not have any *abstract* films to show Rebay – he was quite resolved to go home and make some abstract films specifically for her. On this latter point McLaren's various accounts emphatically concur.

216 McLaren as quoted in Collins 67.

217 McLaren as quoted in Collins 67.

218 The events in the sequence that McLaren describes are seen to be following immediately upon one another. However, McLaren is also on record as saying that the arrangements with the Director to make *Dots* and *Loops* took one month (McLaren as quoted in "Interview" Scottish Arts Council 13). If this is so then the account would appear

Then I discovered the Guggenheim. I saw this museum with thick carpets and drapes and beautiful Bach music in the background.[209] I discovered that all the pictures were abstract.[210] It had *nothing but* abstract paintings – not a single figurative painting, which was unusual in that period.[211] I decided to see the Director, a woman.[212] I asked the girl at the door if I could meet the directress. Upon meeting her I introduced myself by saying "I make abstract films". She replied "Oh you don't say 'abstract', it's 'non-objective'." She went on to add "That's very interesting. We have some early German non-objective films, and some Swedish, some Eggeling, some Oscar Fischinger, and Richter films".[213]

The 'Directress' of whom McLaren spoke was a Baroness Hilla von Rebay. Rebay was a German who "... had devoted herself wholeheartedly to the promotion of non-objective art".[214] Indeed, she had a collection of European abstract films at the Guggenheim (then known as the Museum of Non-Objective Painting). McLaren's presence at the Museum was not purely chance. He went in the hope of presenting himself and his work, for he did have his own films with him.[215] The young filmmaker however, was selective in his presentation of his films to the museum. Even if he did have his recent abstract films with him – and it is difficult to understand why he would not have had them with him – they did not play a part in his approaches to the museum.[216] One can only conjecture that, being somewhat overwhelmed in a museum of abstract art, his diffidence prevented him from presenting his earlier abstract films. His representational films however, contained abundant evidence of his imagination and his approach to film. *Love on the Wing* for example, would not only have displayed his wit, but also his economic, pragmatic and fundamentalist approach to film. McLaren screened his films for Rebay. She liked them. McLaren saw his chance: "This prompted me to ask if she'd be interested if I made an abstract film. She indicated that she'd like to see it anyway. That was enough for me. I rushed home, bought some film and did *Dots* and *Loops*."[217] Although this account of events may be a precis of a more complicated sequence,[218] the mixture of opportunity, persistence and some luck that it reveals is accurate.

Having such an incentive, McLaren entered another

THE FILM WORK OF NORMAN McLAREN

two basic differences from the earlier work commissioned
in New York: the *NBC Greeting* film. Firstly, his two new
films were both abstract. Before his arrival in America
McLaren had made only one abstract film – that first film
of 1933 which was worn out and destroyed by repeated
projections. As well, he had become interested in surrealism which, being originally a literary movement and relying
on works coming from the subconscious through dreams
and through improvisatory expression, tended to be figurative. McLaren, however, retained his love of music and
had also retained a love of abstract art. The collection of
non-objective works in the Guggenheim impressed him
and confirmed the direction he had taken with his recently
completed private works *Stars and Stripes* and the *Allegro*
films. The museum also contained Fischinger's films. One
of these films, *Study No. 7*, had first excited McLaren back
in his Glasgow days as to the potential of film for creating
a visual, abstract, temporal, art form; one that had the same
base as music. It was natural, therefore, that McLaren
should desire that his new abstract films should have a
music track. To achieve this, McLaren needed to buy a
sound-track; that is, he needed to pay to have music recorded onto a film sound-track. But he had no money for
a sound-track, nor did he have any prospect of getting any
money until he had finished the films. Of his private films,
Stars and Stripes used a pre-recorded version of Sousa's
music as an accompaniment. This method however, poses
copyright problems for public screening of films. As well,
the pre-recorded sound would require for professional
screening further recording onto the film's sound track –
a process requiring money which McLaren did not have.
For his other New York private films, the *Allegro* works,
McLaren used a much cheaper method of sound generation. The *Allegro* works in turn marked a revival of an idea
he had worked on for the GPO film *Book Bargain* but which
had been rejected for inclusion in that film. For his new
films therefore, McLaren decided that he would draw not
only on the picture-track, which of course was also an
economic necessity, but also on the sound-track. This was
the second fundamental difference between *Dots* and *Loops*
and the NBC *Greeting*.

The method McLaren devised for drawing sound on
film was clearly explained by him (Fig. 38).

The sounds that McLaren produced for *Dots* and

to be a condensation of several visits that took place over a one-month period (and this confirmed in a McLaren letter of 7 October 1940, cited in Lukach 217) in which case there are several possibilities: perhaps McLaren did not have his films with him on his first visit; perhaps the screening of his films took time to arrange; perhaps McLaren's offer to make an abstract film was a little more premeditated than the condensed version suggests. The differences between the two versions of events, however, are not fundamentally great. In the condensed version McLaren is a film-maker calling prepared to show his films, who, with the unfolding of oppor-tunities took advantage of his fortune. In the stretched version a fortuitous encounter, when he called at the Guggenheim apparently without his (abscract) films, presented an opportunity which, over time, was persistently followed up.

```
     Technical notes for Sound on "DOTS" and "LOOPS" (1940)
```

The percussive, semi-musical sounds were made by painting and drawing with black India ink on clear 35mm. film.

The sounds were placed in the sound track area adjacent to the picture; in this case, on the same piece of film on which the visual images were drawn. For synchronization during projection, the track was positioned 20 frames ahead of picture it was intended to synchronize with.

The sound track was later transferred to normal variable area format for release.

Almost all the sounds were in the form of 'notes' having an abrupt beginning or sudden attack, and a tapering-off or decay, where possible, with an exponential shape or envelope:

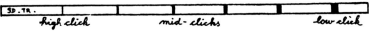

Each note was made up of a number of strokes of the pen or brush.

CLICKS WITHOUT PRECISE PITCH

Just one stroke across the track made a clicking sound:

high click   *mid-clicks*   *low click*

VOLUME OF CLICK

The loudness of a click depended on how much the stroke stretched across the sound track. For example:

loudest   *less loud*   *quieter*   *quietest*

Volume could also be controlled by the slope of the stroke:

SOUNDS WITH PITCH

At least six strokes, if <u>evenly</u> spaced, were enough to make a sound with a <u>definite</u> <u>pitch</u>; the closer together the strokes were the higher the pitch, the further apart, the lower the pitch.

For high sounds a crow-quill pen was used:

very high pitches   *high*   *less high*

For notes in the middle-pitch range, an ordinary broad pen was used:

For deep notes narrow and broad brushes were used:

Loops are distinctive. They range in pitch, volume and duration, but not in their timbre or their attack and decay. Thus each of the sounds also possesses a similarity of attack and decay, and, to a varying degree, a 'kissing' resonance – with a hint of 'raspberry'. This latter characteristic alone gives the films a whimsical quality – particularly in the context of 'serious' art, such as that found at the Guggenheim Museum.

A closer examination of *Dots* reveals that the cumulative structuring of these films is intrinsically linked to McLaren's methods of making the films – he drew the films starting at the beginning and proceeded bit by successive bit until he reached the end.

The musical structure of *Dots* is one of continuous variation beginning with slow, separated, simple sounds – almost sawtooth wave sounds, in electronic music terms, or kissing 'smacks', in more descriptive terms. These are initially heard in groups of four single notes (beats), which establishes a common time, or 4/4 metre, in the work. Next, two notes per beat are heard and repeated and then more complex rhythms occur within the beat and are repeated. Eventually, the rhythmic patterns become more fragmentary and virtuosic, but the underlying feel of the beat is not lost.

In working out the sound for *Dots*, McLaren worked from the beginning of the film drawing the sound in conjunction with drawing on the picture-track. "[The sound was drawn] at the same time. I drew a foot or two's worth of images then immediately afterwards I drew on the sound. It fascinates me to realise that I was capable of drawing on the sound-track without being able to hear it."[219] As well as not hearing the sounds, neither did he notate them before-hand using conventional notation. Thus it is not surprising that the sound structure begins simply and then progresses from section to section to ever more elaborate configurations. McLaren had not only worked out the relationship of the pitch frequencies to the frames of the films, he had also worked out the rhythm of the film in terms of the frame count. "I start slowly. Approximately one rhythm per sixty frames. Then I start on another rhythm. It is simply mathematics based on the frames."[220]

A high degree of synchronization exists between the visual and aural components of the film. The pitch of the sounds and the size of the visual dots correspond: the larger the dot-shape on screen, the lower the sound. Looking at McLaren's technical notes for the film (Fig. 38), one can see that drawing shapes on the sound-track that correspond in size with the simmutaneously presented images of the

219 McLaren as quoted in "Interview" Scottish Arts Council 14.

220 McLaren as quoted in "Interview" Scottish Arts Council 14.

picture-track produces this direct relationship between visual size and pitch. More important structurally, the rhythm (duration and spacing) of the sounds corresponds to the occurrence of the visual images. That is to say, the aural images together with their visual equivalents occur simultaneously. The main divisions of the beats, or later the overall phrases, are marked by the lowest sound (which acts like a tonic note), and by the largest, blot-like shape or dot. Synchronization is most effectively manifested in the contrapuntal parts where there is the juxtaposition of patterns of small dots set against larger shapes and, in the music, a higher 'melodic' line is heard against a lower, and slower, moving bass line. These descriptions of the film offer explanations of McLaren's approach, his ingenuity and his indebtedness to music but they do not convey the film's over-riding characteristics. It is important keep in mind that the essential theme of *Dots* (as well as *Loops*) is that of whimsy and fun.

In making use of a simultaneity between the visual and aural aspects of film, McLaren was adopting the practice that had been developed by commercial animators during the 1930s, so much so that the technique is known as 'Mickey Mousing'. In commercial cel-animation the animator's frame-by-frame control over the visual component of film allows the visual image to be fitted with precision to the sound-track. By adopting the drawn-on sound technique, McLaren gave himself even greater control over the two components of film. By working frame-by-frame on both the picture and sound-tracks, he was able to not only fit picture with sound, but also to fit sound to picture as he worked. This element of control that his process offered him had great appeal to McLaren. It was even more important to him than the new sound qualities that the drawn-on sound process enabled him to create. "I did not make them [my synthetic sounds] to explore new sounds, but simply for my own needs. I wanted to control the sound-track precisely and personally."[221] In these totally direct-drawn films McLaren had control over the correspondence between the two elements of film. Particularly in *Dots*, the degree of correspondence gives the sound-track a prominence that is near, if not equal to, that of the film's visual component. While watching *Dots*, one's attention oscillates between the aural and visual images. This in itself is a fascinating experience. Just as intriguing, if a little more taxing, is the resulting on-going comparison and

221 Norman McLaren in answer to Ivan Stadtrucker questionnaire, March 1975, NFB Archives, McLaren Files, 1184 D112, p.3.

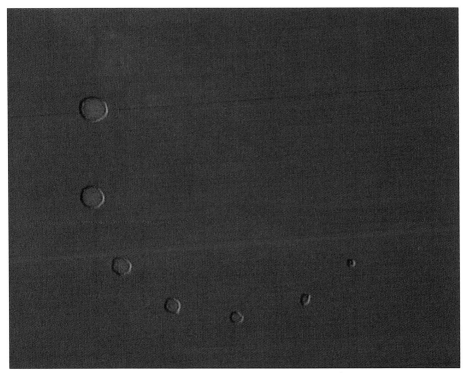

evaluation of McLaren's visual and aural expressions of a single temporal pattern.

The visual and aural components of *Dots* are not, however, identical. The sound component does not have an equivalent of the screen-space in which precise movements and formations may be exercised. The sound-space, especially as reproduced in those days of monaural technology, is much more limited. Variations in loudness, or even pitch, can suggest a depth in space, but in these films a sense of lateral sound space is non-existent. The dots, however, appear at various points on the screen and move around the screen. These, then, are visual embellishments to the sound-pattern, but McLaren has used them in such a way that they support the various levels of energy contained in the sound-track. Thus these visual variations do not appear to be incongruous – they are well integrated.

Mention should be made about the colour in the visual-track of the present releases of *Dots* and *Loops*. Colour is, of course, another aspect of the visual component of the film which lacks a direct equivalent in the sound-track. The original New York versions of *Dots* and *Loops*, however, did not have colour. They were black and

Fig. 39. Dots. The larger the shape, the lower the sound. [NFB.]

white. The present colours of the *Dots* and *Loops* were achieved later in the laboratory using the same methods that were used to colour his later film *Hen Hop*. This process is described below in the chapter on McLaren's technical processes. The laboratory charges for obtaining colour through the multiple printing processes were not within McLaren's reach at that time in New York.

Although these films are supposedly abstract, they do have surreal overtones which, considering McLaren's sympathies and method of working, is not altogether surprising. There are several features which contribute to this quality in the films. Firstly, the dots in *Dots* and the loops in *Loops* appear to move in a three-dimensional space. They appear to recede from and advance towards the viewer. As well, they enter and leave the screen area from the edges, thereby implying a space beyond the screen. The illusion is therefore created of the screen being a mere window into a world which is part of the viewer's world and which obeys the same rules of gravity and physics. Secondly, especially in *Loops*, the shapes metamorphose, often of their own volition. Taken by itself, this is not necessarily surreal, but given that the shapes appear in a three-dimensional world, which is an extension of the viewer's world, the surreal undertones begin to emerge. Thirdly, the types of movements used in the films are emphatically anthropomorphic: the dots (and loops) move, collide, bounce and recoil as if endowed with life. The reasons may be more of a product of McLaren's empathy with his subject than with surrealism. "The objects that play between themselves in my films are all me or part of me. In other words while animating an object, I feel I am it, otherwise I would not know how to make it behave."[222] Be that as it may, in a space that appears to be an extension of the viewer's world, energetic life-like behaviour is being performed by dots and loops. This is a surreal scenario.

The surrealist overtones of these films, however, are not a result of an intention on McLaren's part to make a statement in surreal terms. They are primarily a consequence of his suddenly re-adopting abstract imagery while continuing to employ a process of kinesthetic identification. The images being manipulated thus produce anthropomorphic movement, which obeys, to a large extent, normal laws of physics. These images also exist in a world which seems an extension of the viewer's but which is, in the first place, an extension of McLaren's world that existed

[222] McLaren quoted in Stadtrucker questionnaire 2.

for him while creating the images. This is not to say that McLaren would not have denied the surreal content of the films, for he had worked in an improvisatory way, letting, as he has said, the subconscious express itself.[223] For McLaren, surrealism's main quality was its emphasis on this attitude of mind.[224]

The improvisatory qualities in *Dots* and *Loops* are clearly evident. The direct process of creating the image made improvisation easy. The process also gave each of the films a 'drawn-on' (or, to borrow a term from the visual arts, a painterly) quality. That this quality also pervades the sound-track in each of the films, and that the aural and visual aspects of the film share this quality, further enhances the unity of expression in both *Dots* and *Loops*.

With *Dots* and *Loops* finished McLaren returned to Hilla von Rebay. The Director bought the films for $100 each.[225] McLaren subsequently sold copies of several of his other films to the Guggenheim. One was *Boogie Doodle* which, judging from its absence from McLaren's 14 November 1940 list of films[226] and its attribution of a 1940 date, was made shortly after *Dots* and *Loops* in late 1940. *Boogie Doodle* was made to fit with, and express visually, the jazz of Albert Ammons. Although it is ostensibly abstract, the movements in this film are even more decidedly anthropomorphic than those in *Loops*. Another work to be sold to the Guggenheim was the previously mentioned *Allegro* composite. It will be recalled that for this work McLaren drew both the sound-track and the visuals, which were abstract. This work, judging from the early date assigned to it (before November 1940[227]), marked McLaren's return to abstract imagery. By his use of the word 'pigment' in describing what he applied to the film stock,[228] it would seem that McLaren made *Allegro* in colour. This would explain why no copy was made of the work – colour printing would have been too expensive for the still struggling McLaren. *Allegro* suffered the same fate as his very first film. It was worn out through repeated projection (at the Guggenheim) so it is no longer possible to see the *Allegro* work. In this regard it is fortunate that a good proportion of McLaren's work of this period was originally black and white thus enabling him to afford to have copies struck. Another film project of this time was *Rhumba* (1939?[229]) of which only a drawn sound-track survives. Bearing in mind McLaren's successful *Dots* and *Loops* working process of developing both the sound and visual

223 McLaren as quoted in "Interview" Scottish Arts Council 14.

224 McLaren as quoted in "Interview" Scottish Arts Council 14.

225 McLaren as quoted in Collins 67.

226 McLaren as quoted in Lukach 217–218.

227 McLaren letter of 14 November 1940, as quoted in Lukach 217–218.

228 McLaren letter of 14 November 1940, as quoted in Lukach 217–218.

229 The date emanates from Martin's *Norman McLaren* which has proved somewhat unreliable.

Fig. 40. Stars and Stripes. *The energy of McLaren's film is evident even in this still frame.* [NFB.]

230 David Verrall, NFB memo to Doug McDonald, 9 January 1984. Don McWilliams, NFB memos to David Verrall, 5 January 1984 and 6 January 1984, all NFB Archives, McLaren File – Techniques.

231 Replicating the mistake which appears in Martin, Collins 28 asserts that *Scherzo* was the first title for *Dots*. The same mistake was repeated in Scottish Arts Council 58.

tracks simultaneously and thereby achieving a high degree of sympathy between them, the prospect of adding a visual-track to an already complete sound-track would have held little promise of achieving that same high degree of sympathy. So, athough this work was commissioned by the Guggenheim, visuals were never added to *Rhumba*. A print of *Scherzo*, a lost film of McLaren's New York period, was found in the National Film Board of Canada (NFB) vault material in 1983.[230] While *Scherzo* is a distinct work, it does have strong affinities in both technique and outcome with *Dots* and *Loops*.[231] This would explain why *Sherzo* apparently was not offered to the Guggenheim. Incidentally, like the original *Dots* and *Loops* work, the found print was in black and white. A copy of *Stars and Stripes* (1940), which already has been briefly mentioned, was among those prints that McLaren sold to the Guggenheim. *Stars and Stripes*, a directly drawn-on film, has some interesting connotations.

In *Stars and Stripes*, set to a part of a march by John Philip Sousa, McLaren uses the component parts of the American flag, metamorphosing and moving them so that they cavort, dance and erupt in a pyrotechnic celebration. Earlier that year, in fact in February of 1940, Rebay had commissioned a film from Oskar Fischinger. The German

Fischinger had also migrated to America (to California). It will be recalled that it was Fischinger who had made that early abstract film (*Study No. 7*) which had been a seminal influence on McLaren – providing McLaren with the inspiration to make music visible through film. Several months before McLaren's arrival in New York, Fischinger, in his own hunt for sympathetic patronage, was also to discover the Guggenheim and the Baroness. The film Rebay commissioned from Fischinger in February 1940 was, like McLaren's film, based on the American flag and set to the music of Sousa (*Stars and Stripes Forever*). For his film, called *American March*, Fischinger chose to use cel-animation in what could be construed as a technological tilt at Disney:

> Fischinger used the common Disney style of hard-edged, outlined figures painted on cells, but he carried the technique far beyond Disney's limits and made it an integral part of the meaning of the film. Fischinger has chosen to discuss the idea of America as a melting pot, and he shows this literally by causing the elements in the film – form and colour – to melt.[232]

The extension of the cel-animation technique, an extension that melts the Disney style of hard-edged forms, is a triumphant achievement which, given Fischinger's then recent and disastrous confrontations with Disney during the making of *Fantasia*, has an ironic justification. By comparison, the simple playfulness and energetic fun of McLaren's *Stars and Stripes*, reveal McLaren's more physically kinetic domain of artistic expression. In those internationally sensitive times, Rebay's purchase of these two thematically similar abstract 'marches', one by McLaren and one by Fischinger, were consequential to her efforts to demonstrate the patriotism of herself, a German, and the often foreign-born artists who were recipients of Guggenheim benefaction. McLaren and Fischinger fall into this category. The Scottish immigrant and German immigrant each came to make vivid filmic celebrations of America, patriotic celebrations using the American flag and Sousa's American march music. In doing so, they in turn became at least temporary ingredients of the American melting pot. Unfortunately for McLaren, at least in the short term, the American dream did not materialize for him. The various payments he received from the Guggenheim for his films were only temporary respites.

232 Moritz 155.

McLaren's continuing search for work investigated almost all sorts of film organizations. Even his initial search, on arriving in New York, included such film organizations as Paramount News, National Geographic (which even in those days was a maker of educational films), TV companies, other companies the filmmaking preferences of which were unknown to McLaren, and Terry Toons. McLaren was prepared to do documentary film work, to do animation for diagrams, maps and titles, to animate puppets, to edit film, to process film, to shoot film.[233] He did feel uneasy about some of the work for which he applied. Of his approach to Paul Terry, an 'east coast Disney', McLaren talked of it being 'not without a stroke of bad conscience' and being occasioned merely by his increasingly desperate quest to fill the pot.[234] He had even greater misgivings about what he termed commercial publicity ventures. On being given a list of advertising people, McLaren said "I have done nothing along this line as yet, keeping it as a last and unpleasant resort".[235] Thus the function, that is to say commercial or public purpose of the filmmaking, was of greater importance to him than the precise role he may have been asked to play in the making of a film. This is borne out by McLaren's subsequent employment in New York.

The continued search for work and Grierson again

After the Guggenheim projects, McLaren's searches for work resumed their former frustrating pattern. By this time he had been living from intermittent commission to intermittent commission for over a year. "People were very nice but there was just no work. I don't know how I heard about Caravelle Films but I went there and I showed my films and they said: 'Okay, you're hired'."[236] As McLaren succinctly put it: "Caravelle rescued me from hunger".[237] Caravelle was a company that produced industrial, public relations and advertising films – McLaren's desperation had forced him to accept a position in a company which produced advertising films. Caravelle's animation department had about ten people working in it. The animation process used was the commercially-oriented technique of cel-animation: separately drawing backgrounds and foregrounds on transparent sheets of celluloid and then overlaying the sheets. McLaren started at the bottom as an 'in-betweener'.

233 McLaren letter to Grierson 6 December 1939 1.

234 McLaren letter to Grierson 12 December 1939 1.

235 McLaren letter to Grierson 6 December 1939 2.

236 McLaren as quoted in Collins 68.

237 McLaren as quoted in Collins 68.

Fig. 41. Norman McLaren Guy Glover pastel drawing, 1940s. [McLaren Archive/NFB.]

This almost mindless task consisted of doing in-between drawings. The more senior people drew the main stages of a sequence and the dozens of drawings required between these main drawings, the transitional stages of the sequence, were done by the juniors. After two or three months, McLaren was promoted to the more senior echelons. He was even given his own project to work on – a film on plastics.

On his arrival in the USA, McLaren had kept in touch with Grierson, who was in Ottawa as the Commissioner of the newly-formed National Film Board of Canada. In fact, McLaren's first letter to Grierson is dated 22 October 1939, just two days after Norman's arrival in New York.[238] In the letter, McLaren expresses the wish to see Grierson on the latter's forthcoming trip to New York. His awareness of the trip indicates that McLaren was already in some form of contact with Grierson. The letter as well as other evidence, also indicates that Grierson was not an infrequent visitor to New York.[239] McLaren's contact with Grierson during the early months in New York was primarily concerned with the exchange of filmic information and advice. The months just after McLaren's and Glover's arrival in New York, however, were sufficiently desperate for them

238 Norman McLaren letter to John Grierson, 22 October 1939, Grierson Archives, University of Stirling Scotland, G4 23:12.

239 Ross McLean letter to H. Clegg,12 July 1941, British Library of Information NY, NFB Archives, Production Files.

to consider moving to greener pastures. In his letter to Grierson dated 12 December 1939, McLaren concludes with the following reference for Guy Glover:

> As a possible recruit to the movement, I am sending to see you a young fellow, Guy Glover – a Canadian. It is as a very intelligent handler of actors and enacted material, and as a dialogue writer, that I think he may be of value. For some years I have known his work in London where he has produced several left-wing plays, notably introducing Clifford Odets to the professional stage there. Previous to that he had worked as a semi-amateur in Canada where his acting and directing of "Waiting for Lefty" won much appreciation. As an actor, I know that Robert Flaherty thinks a lot of him.
>
> He has a genuine interest in realism and the interpretation of fact and, though he has done this up till now in the theatre, he has for some time past been wishing to change his medium to film. Being a Canadian, and at the same time having an understanding of the documentary movement as we know it, he may be of use to you. He is to be in Ottawa towards the end of this week, and I have asked him to telephone you.[240]

In the same letter McLaren makes an oblique reference to his own suitability for work at Grierson's NFB. One of his many job interviews produced not only the usual rejection, but prompted a well-intentioned suggestion of where McLaren might successfully look for work. McLaren reported the interview to his mentor, Grierson. "He liked my work, could not use me at present and told me that *you* were the person to see".[241] The irony of the situation would not have been lost on Grierson, who was at that time beginning to build his staff of filmmakers at the NFB while McLaren was unable to find work a few hundred miles away in New York. In the same letter, McLaren expressed a desire to make films of greater substance and import than the *NBC Greeting*. "I very much regret that I seem to be getting caught up in work of such insignificance of subject and substance when there are so many serious things to be dealt with in film."[242] The letters indicated that, had Grierson called McLaren at that stage, 1939, McLaren would have gone to Canada. He would have been both disposed to go and free to go. McLaren made it clear to Grierson that work at the NFB, making films of

240 McLaren letter to Grierson 12 December 1939 1–2.

241 McLaren letter to Grierson 12 December 1939 1.

242 McLaren letter to Grierson 12 December 1939 1.

'serious' purpose, would be welcomed. The proposed Glover-Grierson meeting would have provided further opportunities to explore the employment prospects at the NFB for experienced, as well as aspiring, filmmakers.

Grierson's response to McLaren's letter was immediate and emphatic. Three days after McLaren's letter was written, Grierson wrote back informing McLaren that there was "... no great prospect for anymore outsiders ..." for work at the NFB.[243] McLaren's letter was written on the Tuesday, Grierson's reply was written on the Friday, that is at the end of the week when Glover was going to telephone him. It is unclear if Grierson had seen Glover and written his reply as a consequence, or if he had not received Glover and had written his letter as an explanation.

Whether the Grierson-Glover meeting took place or not, whether McLaren was discussed or not, makes little difference. An astute man like Grierson would have noted the plight McLaren was in. Grierson's emphatic rejection, however, should be seen in the larger context. Just as September to December 1939 had been desperate and precarious months for McLaren, for Grierson they had been months of hectic achievement. In the fall of 1939, the Grierson-conceived National Film Board of Canada came into tangible existence with the appointment of the first Board members.[244] Despite some misgivings about the appointment of a non-Canadian, Grierson was the only feasible candidate to head the organization and so in October 1939 he was appointed temporary Film Commissioner.[245] Through October, November and December, Grierson was busy outlining his plans to the government and preparing for a trip to Australia and New Zealand.[246] Grierson's recruitment of staff at that stage was focussed on what he saw as the three or four key positions [which were to be filled by Stuart Legg (theatrical series), Stanley Hawes (non-theatrical series), Raymond Spottiswood (technical aspects and teacher) and J.D. Davidson (camera skills and crafts), and neither McLaren, the unorthodox animator, nor the inexperienced Glover, were likely candidates. In short, McLaren's timing was wrong. At that point in time, Grierson simply was not in the market for hiring them.

September 1941

Eighteen months later the situation had changed. McLaren was working for Caravelle Films. A home movie of 1941

243 John Grierson letter to Norman McLaren 15 December 1939, Grierson Archives, University of Stirling, G4 23:56.

244 Gary Evans, *John Grierson and the National Film Board: The Politics of Wartime Propaganda* (Toronto: University of Toronto Press, 1984) 55.

245 Evans 55.

246 Evans 58–60, 70. This trip was connected with Grierson's attempt to set up a worldwide network for documentary films and resulted in the establishment of government film organizations in both Australia and New Zealand.

in which McLaren uses such camera effects as fast motion, reversed motion and pixillation, shows a small group of McLaren's friends (and McLaren himself) having a Fourth of July Holiday frolic in the country.[247] Appropriately called *An American Home Movie*, it shows that McLaren's life in New York was becoming more secure and that he had made friends. Some of these people were to become close friends and were to remain so long after McLaren's move to Canada. Against this happy scenario is set the awful unfolding of war in Europe. From April 1940 the Nazi forces overran Norway and Denmark, followed quickly by Belgium and Holland. France fell soon after (22 June, 1940). Thus, by mid-1940, most of Europe was under either Nazi or Fascist rule. Britain held out, but her North Atlantic supply lines came under Nazi submarine attack. In June 1941, the Nazis attacked the USSR, and by early winter of that year were winning tank battles on their advances across the Russian plains to threaten both Leningrad and Moscow. Thus, by September 1941, the war could be regarded as little more than a series of disasters for the anti-Nazi forces. The war outlook in Europe was desperate. Britain was in dire peril. Back in 1939, when in the geographically-removed haven of England, McLaren had reacted passionately to the news of the Nazis' invasion of Poland. He created a dark and sombre pastel drawing labelled, appropriately, *"Drawn the Night Hitler Invaded Poland"*.[248]

Even though McLaren was geographically removed from the war, in the sanctuary of the as-yet non-belligerent USA, the events in Europe were, in a sense, even closer to him than the events in Poland had been. His family, with whom he always remained on close and endearing terms,[249] were in Scotland experiencing the privations of war and, along with the rest of Britain's inhabitants, under threat of Nazi occupation. The fact that he retained his pacifist principles prevented him from returning to the UK. Whatever anxieties McLaren felt were not expressed at that time in his films. He continued to work at his animation table at Caravelle Films, making the film about plastics.

McLaren's so-called 'independent period'[250] as a filmmaker in New York had seen him begin by making a 'greetings' film, the significance and substance of which McLaren questioned. By 1941 he was employed by a commercial and advertising film company to do descriptive cel-animation for industrial films. While he had made some

247 Included in *Creative Process*, 1st Assembly (film) dir. Donald McWilliams.

248 Donald McWilliams and Susan Huycke, *Creative Process s: Norman McLaren* dir. Donald McWilliams, National Film Board of Canada, 1991, script 25.

249 John McLaren, personal interview 5 September 1991. John McLaren, Norman's brother, holds thirty years of Norman's letters to the McLaren parents.

250 Glover 10.

remarkable films under trying circumstances for the (Guggenheim) Museum of Non-objective Painting, his long-term prospects in film looked bleak. The only source of sustained income through filmmaking was at such institutions and in such positions as he occupied at Caravelle Films – and both the institution, implicated as it was in the production of advertising films, and the mechanical nature of the work, were anathema to him. Nevertheless, McLaren remained at his Caravelle animation table, painfully aware of the consequences of the alternative. The lesson taught by his experience of his own poverty was to have a long-lasting effect on him.. That effect, however, was to be realized not in the USA but in Canada.

On 2 July 1941, a meeting in Ottawa between four public servants started a two-month chain of events that would have a profound impact on Norman McLaren's future. One of those officers was John Grierson.

Chapter Five

Canada

National Film Board
Canada
Ottawa, July 2, 1941

At a meeting today with Mr. Budden, Mr. Mainwaring and another who should be identified (Mr. Mansur) there was discussion of the use of films in connection with war savings. They were very ambitious.[251]

So began a memo written by John Grierson, the head of the National Film Board of Canada. Even Grierson could not, at that stage, have realized how modest those ambitions were when compared to the consequences of a subsidiary suggestion he made at the meeting. That suggestion was to result in Norman McLaren moving to Canada to begin a career with the NFB, a career which would, through the ensuing decades, focus attention not only on the films McLaren would make, but also on the NFB and Canada itself.[252]

The offer

The sequence of events that followed Grierson's suggestion is worth considering for two reasons. Firstly, and obviously, the events reveal in detail how McLaren came to Canada. Secondly, they give an insight into the sorts of processes involved in getting a film off the ground in a public organization.

The purpose of the 2nd July meeting was to explore ways in which the NFB could best help the War Savings Committee in its efforts to raise money for the Canadian war effort. Several strategies were considered. The one of interest here concerns the proposal Grierson had for creating greater public interest in the Committee's efforts. At

[251] John Grierson, NFB memo 2 July. 1941, National Film Board of Canada Archives, Production Files.

[252] A simple glance at the sources of the literature on McLaren, and the awards he received, confirms the scope of the attention. However, the wider implications of this statement will become apparent as the text unfolds.

*Fig. 42. John Grierson
at the NFB.
[NFB.]*

253 D.B. Mansur, War
Savings Committee
letter to John
Grierson, 15 July 1941,
NFB Archives,
Production Files.

254 Grierson memo, 2 July
1941.

255 John Grierson letter to
John Devine,
American Film Center,
2 July 1941, NFB
Archives, Production
Files.

256 McLaren in Gavin
Millar, *The Eye Hears,
The Ear Sees*,
NFB/BBC Film, 1970
and McLaren in Guy
Glover, *McLaren*
(Montreal: National
Film Board of Canada,
1980) 10.

257 McLaren's recollection
in *The Eye Hears*.

the meeting, Grierson confirmed "that by the middle of the fall, the public will have been subjected to a great many films dealing with the production of munitions and supplies".[253] He, therefore, suggested that they try a different approach. Remembering the impact Len Lye's graphic films made during Grierson's tenure with the GPO Film Unit, he suggested to the Committee a similar change of emphasis. Grierson tersely recalled, "I also suggested getting hold of the Len Lye poster films, with a view to getting McLaren from New York to do something similar".[254]

On returning from the meeting, Grierson immediately fired off two letters to New York. One was to the British Library of Information asking them to send to him any Len Lye films they held. The other was to the American Film Center, the same organization that held McLaren's films for McLaren on his arrival in New York. In the AFC letter, Grierson asked the centre to get hold of some of McLaren's abstract films and send them to him as soon as possible as he was "... considering a project to getting McLaren to do some for us here".[255] McLaren received a phone call from Ottawa.[256] It is entirely consistent that the call was made on this day. Grierson's call to McLaren was typically direct: "Come up to Canada to make films for us".[257] That following weekend was the 4th of July weekend, during which McLaren shot his *An American Home*

Movie. If McLaren's confidence, if not prospects, had been given a boost by Grierson's offer, then the weekend would indeed have been a happy one, which, judging from the film, it was. On the Monday after the weekend, that is 7 July, things started moving. On that day, Devine at the AFC received Grierson's 2nd July letter and immediately spoke to McLaren. McLaren told Devine that he would send two films off to Grierson immediately.[258] McLaren had, however, informed Grierson when they had talked on the phone that there was an insurmountable problem. "I told him [Grierson] that I was in the midst of directing a film which would take at least six months, and that my employers would insist I completed it."[259] The following weekend, from Friday 11 July, Grierson is documented as being in New York.[260] McLaren's recollection that Grierson came to New York and spoke to him about the nature of the job coincides with this schedule.[261] McLaren had some further misgivings about the offer. Two years earlier, on his arrival in New York, McLaren's attitude to reuniting with Grierson was conditioned by the circumstances of the time. The Second World War, although ominous, had barely begun. The NFB had only just been formed and was yet to start production. Thus, the possibility of making pro-war propaganda films did not concern McLaren at that time. By 1941 the situation had changed. The NFB was in production and making films – and the war had intensified. Because of his pacifist convictions, McLaren explained that he did not wish to come to Canada if it meant making hard-sell war-propaganda films.[262] Grierson was reassuring. He told McLaren he would be free to do what he wanted.[263]

Grierson's view of McLaren's position in the NFB was clear from the start:

> He [Grierson] had an overall picture of the Film Board's function. It was making a great lot of very factual documentary films and it needed a variety in its programming – a little lightness and fantasy. And that's where he saw me fitting in. That's why he said, 'Come and do what you want.[264] ... you will see that you can make cinema as you understand it. As for your employers, leave that to me.'[265]

Grierson was as good as his word. He used his contacts in government circles to decisive effect. "Grierson, through diplomatic channels, brought strong pressure to

258 John Devine, letter to John Grierson 7 July 1941, NFB Archives, Production Files.

259 McLaren as quoted in Guy Glover, *McLaren*, (Montreal: NFB, 1980) 10.

260 John Grierson letter to John Devine, 9 July 1941, NFB Archives, Production Files and Ross McLean letter to British Library of Information, 12 July 1941, NFB Archives, Production Files.

261 McLaren speaking in *The Eye Hears*.

262 McLaren in Glover 10.

263 McLaren in *The Eye Hears*.

264 McLaren speaking in *The Eye Hears*.

265 McLaren quoting Grierson in Glover 10.

bear on my employers. A few days later they called me in and, to my astonishment, said 'You are free to go to Canada'."[266]

Meanwhile, progress was being made in the Canadian bureaucracy. By August, the films McLaren had sent to the NFB to help Grierson sell the idea of McLaren's work to the decision-makers in the War Savings Committee had been returned to New York. With hindsight, it can be deduced that the films had served the purpose for which they had been sent to Ottawa – funding had been acquired for McLaren to make a directly-drawn film for the NFB in their programme for the War Savings Committee.

Early work for the NFB

McLaren was working on the film even before he left New York for Canada. He had called into the New York office of Technicolor Motion Picture Corporation and was checking on the suitability of the colour-film processing services the company offered. McLaren's direct animation films were usually drawn in black ink on clear film, then, by getting the laboratory to use filters when making prints of the film, single-coloured versions were obtained. A multi-colour version could then be struck by superimposing two or more single-colour prints. McLaren had thereby developed a technique which provided him with colour without compromising the simplicity, directness or speed of the drawing-on-film stage. McLaren's visit confirms that the technique to be used in his first film for the NFB had already been decided. That it was the direct-animation technique is not surprising, since this was the technique used in each of the films McLaren had earlier sent for demonstration purposes to Ottawa.[267] The addition of colour to McLaren's direct-animation films increased their impact on the senses. As well, the difference between McLaren's films and the stark black-and-white NFB documentaries of such things as munitions factories was heightened.

McLaren arrived in Canada on Sunday, 7 September 1941.[268] It has been reported that he then came and 'hung round' the NFB with no specific duties, for almost two weeks.[269] However, as has been seen, even before he departed for Canada McLaren had been engaged in preparation for his first film, and, within days of officially starting work in Ottawa, an itemised production estimate for his

266 McLaren as quoted in Glover 10.

267 These were *Love on the Wing, Allegro, Scherzo*, and *Loops*. Massé-Barnett Company letter to the NFB, 19 August 1941, NFB Archives, Production Files, and Ross McLean letter to Massé-Barnett Company, 21 August 1941, NFB Archives, Production Files.

268 Acting District Superintendent of Immigration letter to Ross McLean, 17 September 1941, NFB Archives, Production Files.

269 Marjorie McKay, History of the National Film Board, unpublished ts., 1965 28, NFB Archives.

first War Savings Trailer (*Five for Four*) had been prepared and presented.[270] The film was estimated to take six weeks for McLaren to make, plus laboratory-processing time. The film was to be two minutes long – i.e. 200 feet long. This meant that over 3,000 separate drawings had to be drawn onto the film stock, and one week had already been used in preparation. Nevertheless, the project was feasible. McLaren was indubitably busy but, given his subsequent schedule, it is little wonder that those first preparatory weeks could be retrospectively viewed as a period of calm – Grierson had a new proposal that would engulf McLaren's NFB baptism in flames of a minor frenzy. And Grierson had a way of putting proposals that would sweep the listener along. Refusal was hardly contemplated, particularly if the listener began to believe that he or she had generated the proposal. Not that McLaren needed firing with enthusiasm for the project. The time-scale Grierson imposed, however, was a daunting one. It was early October when Grierson called on McLaren with his new proposal.[271] He wanted McLaren to make a film on 'mailing early' for pre-Christmas release. As he was leaving, McLaren asked how soon it was needed. Grierson calmly said, "Two weeks".[272]

The two-minute film would require over 3,000 drawings. McLaren's current film proposal had scheduled five or six weeks to complete a similar number of drawings. One is tempted to say McLaren was undaunted by Grierson's request. Daunted or not, he proceeded to draw on film, image by three-thousand image. His work was hectic to the extent that not only his ideas suffered but also the work became a blur. "I didn't have time to develop a good idea. I had the impression that I was repeating myself. Once the film was finished, I was not happy with it."[273] What was important at the time was that McLaren finished the film on schedule. *Mail Early* (1941) was released for the Christmas period that year. McLaren had proved his worth. He had produced a two-minute film at a fraction of the normal cost of such a length of film. His process eliminated scripting, shooting, development of the negative print (since he worked directly on the negative stock of clear film), and editing. This process thereby saved on both equipment and labour costs. Thus, for the cost of one person's salary, plus a little for the necessary printing of the film, and the provision of one room for the filmmaker to work in, the NFB got a continuous flow of films from McLaren, four

270 Estimate for War Savings Trailer *5 for 4* document, 12 September 1941, NFB Archives, Production Files.

271 On 2 October McLaren was still trying to sort out the printing process for his initial project. McLaren letter to Ross McLean, 20 October 1941, NFB Archives, Production Files.

272 McKay 2.

273 McLaren as quoted in "Interview", *Norman McLaren: exhibition and films* (Edinburgh: Scottish Arts Council, 1977) 16.

films in his first year alone.[274] Even the room did not initially cost much, since, for the first few films he made at the NFB, McLaren worked in the drying room of the NFB laboratory.[275]

McLaren had originally moved to Canada on a temporary visa of one month. This was extended, first by three months, then by six.[276] The extension of McLaren's temporary stay was granted on the grounds that he was doing "... valuable work in the production of war films for the National Film Board" and that his services were "... urgently required in the national interest ...".[277] McLaren's services were being retained by the NFB. It was not just because his costs were cheap, his work was also valued. How did McLaren fit in such an organization? What sort of organization was it?

The National Film Board of Canada

The National Film Board of Canada was set up and, for its first five years, run by John Grierson. As such, the organization shared many of the objectives and the features of Grierson's early film units in the UK, most notably the GPO Film Unit. The NFB had the task of making documentary films. Having Grierson's hand at the tiller meant that the NFB headed in much the same direction as the old GPO Film Unit. His personality permeated the institution, not only directly, but also through the recruits he took on at the NFB. The first people Grierson recruited were, in fact, all formerly employed by him at the GPO Film Unit. Thus, the NFB endorsed the same concept of public service, the same spirit of social concern and the same forthright approach in expressing the same social conscience in filmic terms. There were, however, two major differences between Grierson's units and the NFB.

Firstly, the NFB was a Canadian institution. This implied more than a flavouring of the film output with prairies, mounties and the like. A part of the NFB Act of Parliament stipulated that the films it commissioned and distributed were to be "... designed to help Canadians in all parts of Canada to understand the ways of living and the problems of Canadians in other parts".[278] The geographical and cultural diversity of Canada had, since the country's inception, been a potentially fracturing force, hence the creation of the railways from the Atlantic across to the Pacific coasts and the creation of the Canadian Broadcast-

[274] Glover 12, quotes McLaren's starting salary at $40 per week whereas RJS [Spottiswoode] "Estimate for War Savings Trailer *5 for 4*", 12 September 1941, quotes it as $75.

[275] McKay 29.

[276] Acting District Superintendent letter to Ron McLean, 17 September 1941. Director of Immigration letter to A.G.McLean, 3 January 1942. A.G. McLean letter to Acting District Superintendent of Immigration, 27 December 1941, NFB Archives, Production Files.

[277] A.G. McLean letter to Director of Immigration, 27 December 1941.

[278] Canada, *An Act to create a National Film Board,* in *Statutes of Canada,* 3 George VI, Ch. 20 (Ottawa: Joseph Oscar Patenaude, 1939) as quoted in D.B. Jones, *Movies and Memoranda: An Interpretative History of the National Film Board of Canada,* Canadian Film Ser. 5 (Ottawa: Canadian Film Institute, 1981) 22.

ing Corporation, disseminating Canadian voices, and later also faces, to Canadians across the country. The NFB was the third member of this unifying triumvirate. From the awareness of other Canadians, provided by the railways, the CBC and the NFB, came a greater appreciation of differences across the country and of similarities within the country. As the NFB grew, so did its distribution network grow to include other countries. The NFB contributed to the way the rest of the world perceived Canada. Thus, as a national institution, the NFB had an overriding function the GPO Film Unit never had.

Secondly, the NFB's formative years were war years. Just as the issue of the war dominated other aspects of Canadian life so it dominated the NFB. The war provided a sense of purpose for those who worked at the NFB. It even lessened the traditional factionalism between government departments. Grierson's presence was also a considerable factor in this regard, but then the war was responsible for that too. Having submitted his proposals to the Canadian Government for the establishment of the NFB, Grierson had left Canada when the war broke out, curtailing his travel plans. He was in Washington when he received the request to head the NFB. Thus, Grierson's greatest gift to Canada also became, by chance, his greatest gift to himself.

Another consequence of war was the frugality it imposed on the new organization. Money was not plentiful, and the accommodation was improvised. Grierson possessed a developed sense of the duties and responsibilities of being a public servant. This moral attitude was the accepted one at the NFB. McLaren, for example, was scrupulously honest when preparing any expense account, always aware that his position as a public servant was a position of trust which should not be abused.[279] Thus, McLaren's ethical beliefs governed even the mundane aspects of his life at the NFB, as well as being a factor in his move to Canada, since he had been reassured by Grierson that he would not be asked to make hard-sell propaganda.

McLaren and war propaganda

McLaren accepted Grierson's assurances regarding war propaganda. Did Grierson keep those assurances? On the face of it the answer is unhesitatingly, yes. After all,

[279] Réné Jodoin, personal interview, 5 November 1990.

McLaren stayed at the NFB throughout the period of the war (and long after). Had the NFB attempted to break those assurances one would have expected McLaren to decline to participate and, if necessary, leave the NFB, for McLaren had a history of taking strong moral stands. He joined the Communist Party on the moral issue of social equity. He left it when Stalin made a pact with Hitler. As a pacifist, he left the UK rather than be compelled to fight in the war. Of the films he made for the NFB during the war, McLaren never expressed any reservations about their propaganda content. Thus, he at least, was of the opinion that he did not make hard-sell propaganda. But, what did McLaren mean by 'hard-sell'?

The term 'hard-sell' carries two connotations. One refers to the means of expression. Put simply, 'hard-sell' communication is direct and carries no hint of subtlety. The second connotation refers to the message's meaning. A 'hard-sell' message is one that has an extreme meaning. It was the second sense of the phrase that was uppermost in McLaren's mind when he expressed his reservations to Grierson. McLaren, the pacifist, did not wish to be associated with messages that contributed to the violence of the war. For example, he would not have wished to make films that advocated joining the forces or killing the enemy. Of course, these pacifist views could be seen as extreme by those whose opinions supported the war. Thus, McLaren used the term 'hard-sell propaganda' to cover a particular set of beliefs. The NFB was a publicly funded organization, the resources of which were focussed on the national war effort. In such an organization, how were McLaren's restrictive parameters of filmmaking accommodated? In other words, how was it that McLaren was exempted from making hard-sell propaganda films?

McLaren's rôle at the NFB provides the source of the answer. McLaren was employed to make happy, jolly films which were intended to act as a relief on film programmes that were otherwise full of the more serious and sombre NFB documentary output. The direct-animation techniques being used by McLaren suited this purpose perfectly. It was difficult to see the simple, dynamic imagery, together with its bright colour, as anything other than exuberant. McLaren's technique, therefore, confirmed his special position.

So far, it has been assumed that McLaren was right in believing that the films he made at the NFB during the

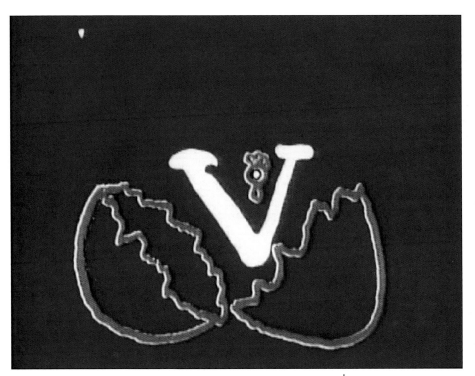

Fig. 43. Hen Hop.
The 'V for Victory'
symbol appears towards
the end of the film.
[NFB.]

war were not hard-sell propaganda. McLaren made a number of war-propaganda films. What purpose do these films serve? Do they, in fact, qualify as hard-sell?

McLaren made five films with war messages: *V for Victory* (1941), *Five for Four* (1942) – this was the film he initially worked on when he first arrived at the NFB – *Hen Hop* (1942), *Dollar Dance* (1943), and *Keep Your Mouth Shut* (1944). McLaren offered an explanation of his war-time films:

> I realized perhaps the necessity of the war because of what Hitler was doing to the racial question. So I cooperated with the war effort, but no more than I had to. No, I wasn't an enthusiastic cooperator, but the kind of cooperation I was asked to do was very simple: make light films with wartime messages like buying savings bonds, keeping your mouth shut.[280]

The message of *Dollar Dance* concerned anti-inflationary measures and, as such, could just as well be a peace-time message. *V for Victory*, *Five for Four* and *Hen Hop* each promote the sale of War Bonds. Since the money from the sale of War Bonds went to the government, and therefore could be used to buy armaments, then an ironic

280 McLaren as quoted in Donald McWilliams and Susan Huycke, *Creative Process: Norman McLaren*, dir. Donald McWilliams, National Film Board of Canada, 1991, script 27.

connection with McLaren's depiction, in *Hell UnLtd*, of the armaments dealer as a personification of evil, could be made. This connection becomes almost tangible if one particular publicity scheme for War Savings Certificates is taken into account. "Our effort to increase the monthly subscription to War Savings Certificates will take the form of establishing quotas for each community. This quota will be expressed in terms of some war weapon rather than in cash."[281] Such specific itemization is, however, in this context, misleading. The buyer of War Bonds had no greater influence on what his or her money was used for, than the individual taxpayer had over other government expenditure. In that sense, the bonds were no more or less evil than general taxation. To be consistent, to be against one government method of gathering and spending money because of the possibility of its being used for armaments, was to be against the other. A similar concept was inherent in both schemes. It was a concept that McLaren, with socialist convictions on the matters of taxation, would reaffirm. That McLaren made films promoting War Bonds does not indicate that he agreed to advocate violence.

The final film McLaren made for the war effort was *Keep Your Mouth Shut*. This film is much closer to the sort of hard-sell propaganda McLaren wished to avoid making. There are several factors which push the film in that direction. First, and most obvious, is the change of technique. The film does not use direct-animation. It mixes live-action with the animation of objects. It is not energetic and fast moving. It is not in colour, it is black and white. The film, therefore, does not have the carefree energy of McLaren's earlier war-time films. It is still humorous, but in a chilling way. The primary factor which moves the film towards hard-sell propaganda is its negative attitude towards the enemy. As well, the enemy is presented in a stereotypical manner. In the film, "Seemingly innocent gossip is given a tragic meaning when it is overheard by a glistening skull who gloats, swastikas gleaming in empty eye-sockets, 'The Axis wishes to thank you ...'"[282] This depiction is a disconcerting feature of the film, even though the film's main objective is the advocacy of absolute discretion – a totally non-violent war-time activity. Using the appropriate original connotation of 'hard-sell', McLaren's depiction of the enemy in *Keep Your Mouth Shut* was an extreme one. In that respect the film veered into the realm of 'hard-sell'. A sense of proportion, however, should be

281 D.B. Mansur, War Savings Committee letter to John Grierson, 15 July 1941, 2, NFB Archives, Production Files.

282 Maynard Collins, *Norman McLaren* (Ottawa: Canadian Film Institute, 1976) 36.

maintained. Seen in the context of other war propaganda of all sides, this lapse by McLaren was minor. It was partly a consequence of McLaren's war-time films becoming increasingly specific. "In my opinion the messages of these war films become more and more precise. At the beginning, the message did not worry me over much, but later I became conscious of its importance."[283] The implication here is that with each war-time film McLaren came to see increasing value in the films' moral and social functions as opposed to their aesthetic appeal. Earlier, McLaren had felt misgivings about making abstract films. "... I felt guilty too. I had sufficient social conscience to realize making abstract films in time of war is kind of idiotic ..."[284] But he accepted Grierson's rationalization concerning the relieving function of such films at the NFB. McLaren expunged feelings of guilt to a sufficient extent as to allow himself to make the war-time films. The trend apparent in the war-time films shows that McLaren's wish to make films containing social statements remained and that he gradually gave way to it. After the abstract indulgence of his New York period, he was shifting the emphasis in his films back to the utilitarian, overtly social-reforming goals of his earlier filmmaking.

The foregoing observations do help to answer the question posed earlier: Did Grierson keep his assurances about not requiring McLaren to make hard-sell propaganda? Grierson, being aware of the range of propaganda used during the war, would be amused by the suggestion that McLaren's diversionary war-time films contained any 'hard-sell'. Yet, McLaren's work did change in emphasis. It became more explicit and direct, and his last war-time film contained some sinister imagery of the enemy. How much this change can be attributed to Grierson is difficult to ascertain. After the initial meetings with Grierson for the *Mail Early* film, McLaren did not see a lot of him. "My contacts with Grierson after that were very few and far between. He spent so much time moving around Canada and maybe abroad."[285] Even though Grierson did not have to be in contact in order to exude the Grierson influence – it often came second hand, through people who worked with him[286] – his principal impact on McLaren had already been made. In his initial, and crucial, justification of McLaren's special rôle at the NFB, Grierson was reducing McLaren's inclination to make socially-aware films. Any move on McLaren's part to revive that inclination was of

283 McLaren as quoted in "Interview", Scottish Arts Council 18.

284 McLaren in transcript of taped interview, 29 February 1976, p.16, Montreal *The Grierson Project,* Cassette VI side I, McGill Archives, Montreal.

285 McLaren as quoted in "Interview", Scottish Arts Council 12.

286 McLaren "Interview", *Grierson Project* 12.

McLaren's making and not of Grierson's doing. However, working in the atmosphere of the NFB with its overriding Griersonian objectives of making utilitarian films, would have revived the dormant guilt of a person with a deep social conscience. McLaren was such a person.

McLaren's formation of the NFB Animation Unit

As the NFB grew, so did its need for more animators. The need was not just for work on animated films alone, but also for work on animated segments in other films, that is, animated titles, maps and diagrams. In 1942 McLaren began recruiting. He brought in a recruit, Guy Glover, who although he did not last very long in animation, was to become a great success in other areas at the NFB. McLaren was inundated with work, but Grierson was away on one of his trips, so, it was the Assistant Commissioner, Ross McLean, whom McLaren approached and asked if Glover might be hired. Since the New York recommendation of Glover by McLaren, Glover had improved his credentials. While in New York with McLaren, Glover had made his own film by drawing directly on the film stock. *Living the Blues* was an abstract film, made to accord with *Andy's Blues* by pianist Joe Sullivan.[287] Not only was Glover hired, but after a short while he was making his own film – another abstract one, this time called *Marching the Colours* (1942). This film uses a series of cinematic wipes of the type employed in commercial cinema. By manipulating the movement (the angle, direction and speed) of the wipes, introducing overlaps as well as colour, and organizing these elements to accord with the structure of the accompanying march, Glover produced a remarkable film, which decades after its inception could still be found in the NFB distri-bution catalogues.[288] "... [W]hen it was screened, Grierson asked who made it. Told that it was the work of Guy Glover, Grierson asked who he was and where he worked. It came as a complete surprise that he was on the staff."[289] Exactly what caused Glover's subsequent move from animation is not clear, for *Marching the Colours* attests that Glover pos-sessed considerable ability in the area of abstract and ex-perimental animation. The general cinematic aptitude revealed in the film was not lost to the NFB, however. Moreover, Glover's move into the live-action section of the NFB enabled him to use his theatrical and literary

287 Donald McWilliams NFB memorandum to David Verrall *Living the Blues*, 5 January 1984, NFB Archives, McLaren File – Techniques.

288 McWilliams memorandum to Verrall, 5 January 1984.

289 McKay 29.

Fig. 44. An NFB photograph of Guy Glover taken in the 1950s. [NFB.]

background. He was assigned to Newsclips and made a film advocating greater vegetable consumption. Then he compiled a film from one-hundred thousand feet of film shot by the Canadian Army Film Unit. Censors had removed most of the exciting sections, but from the remaining shots of sports days and ceremonies, he contrived to make a film which cleverly used those limited resources available. It was called *Letter from Overseas*.[290] Glover had made an excellent start at the NFB and he went on to enjoy an outstanding career with the organization.

Guy Glover would remain at the National Film Board until 1979, becoming, as a director, producer and executive producer, one of the key figures in the development of the National Film Board into the major documentary film unit on the international scene. He was also the first head of French Production at the Board, a post he held, with one interrup-

290 McKay 29.

Fig. 45. Evelyn Lambart in the early days of the NFB. [NFB.]

Fig. 46. Lambart, in May 1944, shortly after joining the NFB. She is working on a map segment for the NFB film Fortress Japan. *[NFB.]*

tion, from 1944 to 1953. The core of his strength as a producer lay in his remarkably developed critical faculty, expressed with a memorable vocabulary, clarity and turn of phrase.[291]

Although McLaren lost Glover as an animation assistant, the latter's eloquent critical abilities were not lost to McLaren. In addition to their personal partnership, which was to last for the rest of McLaren's life, Glover also provided McLaren with consistent, unreserved, yet pertinent, criticism of his work.

Another person who became close to McLaren and who also became part of McLaren's core of advisors/critics

291 Bernard Lutz, *NFB Pioneer Producer Dies Near Montreal,* National Film Board of Canada News Release, 19 May 1988, NFB Archives, Glover File.

Fig. 47. Three of the early recruits to animation work at the NFB, (l–r) George Dunning, René Jodoin and Jim McKay in discussion with Norman McLaren. A photo from the 1940s. [NFB Archive.]

Fig. 48. Grant Munro appearing in Neighbours. [NFB.]

was Evelyn Lambart. She also arrived at the Film Board in 1942, and, like Glover, had an original designation from which she moved. Unlike Glover, she moved to, rather than from, animation. Assigned to lettering and map-making, she was the first to volunteer when McLaren asked for extra help: "It required going up a ladder, operating a camera shutter, shooting some animation".[292] Her rôle as an assistant on many of McLaren's films changed, over the years, to that of film partner.

Over the next couple of years, McLaren was joined by René Jodoin (who was to make several films – *Spheres, New York Lightboard, Alouette, A Phantasy* – with McLaren and who in 1966 set up the NFB's French Animation Unit,

292 Evelyn Lambart, personal interview, (Sutton, PQ, 31 October 1990).

becoming its first head), Jim McKay, George Dunning (who later went to the UK and made *The Yellow Submarine*), Jean-Paul Ladouceur (who was to act as one of McLaren's Neighbours) and Grant Munro (who was to act as the other Neighbour as well as collaborate with McLaren on many his films – *Neighbours, Two Bagatelles, Canon, Animated Motion*).

In the meantime, McLaren had formed the NFB's first animation department. McLaren had made the proposal to Sydney Newman, who, years later, was to become head of the NFB: "I said to Sydney, 'There's a need for an animation department here. We're doing titles for films and starting to use maps. Why don't we join forces with the title department and see if we can get one?'"[293] After discussion with Grierson, McLaren was requested to set up an animation department.

Just as Grierson at the GPO Film Unit had brought in two experienced professionals (Cavalcanti and Flaherty) to teach his young, idealistic filmmakers, it will be recalled that he did the same in Canada. From the UK he brought in the core of his NFB team. Stuart Legg, Raymond Spottiswoode, Stanley W. Hawes and J.D. Davidson became teachers as much as filmmakers. With the growth in personnel in animation, McLaren also found himself in such a rôle. His gradual acquisition of such duties, his undemonstrative personality and, most importantly, his fundamental respect for another's artistic expression, determined McLaren's approach to teaching. He encouraged each animator to find his or her own means of expression. Although he taught the craft of technique, he encouraged experimentation in technique. He was enormously generous with his time. He expected integrity in artistic matters and a similar integrity and sense of responsibility to the employer. McLaren's method of teaching was not based on an authoritarian issuing of directives. He led by example.[294]

The results of McLaren's teaching can be seen in the films made by his pupils, most of whom went on to establish themselves in one sphere or another of animation filmmaking. This is not the place for such a wide-ranging survey, but suffice it to say that the diversity of filmic accomplishments of McLaren's pupils ranges from Pierre Hébert's performances with the drawn-on animation process – e.g. dual screens and live musicians accompanying him in *La Plaint Humaine* – to George Dunning's *The Yellow Submarine*. McLaren's sense of duty compelled him to take

293 McLaren as quoted in "Interview", *The Grierson Project* (29 February 1976) 15.

294 McLaren's various teaching attributes were recalled by his former students who became his colleagues. René Jodoin, personal interview 5 November 1990. Pierre Hébert, personal interview 19 November 1990. Colin Low, personal interview 9 November 1990.

the dual obligations of teaching and heading the Animation Unit seriously. The consequence was that his own film output declined. Yet again McLaren was experiencing a conflict, this time it was between his perceived duty to his colleagues and his desire to indulge his artistic expression. The end of the war was in sight. A post-war optimism was emerging. The Film Board was starting a series of animated films using French-Canadian folk-songs and folk-music – the *Chants populaires* series. McLaren had heard some of the songs and had been stimulated by them. The political aspect of promoting French-Canadian culture also counted in the series' favour, thereby mitigating any social qualms McLaren was feeling about reimmersing himself in film-making. A successor as head of the Animation Unit was found. McLaren felt liberated: "After I had built up the animation department to about six people and one of them took over, I was itching to get back to my own films".[295]

The early post-war films

McLaren did get back to his own films. His films of the immediate post-war period show three tendencies. One is the tendency to react against the type of film that he had just finished making. Initially his enthusiasm for the *Chants populaires* series took him through two films which display similar ethereal moods. The calm, steady movement on *C'est l'aviron* (1944),[296] and the gradual metamorphoses of *Là-haut sur ces montagnes* (1945), are in contrast to the frenetic energy of his previous directly-animated films. The same technique of overlapping dissolves was used in *A Little Phantasy on a 19th-century Painting* (1946) in which McLaren introduced transformations in his monochrome rendition of Arnold Böklin's painting *Isle of the Dead*. McLaren's reaction against the frenetic energy of his earlier films may also have been influenced by Claire Parker's and Alexander Alexeieff's *En Passant* (1943). This film was the first in the *Chants populaires* series. Parker's and Alexeieff's pinboard method[297] of creating and modifying images pro-duced a film of subtle, black and white graduations and a series of flowing metamorphoses much admired by McLaren.

After his three black and white films of calm move-ment, McLaren then reverted to the lively and colourful direct-animation technique for his next film, *Hoppity Pop* (1946). In his following film, *Fiddle-de-dee* (1947), McLaren

295 McLaren as quoted in "Interview" *The Grierson Project* 18.

296 Although *C'est l'aviron* was made in 1944, it is included as a post-war film in that, as one of the *Chants populaires* series, it was part of the new peace-time programme at the NFB.

297 The pinboard screen was, and still is, comprised of thousands of pins which are pushed through the screen. The pins are pushed back to varying heights so that their shadows from a strong and angled light, are of various lengths. The screen is photographed so that only the ends of the pins are seen – it is their shadows that are the subject of the photograph. For the film's next frame the pins' heights are again modified. The process is repeated for each film frame. The technique produces animated film imagery of unusual softness. When the thousands of shadows are seen on film they merge to form a continuum of modulated and subtle greys. Although McLaren greatly admired the technique, he felt that he did not possess the particular type of aptitude required to use it. McLaren used other methods to obtain his subtle effects.

revived his direct-drawn process that he had used in 1933
for his first film. In the context of his post-war output, this
film may be seen as extending the direct-animation technique used in *Hoppity Pop*. It was also the first abstract film
McLaren had made for the NFB.[298] From this shimmering
mass of energy McLaren again reverted to the calm of the
slow metamorphoses provided by his overlapping-dissolve
technique for his next film, *La Poulette Grise* (1947). An
aborted project, *Chalk River Ballet*, next occupied McLaren
(with René Jodoin). For this work the two animators used
circular cut-out shapes which they moved, and shot frame
by frame. The resulting abstract film was considered too
austere in its precise, stark imagery and uniform movement
and rhythm. In 1949 McLaren, with Eve Lambart's help,
made *Begone Dull Care*. This abstract film is allied with, and
an ally of, the accompanying music-track by the Oscar
Peterson Trio. In making this direct-animation film, the
frame divisions were, for the most part ignored, as they had
been in *Fiddle-de-dee*. *Begone Dull Care* has energy, kaleido-
scopic richness and spontaneity, and, as such, is an emphatic contrast to the abandoned *Chalk River Ballet*. In
making these post-war films, McLaren's creative energies
were fully occupied. He was aware of his spontaneous
veering from one technique or style to another: "I remember very little about this film, except that it was a reaction
to the last film".[299] This statement, apart from the memory
lapse, may be applied to most of McLaren's changes of
direction, particularly technical ones.

298 It should be noted that
Fiddle-de-dee does have
a small
representational
components for
example, a fleeting
little butterfly may be
glimpsed in the film.

299 McLaren talking of
Hoppity Pop, as quoted
in "Interview",
Scottish Arts Council
21.

The second tendency in these post-war films concerns their themes. All the films, with one exception, are positive and optimistic in outlook. The brooding, almost macabre, quality of the exception may in part be explained by the fact that the film, along with its subject matter, was commissioned:

> Stuart Legg was preparing to make a film on Germany [Legg's film was never finished] and wished me to give him a sequence of two to three minutes on 19th-century decadent German romanticism. So I read some books on the question. And one day I saw a picture by a Swiss painter, Arnold Böcklin. For me, it *was* 19th-century romanticism.[300]

As well as *A Little Phantasy on a 19th-Century Painting*, three other films of this period had their subjects predetermined. *C'est l'aviron*, *Là haut sur ces montagnes* and *La Poulette grise* were each a result of McLaren's participation in the *Chants populaires* series and so the subjects came with the songs. All the films McLaren made in this period that emanated from his volition alone, were abstract.

The constant switching from technique to technique through this early post-war period illustrates McLaren's

Fig. 50. Norman McLaren and René Jodoin working together in the late forties. They are manipulating the cut-out shapes for Chalk River Ballet. *The film was to be shelved for some years. [NFB.]*

300 McLaren as quoted in "Interview" Scottish Arts Council 20.

propensity to react. Thus, the optimistic thematic trends in his films of the period and the trend toward abstraction may be expected to suddenly change. Further factors considerably enhanced this probability.

In 1944 McLaren had drawn, with Evelyn Lambart, the animated 'wook'-map-segment of an NFB film, *Our Northern Neighbour*. The film attempted to explore the Russian point-of-view of world events. The map, which depicted the tentacles of Nazi aggression coming towards the viewer who was looking westwards from somewhere inside the USSR, encapsulates the film's political angle. Even though the film's stance surprised, and in some circles caused consternation, the film did capture the mood and hopes of many, McLaren included, who hoped the ensuing Allied victory would begin a new world order of peace and international understanding. The development of the Cold War shattered that dream. Nowhere was that dream more quickly broken than in Canada. Within months of the ending of the Second World War in August 1945, the Gouzenko Spy Scandal erupted and with the eruption, anti-communist hatred and bigotry also surfaced. Although McLaren had come to see the Soviet Union as a less-than-perfect society, such an atmosphere was still distressing, even more so when John Grierson became embroiled in the spy controversy – one of his secretaries was apparently suspected of being part of the Soviet information-gathering 'network' and of intending to use Grierson's influence in order to be placed in a more sensitive government department. Grierson denied being connected, or for that matter being used, in any way by the espionage ring. Nonetheless, capital was made of the situation. The NFB had already been faced with the prospect of finding a new commissioner since, well before all the scandal and in keeping with a pledge to look after the NFB only for the duration of the war, Grierson had resigned on 10 August 1945. The spy-scandal became a hunt for communists. It was subsequently alleged that communist cells existed in various government organizations, including the NFB. Eventually, in early 1950, the Royal Canadian Mounted Police gave the newly appointed commissioner a list of thirty-six names of people who were 'security risks'. Commissioner Arthur Irwin, a former editor of *McLean's* magazine, was expected to fire the people on the list. It may be reasonably argued that McLaren, with his political background, was on it. Fortunately, if he was, several factors protected him.

In early 1947, McLaren was interviewed by *Liberty* magazine. In the interview he issued a political disclaimer:

> Once, I took a very lively interest in politics and in the world around me. I saw a lot of things were going wrong and wanted to do something about them. I joined a radical party in Scotland, participated in study groups, and was fair set to become a reforming young zealot. Then, as time passed, my passion for creative work grew to a point where it usurped my active political interests. Now, I feel I can be of more value making an artistic rather than a political contribution to society. Is that bad?[301]

The first part of the statement is an admission of past 'guilt'. The second part, while not being a recantation, does indicate a change of emphasis. The primacy of political activity had been replaced by artistic activity. Such a statement assumes that artistic (aesthetic) activity could be devoid of political content. For McLaren, this was the case. Further, for him, abstract art was, by definition, an appeal to the senses.[302] The predominance of abstraction in the post-war films occurred from 1946 onwards, slightly pre-dating the *Liberty* article. The question arises: Did McLaren deliberately choose to make abstract films in order to avoid making overtly political statements in his films? There is no evidence to suggest that he did. Even his private works of the period, such as his drawing and the film experiment *The Head Test*, while being representational and showing overtones of anxiety, sadness and even pain, are general in scope and do not have direct political implications.[303] Such work is also evidence that McLaren was able to contain this expression of darker emotions within his private world.

The increasing predominance of abstract work, further emphasised his accepted NFB rôle as the provider of 'programme sweeteners'. The assumption was that the provider of such films could not possibly be a security risk.

The earlier-mentioned likelihood of a reactive change occurring in McLaren's work was exacerbated by the atmosphere pervading Canada and the NFB. The social guilt that he felt by fulfilling the menial rôle as a maker of abstract films was becoming as inescapable as the rôle itself, and, with the NFB's predicament, there was no alternative rôle for him. The reactive change, when it came, also helped Commissioner Irwin – assuming McLaren's name had been on that security list.

301 Norman McLaren as quoted in Gerald Hawkins, "Liberty Profile: Norman McLaren", *Liberty* 18 (January 1947).

302 McLaren as quoted in Donald McWilliams, *Creative Process*, proposal, June 1985. Donald McWilliams Collection, Montreal.

303 Norman McLaren, *The drawings of / les dessins de Norman McLaren* ed. Michael White (Montreal: Tundra / Les Livres Toundra, 1975) and Norman McLaren, *The Head Test* included in *Creative Process* 1st Assembly (film).

McLaren was given a year's leave from the NFB in order to do some work overseas for the United Nations Educational, Scientific and Cultural Organisation. Not only had there been McLaren's *Liberty* interview and his abstract, apolitical filmmaking, but now he had more formal international recognition. Even if McLaren's name had been on the RCMP list, to sack him would have invited public ridicule. McLaren was not sacked. In fact, Irwin refused to sack thirty-three of the thirty-six people who were on the list. The NFB was able to continue with its integrity largely intact. In the meantime, McLaren had left for his UNESCO job. In August 1949 he left for China.

Asia

A clear statement of the scope and aims of the UNESCO project on which McLaren was engaged appeared in the preface of the project's subsequent report:

> During 1949 Unesco organized an experiment in West China for the preparation of a wide range of visual aids and their practical use in fundamental education. The work was done in close collaboration with the Mass Education Movement through its Rural Reconstruction College at Pehpei. A single topic was chosen, 'The Healthy Village', in order to allow for intensive preparation and a valid comparison between the different aids.
>
> There were, naturally, two aims in Unesco's action: to carry out a piece of educational work on the spot, and to place the experience of the Chinese project at the disposal of educators elsewhere.[304]

That the second objective was achieved is indicated by the fact that the above was taken from the report which was prepared in order to disseminate the findings. Again, still working in reverse, the contents of the report show that the first objective, the carrying out of the experiment, was also achieved. An enthusiastic McLaren described his part in the planned project:

> I am going to teach a group of Chinese artists how to make animated films, so that they can start making them themselves in order to help educate the people in the backward villages there, who cant [sic] read or write, and who need films made to teach them how to have a *healthy* village. Films on vaccination, hygene

[304] Norman McLaren, *The Healthy Village: An Experiment in Visual Education in West China*, Monographs on Fundamental Education 5, Art Department Report (Paris: UNESCO, 1951) Preface.

Fig. 51. Two frames from a film on hygiene. This film was also part of the series made by Mclaren's Chinese students. Although the technique of drawing with felt pens onto paper has allowed the film-maker to build figures of greater complexity than the direct method would allow, the work nevertheless displays restraint and simplicity. [McLaren Archive/NFB.]

[sic], and all matters about health. I shall be going to the province of Szechwan, which is in the interior in the south. A very backward area. I shall be working with a Mr. Hubbard, an educationist from UNESO [sic], and the project we are working on is called the CHINESE AUDIO-VISUAL PROJECT. What we do with it, is supposed to act as a model for all other member-nations in Uneso [sic] who want to do something about education in their backward areas.[305]

The project went almost to plan. McLaren worked diligently, and taught representative artists from the local population. However, the teaching of filmmaking was only undertaken as a culmination of the Audio-Visual Project. McLaren was unable to teach filmmaking immediately without teaching some preparatory exercises. These exer-

Fig. 52. Norman McLaren presented his Healthy Village Report at UNESCO's Paris Headquarters, on his way home from China in 1950. [Photo by Al Taylor.] [McLaren Archive/NFB.]

305 Norman McLaren, letter to his mother, 1 May 1949, p. 2, Grierson Archives, University of Stirling, GAA:31:63.

Fig. 53. One of the posters made in China under Norman McLaren's UNESCO project. Note the apertures through which a variety of information may be presented. [McLaren Archive/NFB.]

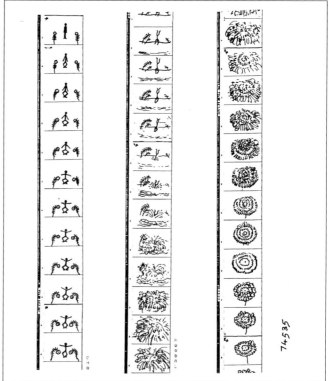

Fig. 54. Three 12-frame sequences from a film made on the energy-giving properties of a balanced diet. This film was one of a cumulative series of works made by McLaren's Chinese students using low-cost animation techniques. This film was made by drawing directly on to the film. [McLaren Archive/NFB.]

cises became useful in themselves. Thus, posters, picture books, scrolls and film strips were made.[306] Simple equipment was used for these stages and also for the film work. McLaren was thus able to pass on other skills in addition to those associated with direct-animation filmmaking. This was not the only aspect of the work that pleased him. McLaren enjoyed being a teacher. For him the process of teaching was not telling others what to do, but drawing it out of them. From UNESCO's point of view, McLaren's project was a success. It was of practical benefit to those Chinese villages, and, through the report, to any other communities that wished to implement a similar scheme. He was doing a job which he felt was socially beneficial. This was the first set of consequences of McLaren's work in China.

Although they were not to become apparent until McLaren's return home to Canada, other consequences also were to flow from McLaren's stay in China. Delayed, or not, these consequences were important as they brought McLaren's political concerns back to the surface.

In 1949, China was in the final stages of its civil war. The place to which McLaren had been consigned, Pehpei (Pei-p'ei), near Chunking (Ch'ung-ch'ing) in Szechwan province, was still in the Nationalists' hands. McLaren half expected Pehpei to be in the midst of political turmoil. Before he left, he was at pains to point out to his mother that he was protected by UNESCO, the work for which organization was apolitical. He casually added: "By July, it is most likely that the war will be over ...".[307] In his first months in China, McLaren observed the people around him. He saw a situation remarkably similar to that which he had observed in Spain in 1936.[308]

> The farmers are all dreadfully in debt, and are forced to borrow money from the landowners and richer folk at interest rates of about 50 per cent, and that is not a typing error for 5, I really mean FIFTY. The landowners take practically all the crops from the farmers, and generally exploit the farmers shockingly by all sorts of practices. When the harvest is in, he will come round to the farmers' houses and expect to be given a great feast in his honor ... at each house, (this, after arranging to take away most of the fruits of the farmer's labor ... as interest on the money he has lent the farmer.). This puts the farmer further in debt, and so the vicious cycle goes on.

[306] Norman McLaren, Diary, 24 October 1949, pp. 3–4, Grierson Archives, University of Stirling, GAA:31:63.

[307] McLaren letter to his mother, 1 May 1949, p. 2.

[308] Norman McLaren, letter to his parents,November 1936, p. 2. Grierson Archives, University of Stirling.

Fig. 55. A McLaren
photo of the Chinese
Communist liberation
being welcomed by
cheerful locals.
[McLaren
Archive/NFB.]

Fig. 56. Norman
McLaren in China.
[McLaren
Archive/NFB.]

The Nationalist government enacted new laws to do
away with thiw, [sic] but the influence of the land-
owners has corrupted the law courts, and so the legal
decisions are all still in the landlord's and money-
lender's favor, even tho they are against the law. The
whole situation is filthy and degenerate and evil; and
there is no wonder the communists are eagerly welcomed with their program of land redistribution and
aboition of usury. [309]

The experience in Pehpei of the Nationalist Army
retreat and the town's preparations for a rapturous, ban-
ner-strewn welcome for the Chinese Red Army liberators
is amusingly described in the article published in *McLean's*
on McLaren's return to Canada.[310] Along the bedecked

309 McLaren Diary, 24
    October 1949, p.2.

310 Norman McLaren, "I
    Saw the Chinese Reds
    Take Over", *McLean's*
    (15 October 1950):
    73–76.

streets the waiting and excited school children had a surprise. Instead of the expected battalions of triumphant Red Army troops, the town's liberators "... arrived in one solitary truck".[311]

McLaren was impressed by the new regime.

> There's much enthusiasm by the country folk for the new regime, for the old government was so evil, corrupt and full of graft; the old authorities lived lavishly and luxuriously, while most of the farming folk are near starvation; the new authorities live very humbly, and are very strict and puritan.[312]

On his return to Canada, McLaren was interviewed for the *McLean's* article describing his experience. The article is a more sober reflection of events than the accounts he related to his parents, particularly in its depiction of life under the new regime. He also resumed his film work, once again exploring new techniques. This time his energies were focussed on creating animated three-dimensional images. He made two 3-D films, *Now is the Time* (1950–1951), and *Around is Around* (1950–1951), for the Festival of Britain. These films, started and completed by McLaren so quickly after his stay in China, show no indication of his experiences, or of his reaction to them. McLaren's next film, exploring yet another technique, was about highway safety. During the making of this film, however, an ironic occurrence of events was to bring McLaren's political tensions erupting to the surface. These events, and the film in which McLaren gives expression to these tensions, *Neighbours* (1952), are examined later.

Towards the end of 1953, McLaren accepted another UNESCO assignment, this time to India. With Edward Ardizonne, an English artist, he conducted two three-month workshops – one in Delhi and one in Mysore. The work was very similar to the UNESCO China project on which he worked:

> ... we will experiment in, the techniques of BROADSHEETS, HANDBILLS, POSTERS, PAMPHLETS, PICTUREBOOKS, CHARTS, DIAGRAMS, MODELS, DISPLAYS, FILMSTRIPS, SLIDES, FILMS (both ANIMATED AND ACTUALITY), PUPPET SHOWS (using traditional Indian methods of rod-puppets, and transparent-parchment shadow puppets, and glove puppets), SONGS, GAMES, DANCES, and DRAMATIC

311 Norman McLaren, "I Saw the Chinese Reds Take Over" 76.

312 Norman McLaren, letter to his parents, 11 January 1950, p. 2, Grierson Archives, University of Stirling, GAA:31:69.

PLAYS WITH ACTORS. Our topics-list reads as follows:- To encourage people to become literate; to tell the stories of Indian Heros [sic] and Saints. To teach improved agricultural methods, and improved cattle-rearing. Health and Hygiene. Civic Rights and duties; improving the occupational methods of city workers; teach about trade unionism; and for women, about motherhood. We will not be able to tackle all on the list of topics, nor all the techniques, and it will depend on the talents, interests and needs of our trainees, just which we will con-centrate [sic] on.[313]

McLaren was more than appalled by the poverty he saw. Worse, he became despairing of the attempts, both Indian and non-Indian, to alleviate it.[314] McLaren even became disenchanted with his own contribution: "I have come to feel certain that this Fundamental Education is no more than giving aspirin for an abscessed tooth. In the long run perhaps a bad thing".[315]

The specific consequences of McLaren's visit to India are not as apparent as those that followed his China work. One reason for this was that the film *Neighbours* had become a huge distribution success. The extent of its impact was such, that, long after the India visit, the film still stood as McLaren's statement on human relationships. This helped to resolve, at least temporarily, some of the anxieties McLaren experienced while in India. It was not until 1957 that McLaren made another film which expounded a parable. The theme of exploitation in *Chairy Tale*, which was made with Claude Jutra as co-director and also with the help of Evelyn Lambart, is applicable to his Indian experiences. The film's use of Ravi Shankar's sitar music supports this Indian connection. However, McLaren has also said the film was motivated by events in his personal life – he was being sat upon by his friends.[316] The Indian connection, if it is existed, was a subconscious one.

The music of India did make a deep impression on McLaren. He became fascinated by its structure: "... [In Indian music] you get one germ in the raga, and that germ is developed and developed and developed. And it builds all the time ... it's just a constant build."[317] This was a significant addition to McLaren's repertoire. It justified the accumulative structure he had used in some earlier films (e.g. *Dots*), and gave him the reassurance to apply this structure to subsequent films. The following description,

313 Norman McLaren, Statement Delhi, 23 November 1952 p. 1, Grierson Archives University of Stirling, GAA:31:78.

314 Norman McLaren, Statement Delhi 1, and letter to Jack and Joan (McLaren), 18 December 1952, Grierson Archives, University of Stirling, GAA:31:86.

315 McLaren, Statement Delhi 1.

316 McLaren "Interview", Collins 72.

317 McLaren as quoted in *Creative Process* script 14.

Fig. 57. Norman
McLaren guides an
Indian student
film-maker.
[McLaren
Archive/NFB.]

by McLaren, of Hindi musical structure also accurately
summarizes his film *Mosaic* or the *Lines* films (see Figs. 58
and 59 on the following pages): "... it slowly keeps building
up by a series of progressively more intricate and more rapid
variations, until a high speed climax terminates the
work".[318]

As for the general consequences of his visit to India,
McLaren's optimism – despite his frustrations before the
enormity of the social and economic problems there –
remained undimmed. However, as his above reservations
on the effectiveness of the Fundamental Education programmes imply, he came to see his most effective contribution to society as being within the NFB.

Apart from visits to animation festivals, the institution of the NFB circumscribed the rest of his professional
life.

McLaren within the National Film Board

As alluded to before, the National Film Board of Canada
has specific objectives which it is legally bound to pursue.
The first aim is "... to produce and distribute, and to
promote the production and distribution of films designed
to interpret Canada to Canadians and to other nations".[319]
This has led to the production of many documentary films
on various aspects of Canada and Canadians.

Being a large, publicly-funded organization, the NFB
follows certain procedures to ensure that it spends the
public's money appropriately. The procedures adopted, in
order to decide what films are to be made, by whom, and

[318] McLaren as quoted in
Creative Process
proposal 10.

[319] Guy Glover, *Creative
Film Making in a
Government
Organization*, text of
address to The New
York Film Council,
New York, 24 April
1962, p.2, NFB
Archives, McLaren
Files, 1184 D-112.

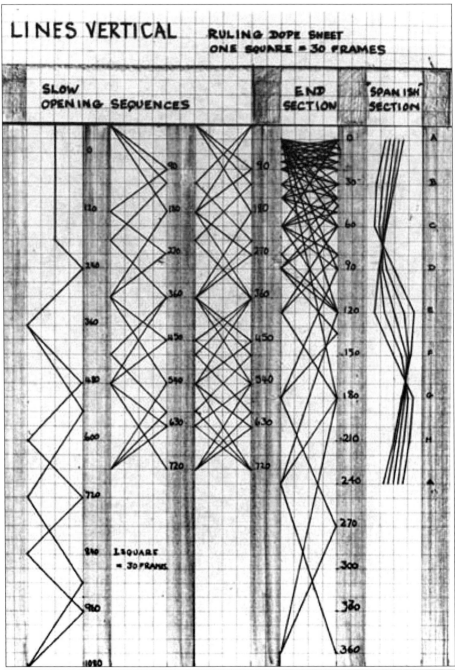

Fig. 58. One of the dope sheets Norman McLaren prepared for making Lines Vertical. This one was for the slow opening sequence, the end section and the Spanish section.
[McLaren Archive/NFB.]

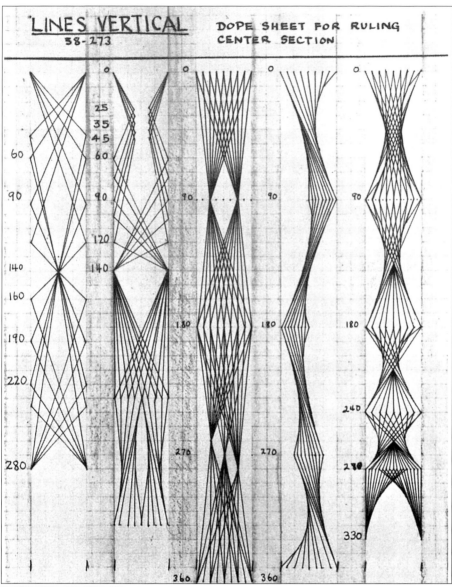

Fig. 59. Another of the dope sheets Norman McLaren prepared for making Lines Vertical. (This dope sheet was one of the starting points for the work. The final centre section is even more complicated. For example, it includes repeats of some of the intricate passages.) The fitting of the complex variations of the centre section between the slow opening section and the rapid dénouement of the end section (Fig. 58), clearly illustrates the raga-like accumulative structure often favoured by McLaren.
[McLaren Archive/NFB.]

for how much, are central ones. While these procedures may vary in detail from time to time, the following description by Guy Glover, who, when he gave it, was Executive

Producer at the NFB, serves as an example of a general pattern.

[Film ideas are received from within the NFB and also the community. These ideas are then put to the Programme Planning meetings.]

Usually each subject proposal is known to one or other of the Executive Producers who is expected to present it. Often he does this on behalf of a filmmaker in his unit who originated it and who, besides putting what he can of it onto paper in brief outline, has discussed it with the Executive Producer in fuller detail. Other proposals are supported by other production or distribution officers – but each proposal must run the gauntlet of the gole committee. If a proposal meets opposition, the members present vote on it.]

[Once the decisions are made at this level they go as recommendations up the various levels, until the Board itself approves, modifies or disapproves, an annual programme.][320]

In view of these NFB objectives and procedures, it is difficult to understand how McLaren fitted into the NFB and how he could justify his films to the Board. To recapitulate a point made previously, John Grierson had earlier given McLaren a special place at the Board as a producer of films that were fun and enjoyable, and as such were a welcome relief to the serious documentaries on an NFB programme. This function was practical at the time and McLaren's films of that time were, ostensibly, functional – they advocated buying War Bonds, or illustrated facets of French-Canadian folk culture. Over the years, however, things gradually changed.

The NFB's films increasingly went to theatrical outlets and were decreasingly in programmes that consisted only of NFB work. In this context, 'light relief' was no longer needed as a programme balance. Such programming considerations were no longer the concern of the NFB, but of the programme compilers of the theatres. When, in the mid-1950s, television became an important element of the NFB's distribution outlets, the programming for 'light relief' became even more an obsolete concept. In addition to these gradual changes, McLaren's films were also changing. An increasing number were abstract. An increasing number were vehicles of personal expression. Thus, fewer

320 Glover, *Creative Film Making* 4.

of McLaren's films could be classified as an "interpretation of Canada" in the utilitarian sense used to apply to other NFB films. How then, could McLaren's non-functional films be justified through the various bureaucratic levels at the NFB, particularly in the context of the redundancy of his special programming rôle?

The NFB had not one, but three specific objectives. In addition to the first one which required the Board to interpret Canada to Canadians and to other nations, there was a stipulation that compelled the board to represent the Canadian Government in any dealings with the private film sector, and, more importantly in this case, the Board was empowered "... to engage in research in film activity and to make available the results thereof to persons engaged in the production of films".[321] It was in serving this objective of the Board that McLaren's work was not only justified but also endorsed as an important and necessary component of the organization. Several aspects of McLaren's work support its value as filmic research. Firstly, McLaren used, and developed, many different animation techniques, ranging from cameraless, hand-drawn work through increasing levels of technology to complex and sophisticated work on the optical printer. He also developed several systems of a visual generation of sound. Secondly, as he worked on a particular technique, McLaren compiled notes which describe in detail the processes he used. These technical notes became the source for many articles written by McLaren and others.[322] In addition, McLaren issued copies of his notes to any person or organization that inquired after them. A third support of the research aspects of McLaren's films lies in the fact that they could be seen as artistic experiments. The subjective nature of evaluating this aspect, however, was not of direct concern since by establishing his technical accomplishments alone, McLaren could justify his place at the NFB: "...apart from any artistic value, my work has been supported [at the NFB] on the grounds that the technical innovations attempted in it have been of potential value to other filmmakers ...".[323]

Although McLaren's place at the NFB was thus secure, the potentially restrictive nature of the Board's bureaucratic method of film-project approval gives rise to some questions concerning the type of position McLaren occupied at the Board. How much freedom did McLaren enjoy? Were any of McLaren's projects declined or modified for lack of sufficient experimentation, inappropriate

321 Glover, *Creative Film-Making* 2.

322 See Bibliography.

323 Norman McLaren, as quoted in Ivan Stadtrucker, questionnaire, 7 March 1975, p. 4, NFB Archives, McLaren Files 1184 D-112.

subject treatment or for any other reason? McLaren answered these questions directly. "When I have an idea for a new film, I follow the standard NFB procedure. I complete a budget form, on which there has to be a three or four-line description of the film's content or purpose".[324] McLaren then described the intricate process of approval, but then concluded, "My proposals have always been accepted, despite the fact it must have been difficult for the committee to visualize the nature of my final film from its three line description".[325] One suspects, therefore, that Glover had McLaren's work in mind when he qualified his account of the approval procedure: "Some of our best films have been accepted at this stage [at Program Planning meetings] as scarcely more than a line of typescript and the gleam in the director's eye which, miraculously, manage to inspire with enough confidence . ..the Program Planning Committee".[326] How was it that McLaren was so generously treated?

In its early days the NFB was a smaller organization and could, therefore, work in a more informal manner. As well, Grierson's allocation to McLaren of the special rôle tended to place McLaren's films in a category of their own. So, although McLaren submitted proposals, even from, literally, his earliest days at the Board, they were essentially formalities.[327] Later, when the NFB was a much larger organization, and the approval procedures more firmly established, McLaren was still regarded as a special figure. As far as his proposals were concerned, these later Planning Committee meetings remained a mere formality. There were four reasons for this generous treatment of his proposals. Firstly, McLaren was the only one of the initial core of British filmmakers brought in by Grierson to remain long-term at the Board. He, therefore, possessed the respect that went with this seniority. Secondly, McLaren earned his standing by a commitment to film and animation, his insight into the discipline and the example he set.[328] Thirdly, the growth in number and importance of film-festivals, together with their propensity to award prizes to McLaren's films, further augmented his position within the NFB. A fourth and very simple reason was that relative to other NFB proposals, McLaren's were invariably modest. His films did not cost much money to make. By the time he was making his final films, committee members felt embarrassment at being asked to review a McLaren proposal.[329] McLaren was able to state, therefore, "Apart

d in

:d in

te for

Fi
Se   NFB
A1   :tion
Fi

.s R
per   :w, 14
N

329 Davi.   ersonal
interv
Novem   ).

from the war time, when I was asked to make films on such topics as Saving Money, Buying War Bond,[sic] etc., but where I was at liberty to treat the themes in my own manner, I have had complete freedom to choose my subject matter, techniques, visual and graphic style, sound, duration of film, etc."[330] To this must be added two further freedoms. McLaren had the freedom to make informal experiments, or film-tests, that may or may not have been subsequently developed into a film.[331] He was also given the freedom to abandon a project if he felt so inclined. This he seldom did. In about 1945, while making *Dans un petit bois*, McLaren fell off his ladder, from where he was operating the animation camera, through the twelve sheets of glass which held the multi-plane set-up he was zoom-shooting. He totally destroyed the set-up and, thereby, any chance of completing the film. "Norman was sitting [unscathed] in this mess of shattered glass, and he got hysterical. He was laughing, and laughing. And said: 'Thank god, now I don't have to make the damn thing'."[332] In 1966, he began shooting a film called *The Seasons*, which, despite his coming back to it several times, remained unfinished. In 1948, he and René Jodoin abandoned *The Chalk River Ballet*. Twenty-one years later McLaren went back to it, did some more work, principally on the sound component, and released the film as *Spheres*.

Despite these freedoms, McLaren did feel pressures. With each new film, McLaren felt the need to surpass the previous films.[333] This need, however, was not directly attributable to pressure being applied by the NFB. It was the consequence of being a filmmaker who was anxious to improve and to progress. There is no evidence to indicate that such ambitions were any less prevalent in filmmakers who worked outside such organizations as the NFB. The only contribution of the NFB in this matter was that it provided McLaren with certain advantages, which enabled him to produce films of remarkable quality and variety, and, as such, made the subsequent standards McLaren sought to achieve that much higher and that much more difficult.

McLaren did enjoy specific advantages at the NFB. Although, particularly in the early years, he did not require a lot of equipment, he could call on the NFB to provide it when he needed it. In 1941, for example, he was able to ask the NFB carpenter to build for him 'Model II' of his film-drawing board.[334] In 1939, in New York, he had built

330 McLaren, Stadtrucker questionnaire 4.

331 *Creative Process* 1st Assembly contains numerous examples such as *The Head Test, Tanguy Landscape Teat,* the *Leap-frog Tests* and the *Blurr Tests.*

332 Grant Munro as quoted in *Creative Process* script 24.

333 Colin Low personal interview 9 November 1990

334 Guy Glover et al., *Technical Aspects of NFB Animation Chiefly in the 1941–51 Period,* 1981, NFB Archives.

Fig. 60. One of McLaren's film-drawing boards. This model is designed so that it can be built and used with very little technical expertise or equipment. [McLaren Archive/NFB.]

'Model I' by improvising with such items as a coat-hanger, which was, perhaps, McLaren's version of the New Zealand fix-it-all material, No. 8 fencing wire. As well as equipment, the NFB provided McLaren, when the need arose, with assistants to help with the camera, to help manipulate objects being animated, or even to act as the objects being pixillated. Although these assistants tended to come from among McLaren's fellow animators at the Board, they nevertheless still provided a service which was coming through the auspices of the NFB. An invaluable service provided by the NFB to Norman McLaren was to distribute his films. Not only did the NFB distribute McLaren's films all over Canada but, through Canada's diplomatic network, McLaren's films, along with other NFB films, were distributed throughout much of the world. The distribution people sometimes were at a loss where to distribute McLaren's films, since they were so different from the live-action documentary work that was normally handled. They learnt that an audience did exist for McLaren's work. On McLaren's production files 'Distribution' is usually indicated as 'Festivals' or 'Ciné Groups'.

Another important benefit McLaren enjoyed was financial security. He was paid regularly, his salary being independent of any returns his films obtained. Freedom

from money worries is an enviable position After his experiences of poverty in New York, McLaren was apprecia-
tive of the security the NFB provided. That he continued
to work at the NFB for a total of forty-three years indicates
an awareness, on McLaren's part, of the long-term financial
and artistic security he enjoyed. With the advantages of the
readily-available equipment, help, distribution and the
provision of security he found at the NFB, McLaren was
able to concentrate more fully on, and devote more time
than would otherwise have been the case to his filmmaking.

The privileged position McLaren occupied at the
NFB has also been seen as a handicap for him:

> But Norman is not a person who is tragic. Well, he
> suffers a great deal. But to suffer is not to be tragic.
> He suffers a great deal because, like all artists, he finds
> it difficult sometimes to get what he wants or to get
> the effect he wants. He finds perhaps that the very
> ease of his life at the Film Board makes his esthetic
> life difficult. He is the most protected artist in the
> history of cinema. That means that he's under no
> great pain and suffering. And that makes him suffer.
> That's one of the paradoxes. The very certainty of his
> life, the security of his life, the cosiness of his life may
> not be good for him. I don't know.[335]

Grierson completely overlooked the extent to which
McLaren did suffer over the plight of his fellow human-
beings – be they in the slums of Glasgow, in the ruins of
Madrid or under the yoke of usury. To allude to such
people and circumstances, would bring a grimace to
McLaren's face and even a tear to his eye.[336] Associated with
these emotions was the feeling of guilt that he could or
should make more direct filmic statements to help such
people. Contrary to Grierson's assertion, McLaren's suffering did not emanate from having nothing to suffer. It
emanated directly from his empathy for his fellow human-
beings and from his guilt at not doing more to help them.
The Grierson comment does make one thing abundantly
clear, however: McLaren did occupy a position of privilege
at the National Film Board, as the "most protected artist in
the history of the cinema".

335 Grierson as quoted in
Creative Process script
30.

336 Colin Low, personal
interview 9 November
1990 and Donald
McWilliams, personal
interview 24 October
1990.

Part Three

Chapter Six

Technical Processes

McLaren used many different themes for his films and made use of a wide part of the continuum between representational verisimilitude and abstraction. Even had these two factors been kept absolutely constant from film to film, McLaren's work could still be viewed as, at best, an astonishing variety of filmic expression, or, at worst, an inconsistent series of films and an unstructured body of work. In this respect, a parallel with the infamous film of McLaren's Glasgow days, *Camera Makes Whoopee* may be seen. This film, it will be recalled, was, much to the young McLaren's distress, lambasted and dismissed from contention in the Scottish Amateur Film Festival Awards, by Grierson. In the film McLaren attempted to use every trick in the cinematographers' manual and as a consequence the film was an uncoordinated and confused expression. It lacked unity. However, the output of an entire career consisting of nearly fifty films is not a single work of art. Any unity it has, or does not have, is not an overriding judgement which condemns, or otherwise, each individual work within that body. The reason for looking at a total output is that relationships and developments may be apparent which give greater insight into the individual works. The negativism implied in an assertion that, for example, McLaren's films lack technical consistency, springs from a failure to appreciate the relationships and developments in his film work.

The extent of McLaren's technical invention is extraordinary and can be glimpsed in the following account. His major technical achievements, together with their implications, are examined. In order to convey the

nature and frequency of change from film to film, a modified chronological sequence is followed. Although some techniques recur in subsequent films, the main discussion of them centres on their initial occurrence.

Drawn-on film

As a student in 1933, without equipment or money, McLaren begged an old commercial 35mm print, stripped the film clear of its emulsion, and then applied coloured inks and dyes to the clear film. The resulting film was projected so often through the school's dilapidated 35mm projector that it, the film, soon wore out and was destroyed. The working pattern established at this point by McLaren proved more durable than the pattern on his unfortunate piece of film. Just as shortages of equipment, material and labour were concerns of his right until the last few years at the National Film Board of Canada, so he continued to find solutions that not only addressed the immediate problems but produced films with startling new effects. In *Love on the Wing*, through his New York work and most of his early work at the NFB, including *Hen Hop* (1942), McLaren drew images directly on the film, frame-by-frame – a difficult task. The filmmaker is drawing in a rectangle

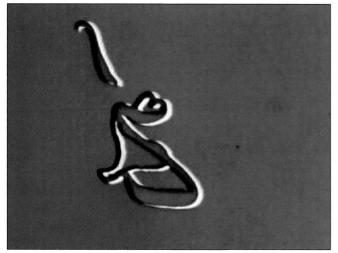

Fig. 62. Loops. This frame is an example of the bold and simple linear style of McLaren's drawn-on-film work. [NFB.]

2.2 cm (seven-eighths of an inch) across. The artist therefore is unable to go into a lot of spatial detail. Moreover, the simplicity of the image looks even starker and its lines even bolder when it is projected, magnified, onto the large screen. In addition, even the most skilled placement of successive images will be revealed on the large screen to be slightly misregistered. The resulting jumping, trembling image (known as 'boiling'), such as appears in Hen Hop, for example, has enormous energy.

The technique of direct-drawing on the film stock permitted McLaren a spontaneous approach. Direct-drawing also was in accordance with his initial approach to filmmaking, which eschewed extensive and detailed planning.

It gave him an intimacy with his work which is revealed in the freshness and liveliness of his direct-drawn films (like Dots, Loops and Hen Hop). This aspect of the association of the technique with spontaneity has been discussed earlier.[337] What has not been examined is the reason for McLaren's use of the technique. On the one hand (to coin a phrase) McLaren has extolled the technique because it put him in direct contact with the film-stock and thereby allowed him to make his films with spontaneity and a high degree of expression, relatively unadulterated by technical processes:

> I try as much as possible to preserve in my relationship to the film the same closeness and intimacy that exists between a painter and his canvas. In normal filmmaking, everybody knows, there's an elaborate series of

[337] Chapter Four, New York Interlude.

optical, chemical and mechanical processes. And these stand between an artist and his finished work. How much simpler it is for an artist with his canvas. So I decided to throw away the camera and instead work straight on the film with pens and ink, brushes and paint. And if I don't like what I do, I use a damp cloth, rub it out and begin again.[338]

On the other hand, McLaren has stated that in New York he used the similar technique of directly drawing the sound-track because of necessity: he could not afford to pay for the process of laying sound on the track by the normal recording methods. By implication, the direct visual images had a similar appeal, especially in those poverty-stricken years in New York. McLaren has asserted that the advantages of the direct method of animation were its cheapness and simplicity:[339]

> I had a terrible time during my first trip to New York in the thirties. I made those Guggenheim films while I was nearly starving in a little room on 125th Street and Riverside Drive. All I had was a pen, some dye, a plain table, a sloping bench with a groove for sliding film and a wire coat hanger.[340]

Thus McLaren has cited two reasons for adopting the drawn-on process: economic necessity and the direct contact with the film stock. Examining both these reasons, their contents and the chronology involved in McLaren's use of the drawn-on film technique, reveals an interdependence which refuses to yield a priority of one reason over another. McLaren first drew directly on film in 1933 because he had no camera. In spite of having other animators' techniques available to him he resumed the practice in 1939 for *Love on the Wing*, and revelled in the freedom for spontaneous and lively expression the method gave him. A year or so later in New York, he once again had no choice but to use the technique as he had no access to equipment such as an animation camera.

His early NFB films also were made using this technique and again economy of means, intrinsic to the method, was an important consideration during these war years. Subsequently, however, McLaren returned to the technique from time to time. *Hoppity Pop* (1946), *Fiddle-de-dee* (1947), *Begone Dull Care* (1949), *Blinkity Blank* (1955), *Short and Suite* (1959), *Serenal* (1959), *Mail Early for Christmas* (1959) and *Lines Vertical* (1960) are each films

338 Norman McLaren as quoted in Donald McWilliams and Susan Huycke, *Creative Process: Norman McLaren,* dir. Donald McWilliams, National Film Board of Canada, 1991 script 6.

339 Norman McLaren as quoted in "Interview", *Norman McLaren: exhibition and films* (Edinburgh: Scottish Arts Council, 1977) 15.

340 McLaren as quoted in *Creative Process* script 5.

Fig. 63. Hen Hop. McLaren drew the original imagery as black ink-lines on clear film. The colours were obtained later in the film-processing lab. [NFB.]

which use the technique of drawing, or scratching, directly on film. Moreover, McLaren had other animation techniques and equipment available to him through these post-war years at the NFB. The method of direct-animation, therefore, continued to appeal to McLaren, even when one of the reasons for adopting it – its cheapness and the consequence that it was the only method available to him – had ceased to apply. Thus, the ease of spontaneity the process offered him, in later years became the technique's *raison d'être*. Added to this, however, was another increasingly important reason for using the technique. McLaren

Fig. 64. As well as painting on a transparent sound track, Norman McLaren also engraved marks on black film. Here he is engraving sound for his 1956 film Rythmetic. [NFB.]

Fig. 65.
On these two pages is a longer twelve-frame sequence-cluster of single-frame images from Blinkity Blank. *The contrasting single-frame presentations of the angular bird range from bold, to suggested outline, to a negative image. These images when run through the projector at normal speed, produce a blinking, shimmering effect.*
[NFB.]

341 "Interview", Scottish
Arts Council 14.

found that within the basic technique of directly working on the film stock, there were many technical variations. The later films explore direct animation through frameless, scratch and the intermittent techniques. These processes will be examined below as will McLaren's instigation of the technical variation.

Black and white into colour

The colours of drawn-on films like *Hen Hop* are a further example of McLaren's use of alternative production methods. This particular technique, associated with converting black and white film-images into colour, was developed by McLaren earlier in the war years. The images were drawn in black and 'white', i.e. black on clear film. Colour was obtained chemically in the processing lab using first a colour positive print and then superimposing a negative print of a different colour. This process not only produced a multi-colour film, it also varied the film's linear imagery. The two prints were not a perfect match. The positive print was a little smaller, and so when the superimposed image was obtained, a thin white line occurred around the components of the image. This effect was discovered accidentally by McLaren when one of his print copies dried and shrank a little before being sent to the laboratory.[341] Recognizing that accidental effects were sometimes successful meant that McLaren felt obliged to try all the possibilities and even impossibilities of the processes of animation. However, economy of means remained the main spur to his use of unorthodox processes.

Sound

It will be recalled that McLaren had independently discovered the possibility of creating sound with visual marks on the optical sound-track some years before his move to the USA. He painted (or scratched) directly on to the sound-track. The result was a series of sounds unique in character. As well, McLaren the composer had a particularly tight control over the rhythm and tempi and their relation to the visual component. As he also drew the visual track of these films, frame-by-frame, he had maximum control of the visual/audio relationship. Another attraction of the process of painting on film, sound or visual track, was that it gave McLaren a closeness with his film which was, as he put it, comparable to that which exists between the painter and the canvas. It is not surprising to find, therefore, that McLaren's directly animated films have an expressive, painterly quality – the marks of the pen or brush are visible. Another advantage of the method was that it allowed immediate feed-back. To see how a sequence or movement was working, he did not have to wait days for film to be processed in a laboratory. He could simply run it through a moviola as he worked. This allowed him two further luxuries. Mistakes could be corrected immediately and he could shape the film as he worked. He had no script, no storyboard, usually only the vaguest of ideas of the whole film. Normally only the next ten or twenty seconds from the point at which he was working took any definite shape in McLaren's mind. Perhaps because of his awareness of the danger of an overly confusing structure resulting from this approach, McLaren's films each have a simple structure. They also had a quality difficult to detect in traditional animated films: spontaneity.

With Evelyn Lambart's help, McLaren also developed a card system of producing sounds. This method was based on Pfenninger's pre-war research. McLaren and Lambart made cards, each of which had a certain frequency of striations on them. Each frequency, when photographed onto the sound-track, was capable of producing a particular pitch. The volume could also be controlled. McLaren used this process extensively in his film *Synchromy* (1971). In this film McLaren was to go one step further by putting the sound-track striations also onto the visual track, but more of that anon – in Chapter Seven.

Intermittent images

For his film *Blinkity Blank* (1955), McLaren used visual intervals, that is, instead of drawing every frame he drew a cluster of four or so frames, sometimes more but sometimes perhaps only one or two, and then left a dozen or so frames blank before another cluster of related images was drawn. This spacing of the images was continued through most of the film. The effect is of a stroboscopic movement full of surprise. The *Blinkity Blank* technique was a reaction to, or development of, the films he had made by drawing or painting on the clear film. As McLaren said "I had made several films by drawing on a blank film. I wondered if I couldn't do the opposite: scratching on black."[342] McLaren also said that working in clear film caused continual problems with dust particles being visible on the film.

342 McLaren as quoted in "Interview", Scottish Arts Council 32.

I had set out to engrave a film on black; I had no idea
what it was going to be about; when I was drawing
directly on clear film, I had to be so careful about
being clean. I thought how wonderful it would be not
having to be careful about being clean; and to be able
to run it through the moviola many times before
worrying about scratching.[343]

With black film, this problem was almost eliminated.
However, the completely black film used by McLaren
prevented him from seeing the edges of the film frame,
thereby removing the most important guide to registering
the position of the image from one frame to the next.
McLaren continues: "This seemed to me to be an [unsolv-
able] problem. However, I said to myself why use *every*
frame?".[344] The solution was to use single frames of image
separated by stretches of blank film. In *Blinkity Blank*,
McLaren took this almost subliminal signalling further.
Firstly, by arranging the images in clusters, he made use of
the fact that although each image lasted the same length of
time, some were more noticeable than others. The last
image in the cluster persisted longest in the viewer's eye.
The first image was the next most important while the
intermediate images were noticed least. Secondly,
McLaren managed to not only imply the continued existence of the image in the blank stretches between the
clusters, but also to suggest the movement of and within
the image, movement of an explosive and almost bewilder-
ing energy.

Cut-outs

Sandwiched between films that required drawing directly
on film, or drawing in pastel, or manipulating a chair,
McLaren explored a contrasting technique. Animating
through the use of cut-out shapes is a calm, clean process
requiring precision. This process, in the context of the
immediately preceding work, was an appealing one. Thus,
he was attracted to use the process that had already been
used by other animators within the NFB. In *Le
Merle* (1958), McLaren and Evelyn Lambart created movement by moving white cut-out paper shapes, frame-by-
frame, under the animation camera (see Figs. 69–70). In
Rythmetic (1956), and *Spheres* (1968 – the visuals were made
earlier, in 1948, and were also used in *A Phantasy*, 1948),
McLaren used this method, augmented by cut-out
'replaceables'. If it was necessary for an object to appear to

343 McLaren as quoted in
    Donald McWilliams,
    Creative Process
    proposal National
    Film Board of Canada,
    July 1985, p.24.

344 McLaren as quoted in
    "Interview", Scottish
    Arts Council 32.

not only move, but also to change size or shape, then, not only displacement, but also replacement of the cut-out object with one that was correspondingly bigger/smaller or different in shape, was required.

3D films

McLaren was fascinated by the illusion of depth achieved through stereoscopic vision. He did many drawings and paintings which, when viewed through a system of mirrors that he devised, contained the illusion of depth. In 1950–51, McLaren made two 3D films for screening at the 1951 Festival of Britain.

For one film, *Now Is the Time*, the sets of imagery were derived predominately from paper cut-outs and drawn-on animation. For *Around Is Around*, McLaren photographed the moving image of an oscilloscope. In his article, "L'animation stéréographique"[345] published a year after he made these two films, McLaren listed no less than six different ways of creating a 3D image through animation – all but one of which (actually drawing two different images, one for the right eye and one for the left) he used in his two films. The techniques McLaren used are each attempts to short-cut the even more laborious process of animation when the aim of a 3D illusion requires double the number of images – i.e. a set of images for each eye.

One technique in particular displays McLaren's ability to make maximum use of the materials he had at his disposal. He achieved an illusion of depth by using exactly the same sequences of image for each eye but with a time delay of two frames for one eye. At any one time, therefore, the viewer's left and right eyes were seeing slightly different images which were then interpreted in terms of depth. It should be remembered though, that this technique will only produce the illusion of depth when the movement of the image is in a horizontal direction since our perception of depth is provided by a horizontal displacement of the images seen by each eye – our eyes being side-by-side rather than one above the other. As well, the two-frame staggering of the images would not achieve an illusion of depth if the image itself significantly changed its shape, for in that case frame three (which would be watched with frame one) would be too much altered for the perceptual processes to register the two images as two views of the same subject – the essence of stereographic projection. Instead, the images would be seen as of different subjects and so would not be

345 Norman McLaren, "L'animation stéréographique", Cahiers du cinéma 14 (juillet-août 1952): 25–33.

Fig. 66. Le Merle *i.*
The blackbird's
introduction is as a bird
of very few components
or cut-outs.
[NFB.]

Fig. 67. Le Merle *ii.*
A relatively orthodox
image of the blackbird
from the film.
[NFB.]

Fig. 68. Le Merle *iii.*
A complex and
culminating image of the
blackbird similar to the
one the film-makers'
hands are manipulating
in Fig. 70.
[NFB.]

Fig. 69. Norman McLaren and Evelyn Lambart move cut-out shapes for the making of Le Merle. [McLaren Archive/NFB.]

Fig. 70. A close-up view of McLaren and Lambart's hands adjusting cut-out shapes in the making of Le Merle. [McLaren Archive/NFB.]

346 In "Interview", Scottish Arts Council 26, McLaren implies that the technique was used throughout *Around is Around*. However, the type of movement and the extent of the change of image within the film make this implausible. McLaren in fact was thinking of the drawn-on-film figures from his other 3D film *Now is the time*. Although these figures are superimposed on a perspective rendering of a cloudscape which utilises another method of attaining an illusion of depth (that of manipulating layers of cels), their movements and stability of image enable them to be the subject of McLaren's two-frame displacement method.

reconciled stereographically. McLaren therefore, was able only to use this particular method in parts of his 3D film work.[346] Be that as it may, the essential point is that McLaren did develop an extremely economic system of providing an illusion of depth for only single sets of imagery are required.

Unfortunately, *Around is Around* and *Now is the Time* require special screens and viewing glasses for the illusion of depth to be successfully achieved. As a consequence, they are rarely screened.

Chain-of-mixes

Animating fast movement involves a succession of large

displacements of an image over a short time, that is, through a small number of frames. Slow movement, on the other hand, normally requires tiny displacements over a long period of time, that is, through a large number of frames. Slow movement, therefore, involves not only a lot more time and labour to produce the greater number of frames, but also an almost impossible degree of accuracy of registration of the image from one frame to the next. This is because any misregistration would cause a jump in the image and this jump would camouflage any slower intentional movement (rather like someone trembling with the DTs trying to perform a slow, graceful ballet). The problem of creating slow movement through animation was resolved by McLaren using an extreme and seemingly contrary solution. Rather than increasing the number of images required, he reduced them drastically. He used only one image.

It would be logical to assume that the use of just one image would produce a static image. With McLaren this was not the case. The process is known as his chain-of-mixes technique and is simple, although it did involve risks on the part of the filmmaker. A painting or drawing was placed on a wall and a shot of several seconds was taken of it from a movie camera fixed firmly in front of the painting or drawing. The camera was set so that it faded the image out. Next, the artist made a few alterations to the painting or drawing. The camera operator then rewound the film a little, and shot again, fading in the new take. This produced a dissolve, or mix, from the first image to the second. The second shot, like every other, was also faded out, ready for the next shot's overlapping fade-in. This procedure was repeated many times. The image being shot undergoes a gradual metamorphosis. The procedure had its difficulties. The film could not be taken out of the camera between shots for developing because of the need for the double exposure in the dissolves. The camera images on the exposed film could not be seen by the animator – in this case McLaren – until the reel of film, or the shooting, was finished. The animator, therefore, had to be fully aware of the recent past of the image and its rate of change in order to make the next alteration to the image compatible. A further problem, associated with the proscription of removing film from the camera, was more serious. Slow, gradual change was the reason for using the dissolve technique, but if a single mistake was made either in the shooting or in the drawing, the flow of the film would be lost, possibly ruining the entire film. As McLaren put it, "[When working on the drawings] I am under tension for the least mistake is fatal".[347] A third problem was also caused by the method's lack of feedback to the animator. The exact nature of the transformations could only be imagined until after the shooting was finished. Even an experienced animator like McLaren could have difficulties in this regard, "...I became more and more anxious. Despite the [image transformation] that I was [creating], I had the impression that I was working uselessly. It was then that I decided to be bold. I was rewarded, because things went much better."[348] *La Poulette grise* exemplifies the dissolve technique (see Figs. 71–76). It was made in 1947, sandwiched between two films in which yet another device, which also happens to be a shortcut, was used.

Frameless drawn-on film

McLaren first painted directly on the film stock in 1933 and even at this early stage laid images which ignored (ran across) the frame divisions in film.[349] He returned to the technique in 1947 (*Fiddle-de-dee*), and again in 1949 when he made, with Eve Lambart's help, *Begone Dull Care*. When they made *Begone Dull Care*, McLaren and Lambart worked jointly on short sections of film. Three to four-foot lengths (i.e. fifty to seventy frames), of film were laid on a surface and paint and resists were applied using all sorts of methods – painting, smudging, painting with lace or chains, or letting dust fall on wet paint. Both sides of the film were used to get independent (or supportive) overlays. Scratches and the crazing of drying paint were also effects which were used. Contrary to expectations, McLaren's work using this technique is not a confused mess. There are two reasons for this. Firstly, the music which accompanies the visuals tends to lend them its structure and tempi. As McLaren had discovered in 1933, even the most amorphously strung-together visuals gain a sense of order if they are accompanied by strongly structured music. Secondly, the work on the visual section did not stop once the paint had dried. In *Begone Dull Care* (1949), for example, McLaren and Lambart worked with the music. They had some preconceptions of the effects they could produce on film, and asked the jazz musician, Oscar Peterson, to work with them, which he did. McLaren and Lambart then modified their images to accord with Peterson's music. They also

347 McLaren as quoted in "Interview", Scottish Arts Council 23.

348 McLaren as quoted in "Interview", Scottish Arts Council 24.

349 It should be acknowledged that both Len Lye (e.g. *Colour Box*, 1935) and Harry Smith (e.g. *No. 1*, c.1940) were also early exponents of this technique and produced significant work usng it.

Fig. 71. La Poulette grise *(i).* This is the first of six stages in the gradual metamorphosis of an image. [NFB.]

Fig. 72. La Poulette grise *(ii).* This stage occurs after c.72 frames of gradual change from i). [NFB.]

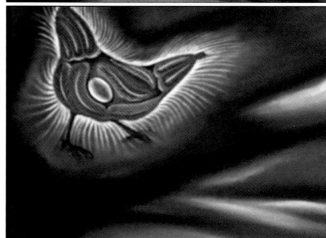

Fig. 73. La Poulette grise *(iii).* This stage is a further c.48 frames of gradual change after (ii). [NFB.]

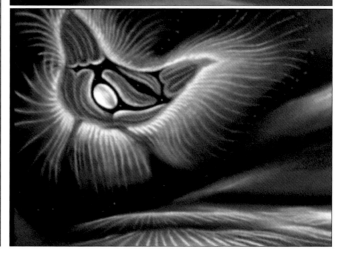

Fig. 74. La Poulette
grise *(iv)*.
*This stage is another
c.48 frames of gradual
change after (iii).*
[NFB.]

Fig. 75. La Poulette
grise *(v)*.
*This stage is yet another
c.24 frames of gradual
change after (iv).*
[NFB.]

Fig. 76. La Poulette
grise *(vi)*.
*And this stage is a
further c.72 frames of
gradual change after (v).*
[NFB.]

edited their images so that the structure of the film's visual and aural components had a strong affinity. In short, the music and the visuals in *Begone Dull Care*, as in McLaren's other films of this type, are carefully matched.

The trio from *Lines*

In a sense, the next piece of technological economy also disregards frame division, and was even pre-empted in parts of other McLaren films such as *Begone Dull Care* (see Fig. 79). If a line or scratch runs vertically down the film, through the frames, the image which appears on the screen is of a vertical line. If the line or scratch is slightly off-vertical, that is, if it starts at the top left corner of the first frame and continues in a straight line down through twenty-four

Fig. 79. In this single-frame sequence from Begone Dull Care a multiplicity of techniques and approaches may be discerned including painting, scratching, use of resist, ignoring frame divisions but also retaining partial frame-by-frame continuity. [NFB.]

350 McLaren as quoted in "Interview", Scottish Arts Council 38.

351 McLaren as quoted in "Interview", Scottish Arts Council 39. Evelyn Lambart has said that "...the lines films were initiated by Norman seeing the relative movement of telephone wires as we travelled past them" (Evelyn Lambart, personal interview 31 October 1990), in which case the idea of rotating the lines of *Lines Vertical* to a horizontal orientation would not have been an unnatural step. Although Réné Jodoin was unsure of the telephone line inspiration for the line films, he felt the anecdote did illustrate the point that McLaren "...retained the joy of discovering new and delightful things." (personal interview 5 November 1990)

352 McLaren as quoted in "Interview", Scottish Arts Council 40.

frames to reach the right hand side of the twenty-fourth frame, then the projected result is of a near-vertical line on the screen which, while retaining its vertical orientation moves across the screen from left to right in exactly one second. As he later recalled, McLaren at first attempted to make a film "... using a single vertical line moving in turn slowly then rapidly. As this film was to be very short it seemed to us [McLaren and Lambart] a feasible experiment. We set to work and discovered that it couldn't exceed a minute in length."[350] The reason McLaren felt that a film with a single line could not be any longer, was fear of losing the audience's interest. So he and Lambart decided to use several lines (dope sheets showing the line variations appear in Figs. 58 and 59). They also added colour. The initial challenge, stemming from the obvious, and easy, use of the vertical line, was to see how far it could be taken. McLaren felt the need for variety. It is interesting to note that, in the search for diversity in the film, he did not alter the thickness of the line. This would have been technically easy. Instead, he decided the film's essence and unity would be better retained if the line was duplicated rather than altered. Finally music was added. Maurice Blackburn, who contributed the music for many of McLaren's films and who had a strong artistic affinity with him, created an ethereal sound track of remarkable quality.

The development from *Lines Vertical* (1960) was simple. As McLaren said, "I was curious to see what the result would be if I moved the lines into the horizontal plane. I was convinced that the result would be completely different."[351] McLaren sent *Lines Vertical* to the laboratory. Using a prism or two, the laboratory turned the image on each frame of *Lines Vertical* ninety degrees. McLaren then added strong background colours and asked Pete Seeger, the well-known folk musician, to compose some music which with its energetic strumming further distanced the new film from the original. The cumulative result of these visual and aural variations was *Lines Horizontal*, a film with a completely different ambience from its parent film.

Several stories, which account for McLaren's next trick, are in circulation. In one account, McLaren implies that the discovery was premeditated: "Evelyn Lambart and I worked on a mixture of horizontal and vertical lines. To begin with, I wondered what would happen if we presented them both simultaneously.[352] In another account, the discovery was accidental:

Fig. 80. Norman
McLaren and Evelyn
Lambart working on
Lines Vertical.
[McLaren
Archive/NFB.]

Fig. 81. Evelyn
Lambart scratching lines
through the frame
divisions for Lines
Vertical. Compare
Lambart's work with
Figs. 58 and 59.
[McLaren
Archive/NFB.]

Fig. 82.
Lines Vertical. *This is a typical, more complex frame from near the film's climax. Compare this frame with the dope sheets in Figs. 58 and 59.*
[NFB.]

Fig. 83.
Lines Vertical. *A simpler part.*
[NFB.]

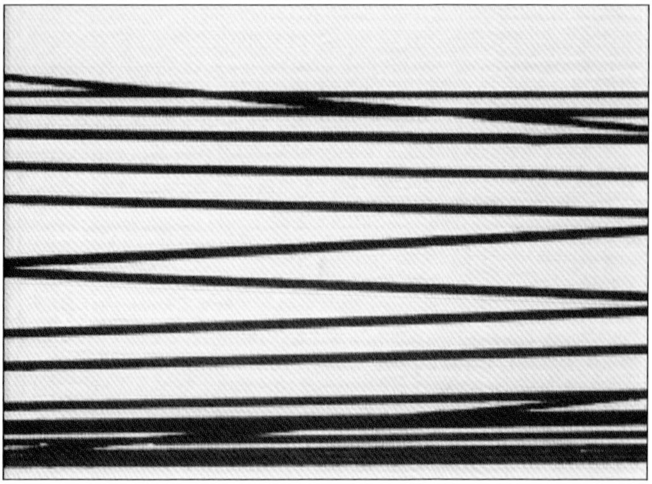

Fig. 84.
Lines Horizontal. *The affinity and contrast with* Lines Vertical *is obvious.*
[NFB.]

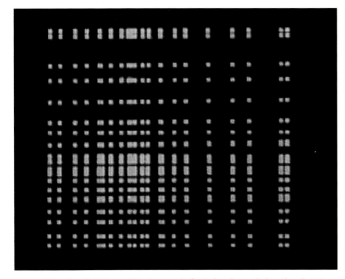

Fig. 85. Mosaic Sequentially combining of the images (such as Fig. 83) from Lines Vertical with corresponding images (such as Fig. 84) from the film Lines Horizontal so that only the intersections of the lines are visible. This gave McLaren the basis for Mosaic in which the intersections (dots) move with an astonishing accord for each other, an accord which mesmerises as the film's complexity increases. [NFB.]

He had *Lines Horizontal* finished and he had *Lines Vertical* finished. And one day he put *Lines Horizontal* in the moviola and was taking it out to put on *Lines Vertical*, and the film got stuck, and *Lines Vertical* was superimposed over *Lines Horizontal* just before it fell to the floor. He saw this. So that became *Mosaic*. Just a sheer accident.[353]

A third account, is an amusing corollary of the accidental discovery. An eminent British mathematician was visiting the Board and wished to pay homage to McLaren, whom he greatly admired. McLaren arranged a screening of *Lines Vertical* and *Lines Horizontal*. The two projectors, each containing one of the films, were switched on simultaneously rather than sequentially and presented on the screen both the moving horizontal and the moving vertical lines. The effect on the mathematician was dramatic – he swooned.[354] Thus McLaren was convinced that the idea of combining the images was worth pursuing.

The simultaneous projection of two negative (i.e. clear film with the lines in black) prints of *Lines Vertical* and *Lines Horizontal* (1961) meant that only the points of their intersecting lines were visible on the screen. As the now invisible lines moved, so did their *visible* intersections. As the lines multiplied, so did the intersecting points. Once again colour was added in the final stages, as was the music, which, this time, McLaren composed using his synthetic-sound technique. The resulting film is *Mosaic* (1965), which builds to an immensely powerful climax.

353 Grant Munro, personal interview 23 October 1990.

354 Robert Verrall, personal interview 14 November 1990.

Pixillation

The last three techniques to be discussed are each attempts by McLaren to animate people. Each technique, however, produced startlingly different results. In *Neighbours*, his 1952 comment on conflict, McLaren reverted to the traditional animation process of using the movie camera to photograph one frame at a time, but instead of shooting drawings, cut-outs, or puppets, he placed live people before his camera. McLaren developed the technique which had been around since the 1890s in new and exciting ways. For example, McLaren photographed an actor (Grant Munro or Jean-Paul Ladouceur) at the height of his jump, and then moved the actor along a little and photographed him at the height of his next jump and so on, for many more jumps. The effect, when the film was run through a projector and screened, was of the man flying. Other such effects included gliding, spinning, disappearing and reappearing. These devices are not unusual in traditional forms of animation, but in this film, the pixillation technique allows the action to be performed by normal-looking people, who are in a natural setting. It is this that gives the film its edge and which makes the violence of the film so repugnant.

Multi-images

The pixillation of *Neighbours* obtains extraordinary illusions of movement by eliminating movement of the actors which occurs between shots. A contrary process was used in *Pas de deux* (1967). In *Pas de deux*, McLaren allows the camera to shoot live-action normally, thereby recording each component split-second of movement. McLaren eliminates nothing. It is what he has added that makes *Pas de deux* such an intriguing film. The image in *Pas de deux* was multiplied on itself somewhat akin to a photographic multi-exposure, except that the second and subsequent images were not identical to the first but were of preceeding moments (the sports and animal photography of Marey or Edgerton are static examples of this). The multiplication of the image was such that up to eleven successive elements of a movement were screened simultaneously (see Figs. 88–91). Seeing the multi-limbed figures in stills from *Pas de deux* gives the false impression that the figures are like those sculptures of many-armed Hindu gods. On seeing the film, the added but essential element of movement allows the viewer to see the images of, say an arm, as part of the one arm in

Fig. 86. On this and the following page are six consecutive frames from one of the flying sequences in Neighbours. Each frame shows the actor, in this case Grant Munro, in mid-jump and therefore in mid-air. When these frames - together with their adjacent and similar frames - are screened at 24 fps, the illusion of flying is achieved. [NFB.]

Sequence continued from previous page.

Fig. 87. At the climax of
Neighbours, *the
neighbours' wives are
also pixillated. Here
Norman McLaren
adjusts the position of a
wife. Neighbour Grant
Munro who is already
in position for the next
shot, holds his pose
while this change
between shots occurs.
[NFB.]*

graceful motion.[355] McLaren's wonderful sense of timing and structure make the technique of *Pas de deux* a revelation, with its constant unfolding and folding of movement.

The blur

In his last film *Narcissus* (1981), McLaren made extensive use of the blur in the film's climactic section (see Fig. 92). "A blur in movie-photography is very similar to a blur in still photography and I think most people are familiar with a blur. It is not to be confused with a stroboscopic photographic optic which captures all the different positions, but it creates a suffused flow of the action".[356] The blurs which McLaren captured on film, by photographing the dancers and by using various slow shutter-speeds, were further manipulated in the optical printer. Dissolves, freezes, fades and mirror images – including overlapping mirror images – of the blurs were, thereby, achieved. Earlier in film McLaren used various other devices such as image pop-on and pop-off, fade-ins and fade-outs, and image flicker thus helping to make *Narcissus* one of McLaren's most technically replete films since *Camera Makes Whoopee*.

Reasons for McLaren's technical diversity

One: Necessity

There are several reasons for McLaren's use of so many different techniques. Firstly, there were reasons of necessity. When in his student days and his days in New York he had no camera, and, in the latter case, no sound record-

355 Alfio Bastiancich, in his *L'opera di Norman McLaren*, (Torino: Giappichelli,1981) 103, states that the phases of movement are indicative of a disintegration of the dancers. This reading fails to sufficiently consider the overwhelming effect of movement in unifying the images.

356 McLaren speaking in *Creative Process*, dir Donald McWilliams,1st Assembly (film), 1989.

Fig. 88.
Pas de deux (i). The
two dancers at the
beginning of sequence at
the climax of the film.
Note the simplification
of the image by using
just side lighting and
having no background
visible.
[NFB.]

Fig. 89.
Pas de deux (ii). From
the image in a.,
successive images of the
dancers' movements flow
with them as they dance.
[NFB.]

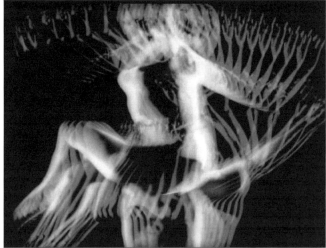

ing materials, McLaren improvised by drawing his imagery directly onto film. He found not only that the results on film were satisfying but also that the method gave him an intimate contact with his film materials. This contact allowed him to express his ideas spontaneously. Three of his techniques were in fact extensions of the direct-animation technique. Frameless-animation, intermittent-animation and the drawn-on-sound technique were each executed directly on the film-stock and so these approaches also possess the advantages McLaren associated with being in direct graphic contact with the film-stock. Spontaneity of expression was a feature of McLaren's approach which was consistently maintained throughout his career, although it

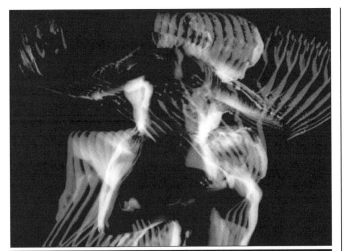

Fig. 90.
Pas de deux *(iii). As the performers continue, the multiple imagery which unfolds after them, creates a vivid enhancement of their dance.*
[NFB.]

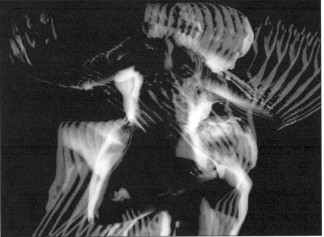

Fig. 91.
Pas de deux *(iv). The dancers pause and their following images merge into them once again.*
[NFB.]

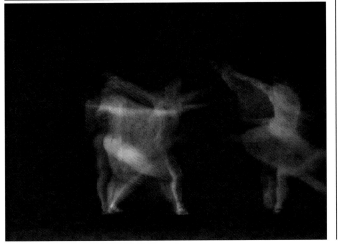

Fig. 92. Narcissus McLaren's blur technique produced a suffused flow of imagery.
[NFB.]

must be said that in those films in which a higher and more complicated technical process is employed, the occasions in the filmmaking where spontaneity was possible became more limited. The technically more complicated films are *Pas de deux* (1967), *Ballet Adagio* (1972) and *Narcissus* (1984). The filmmaking process in these later films was more sectionalized. There were distinct stages of shooting, processing and editing.

> The multiple image effects for *Pas de deux* had to be very carefully worked out frame by frame for every image. If there's [sic] twelve images on the frame, and if you have got twenty-four frames per second, you've got to account for these on a sheet for the optical camera operator, so he knows exactly what to do.[357]
> ... this [particular dance] struck me as being the best for slow motion purposes. We shot it in the next three days with a couple of cameras. It was all done in such a hurry, and it was only after I'd seen it that I realized if we'd had more time we could have changed the choreography around to get stronger parts.[358]

As can be appreciated, in these later films there had to be a greater emphasis on planning, and, although in comparison to the cel-animation process, the creative process in the films was consistently on-going, the constraints emanating from the need to anticipate effects through several stages limited the degree of spontaneity.

Two: Satiation and reaction

The second reason for McLaren's tendency to switch to different techniques arises from the amount of time that was necessary in completing animation films. McLaren's films involved many months, even years, of concentrated effort. The single-mindedness of the operation was heightened by the fact that, in most of his films, McLaren used just a single technique. If a second technique was used at all, then he tended to use it throughout the film, as in the background segments of, for example, *Love on the Wing*, *Spheres*, *V for Victory*, and *Five for Four*. On occasions, a second technique was included in a film as a visual highlight. For example, the cool, vibrating white lines used in the slow, middle-section of *Begone Dull Care*, contrast stunningly with the frenzy of the rest of the film's imagery, and the overlapping dissolves of scratch imagery provide a similar contrast to the rest of *Blinkity Blank*. McLaren has,

357 Maynard Collins, *Norman McLaren*. (Ottawa: Canadian Film Institute, 1976) 79.

358 Collins 80.

therefore, used the two techniques in a film in order to augment structure.

Surrealist concerns also allowed McLaren to introduce a second element and thereby offer a surrealist perspective on the otherwise geometric phenomenon of *Spheres* (the butterfly) and *Mosaic* (live-action shots form both the beginning and the ending). In each case the cohesiveness of the rest of the film added to the incongruity of the second element, enhancing its surreal qualities. McLaren thus made use of a discord within the filmic structure.

McLaren's general concern for unity within a film was also a strong factor in his overall determination to limit the number of techniques used in each film. It was an outcome of the lesson in unity provided by Grierson when he criticized McLaren's technically-eclectic student film's limitations. The limitation of technique was itself also a stimulant to creativity: "I'm a firm believer in the benefits of barriers like this. In my case, the technical and thematic limitations favour creativity. The more limits there are to the way of working, the more the final result is likely to be good and original."[359]

Here, McLaren was talking of the 'controlled spontaneity' of the engraved film *Mail Early for Christmas* (1959), but his remarks are indicative of a general approach. For McLaren, the limits imposed by the technique constrained the work and helped to ensure its unity. Within those constraints the filmmaker was compelled to be as inventive as possible in order to maintain progression throughout

Overleaf:
Fig. 94. Spheres. *In this section just three cut-out sphere sizes have been used. [NFB.]*

Fig. 95. Spheres. *Here the cut-out spheres have been moved or substituted. They have also been added to considerably. [NFB.]*

359 McLaren as quoted in "Interview", Scottish Arts Council 38.

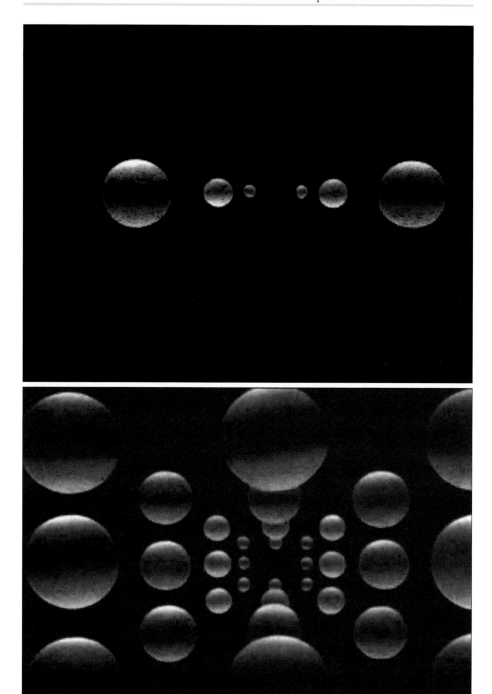

the film. For McLaren, making a successful expression was achieved through manipulating two forces, the unifying force and the experimental force:

> A work of art has to have cohesiveness and consistency, but not so much cohesiveness and consistency as to become boring, and not so much non-cohesiveness as to fall apart. It has to be organically linked, and yet it must have surprises in it that you don't expect, but surprises that are relevant to the whole work.[360]

The choice of a limiting technique meant that McLaren could then focus his attention on being adventurous. As mentioned above, this was an area in which McLaren excelled. Grant Munro relates that:

> Eve, René and I don't need to be reminded ... that we were very privileged ... that we had something to contribute, but by God we worked. Oh, you really did, and you worked day and night, I mean you lived the film and ... sometimes Eve and I felt sorry for ourselves – we were the seven dwarfs (laugh). If you had five different combinations to attempt in a visual, and you knew that two wouldn't work, and you'd say to Norman, 'these two won't work, let's try the other three'. Well, he'd try eight. He was obstinate and you'd discover things.[361]

NFB producer Tom Daly gives an account which illustrates McLaren's ability to perceive a potential in everything, including apparent disasters:

> He was looking at some of his own rushes, and light had got into the camera. So these original rushes were spoiled. But everybody was kind of sad about it, except Norman. Norman was saying, "Oh, but you notice how, when it gets that light colour, it becomes kind of ghostly. And if we should want that kind of thing, I would know what to do now." He was the only one kind of thinking what it was instead of what it wasn't.[362]

This inventiveness was another facet of McLaren's preoccupation with technical processes in a work.

This concentration of technique in a film, sensibly justified though it may have been, had its effect on McLaren. On completion of a film, after many months, for example, of drawing thousands of 35mm-size drawings, or of working on a single pastel drawing, McLaren was more than ready for a change. There were two approaches to this

360 McLaren as quoted in *Creative Process* script 19.

361 Grant Munro, personal interview 23 October 1990, audio cassette.

362 Tom Daly as quoted in *Creative Process* script 19.

problem. One approach was to attempt to avoid it by working on more than one project at a time. McLaren tried this, sometimes working on as many as three projects simultaneously. In about 1963, for example, he wrote of helping in *Christmas Cracker* (1963) with director Grant Munro, working on the music of *Canon* (1964) and helping Eve Lambart add colour to *Mosaic* (1965). At the same time he was also teaching some students from Vietnam and Pakistan.[363] Such a hectic solution to the problem, of course, can have its own demands. The other approach to the problem of saturation was, in his next film, to react, to escape into a completely different technique. McLaren did react and benefited from the rejuvenation it brought.

An advantage to McLaren for changing his technique so markedly and so frequently between films, was that it fulfilled his rôle at the NFB as a researcher in film. It will be recalled that an official justification for McLaren's work at the NFB was that it complied with a requirement in the Board's official objectives: to engage in film research and to disseminate the results of the research. Although McLaren's film work served this end – his writing of his Technical Notes also serves the same purpose – it would be a mistake to regard McLaren embarking on a new technique in order to justify his NFB position. McLaren's position at the NFB was too secure for him to have to worry about such justifications. As well, there were far more compelling reasons for his use of new techniques. His work, through the years, on many techniques did provide an official justification of his position for the NFB. For McLaren, this function at the Board was one that he took seriously, but, happily, it was one that coincided with his reliance on technical exploration, rather than causing such exploration.

Three: Genesis

A third reason for McLaren's diversity of techniques lies in his manner of starting films. The genesis of many of McLaren's films was the technical process to be used. When McLaren had achieved his first technical breakthrough, he had been driven by necessity. His radical technical approach not only enabled him to make a film, but it also achieved startling new filmic results. A second lesson provided by necessity, when he had to create his own soundtrack, confirmed the value of his technical approach. Even when McLaren was provided with a theme or subject for

363 Norman McLaren, letter to his mother, n.d. [1963],p 1–2. Grierson Archives, University of Stirling, Stirling, Scotland. GAA:31:143.

a film, as in the *Chants populaires* series, he turned the filmic problems of expression into one of technique, asking himself how he could animate slow movement. His chain-of-mixes solution endorsed the value of the approach, for it produced not just a solution to the technical problem but also generated a new and exciting visual experience. *Blinkity Blank* is an example of a film which grew solely from a technical challenge. It evolved from an attempt to explore an alternative way of drawing on film which would eliminate some of the difficulties of the method (dust). Inherent in McLaren's solution (to use black film), were other difficulties (of registration of black films); the subsequent solution (to scratch on intermittent frames) provided the basis for the film. As has been seen, technical considerations were also factors in the instigation of the *Lines* films and *Mosaic*. Others of McLaren's films had their origins in technical experiments and in observations he had made some time before the films concerned were created. As Tom Daly's above quote illustrates, McLaren's observation skills were used to detect new technical possibilities in film. McLaren could then store the observation. The idea of manipulating a chair occurred to McLaren some five years before *Chairy Tale* (1957) was made.

> One day at the at the beginning of the filming [of *Neighbours*], Jean-Paul Ladouceur tripped over one of the [deck] chairs, and had no end of difficulties opening it, first getting it the wrong way round, and then forcing it. I said to myself – here's a good idea for a film. A man struggling with a deck chair. I put the idea to one side. Some years later, the idea came back to me.[364]

As McLaren's career progressed, he gradually acquired a series of film tests which had been conducted as ideas came to him. So, it is not surprising that, in his later films in particular, McLaren used ideas from those tests as a basis for his work. The multi-imagery of *Pas de deux*, for example, was first explored by McLaren, with Grant Munro's assistance, in what are called the *Leap Frog Tests* of 1961. Prior to that even, when working with the engraving-on-film technique, McLaren had overlaid the image of a group of scratch-marks over the same scratch-marks as they had appeared earlier, so that the scratches follow and merge with each other. This scratch test was made at the time of *Blinkity Blank* and is remarkably similar to the

[364] McLaren as quoted in"Interview", Scottish Arts Council 34.

Fig. 96. The Leap Frog Tests *of 1961. Grant Munro's original running image without any image repeats. [NFB.]*

Fig. 97. This frame from one of the Leap Frog Tests *shows an image of a running Munro in which the subject is repeated just six times with a moderate-sized stagger between each repeat. [NFB.]*

Fig. 98. This frame is from another of McLaren's 1961 Leap Frog Tests. *Here Munro's image is in the process of being repeated 32 times with just a small amount of stagger between each repeat. [NFB.]*

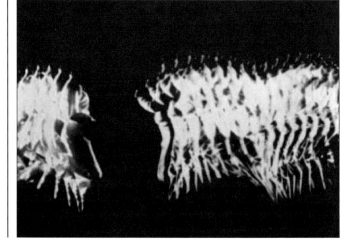

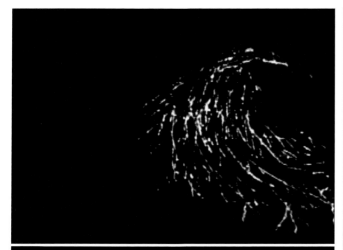

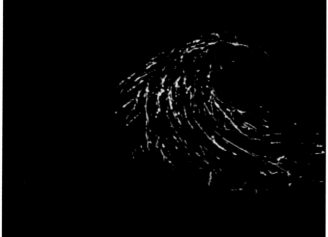

Fig. 99.
Blinkity Blank
*Scratches on the black
film surface were
reproduced in the optical
printer and overlaid on
their preceding frame's
set of scratches. This
process was repeated
through this sequence of*
Blinkity Blank.
*Illustrated are two
successive frames from
this part of the film.*
[NFB.]

gradual metamorphoses in the slow section of that film. He returned to the technique in 1967 manipulating live-action footage (as in his original *Leap Frog Tests*). In the exquisite *Pas de deux*, his use of stark, side-lit imagery on a plain-black background exposed the time-delayed overlapping stages of movement allowing them to describe and embellish the dancers' movements. In his last film, *Narcissus,* (1984), McLaren made use of the blur technique. The technique was first tested by McLaren nearly thirty years earlier when making *Chairy Tale*:

> I often thought it would be nice doing blurs, and we did some tests around the time of making *Chairy Tale*, with the slow moving camera and of course we got blurs.[365] What we did was [we set the] camera with

365 McLaren used the blur technique in part of *Chairy Tale* itself.

Fig. 100. One of McLaren's early blur tests (c. 1957). McLaren himself was the performer on many of these tests. [NFB.]

an exposure of one second so the camera lens was open for one second. Sometimes in one second we would do a whole action. The faster you move, the more diffuse the blur is. The slower you move, the more precise, until it becomes so slow that the movement becomes a clear image, and it's stationary.[366]

A technique, or an associated challenge, therefore, was often the genesis of McLaren's filmmaking. Why did McLaren choose to work in this way? One can see a justification in the method embedded in McLaren's beliefs in surrealist philosophy. Just as some surrealist painters had used, say, smoke stains (*fumage*), or smudged blots (*decalomania*), as a means of invoking images from the subconscious, and thereby initiating the ideas for a painting, so McLaren may have used technology as a starting point for his films, thereby allowing ideas to surface from his subconscious mind. The evidence for this notion is of an associative kind: McLaren espoused some surrealist philosophies, and by extension, he could also have applied this one. It, therefore, remains merely an interesting, if feasible, possibility. The most obvious reason why McLaren chose to work in this way, was that it was successful for him. He found it suited his analytical approach, and produced films that he felt were effective. They broke new ground, and were both visually and aurally intriguing, fascinating and literally excited the observer.

These diverse techniques of McLaren's had in fact been the result of a consistent approach to his work. McLaren's definition of animation was never more than

Fig. 101. A Chairy Tale. McLaren put the blur technique to immediate use in 1957's A Chairy Tale. In this segment, the human protagonist blurs past the watching chair. [NFB.]

movement achieved by projecting a series of static images through a movie projector. Left completely open was how these images could be obtained or sequenced. The technical developments and breakthroughs achieved by McLaren resulted from his ability to identify and abandon earlier preconceptions about the making and ordering of images for animation. For McLaren the technical problem was sometimes how to achieve a particular goal (e.g. very slow movement) and at other times how to animate within limited means. It is worth repeating an earlier quote from McLaren: "I'm a firm believer in the benefits of barriers like [technical limitations]. In my case, the technical and thematic limitations favour creativity. The more limits there are to the way of working, the more the final result is likely to be good and original."[367] For McLaren, technique was not just a means to an artistic end. As he would see it, the relationship between technique and art was symbiotic.

367 McLaren as quoted in "Interview", Scottish Arts Council 38.

Chapter Seven

Confluence and Conflict in *Synchromy*

Conflict

At the "Illusions and Realities in the Nuclear Age" Conference of 21–23 April 1986, Norman McLaren spoke at the inaugural presentation of McGill University's Norman McLaren Award. The Award was to be "... presented annually to the student whose work demonstrates similar social concerns to those of Norman McLaren".[368] McLaren, appropriately, was the first recipient. In his acceptance speech, McLaren alluded to the tensions he felt through his filmmaking career: "I had a lasting social conscience and feeling about the humanity around me and I have felt very frustrated, often, at never being able to do much about it in my films because I've had other tendencies as a filmmaker".[369] One of those tendencies was to make abstract films.

Dissipation and different conflicts within abstract film

Despite the nagging guilt McLaren felt about making abstract films, he continued to make them.[370] In doing so, conflicts associated with, and existing between, his means of expression arose. Since these conflicts recur to varying degrees in many of McLaren's abstract and near-abstract films, an analysis of two films, in which these conflicts are prominent, is presented in this chapter. A clue to the reason for McLaren's pursuit of abstract film in spite of his

368 *Creative Process* dir. Donald McWilliams,1st Assembly (film), 1989.

369 Norman McLaren speaking in *Creative Process* 1st Assembly (film).

370 Donald McWilliams personal interview, 24 October 1990.

conscience lies in his love for dance and music. The abstract art of music provided a theoretical justification, if one was necessary, for McLaren's involvement in abstract film. More importantly than that, however, music provided an example and an inspiration: "By far the greatest influence [from the non-film arts] has come from music".[371] McLaren also said, "So to my way of thinking and working an abstract or non-objective film has *much* greater affinity to music, ballet and dance than it has to any kind of abstract painting".[372] In his early abstract films, McLaren used music not only as a general inspiration, he also interpreted specific pieces of music, in an intuitive yet loosely systematic way, into the visual area of film:

> Music has had a great effect on me and in quite an old-fashioned way since I have found some music "inspiring". Certain music had the power of bringing up before my mind's eye certain kinds of moving imagery and some of my earlier films were attempts to put such imagings onto film. But although I may have once thought that I was, if only intuitively, giving a visual translation of the music in my film in a way that might conceivably have some logical scientific basis, I tend now to consider that naive.[373]

In this statement, McLaren was referring to his systematic linking of sound and image in such early abstract films as *Stars and Stripes, Dots* and *Loops*, even though in the latter two cases, he constructed the music-track himself. It will be recalled that these films were discussed earlier.

371 Norman McLaren in Ivan Stadtrucker, questionnaire 7 March 1975, p. 4. NFB Archives.

372 Norman McLaren , letter to Lorettan Devlin Gascard, 15 April 1981, p. 1. NFB Archives.

373 Norman McLaren, letter to Theo Goldberg, 27 February 1973, p. 3. NFB Archives.

Fig. 103. Oscar
Peterson.
[Photo: Canada-Wide.]

The overriding reason, however, for McLaren's indulgence in abstract filmmaking was that, despite his guilty
feelings, it was a process he enjoyed. He made abstract films
throughout his career, from 1933 through to the climactic
piece, *Synchromy* (1971). He also expounded music in visual
terms in didactic works, such as his film *Canon* (1963),
co-directed with Grant Munro, and *Six Formes Musicales*
(1967), a book and record made with Maurice and Marthe
Blackburn (NFB composer Maurice Blackburn's affinity
with McLaren has previously been mentioned, see page
178). The following account gives a good idea of the
optimism, anxiety and fun involved in making his energetic, visual interpretation of jazz in the film, *Begone Dull
Care* which, with Evelyn Lambart's help, he made in 1949:

> I had heard a record by Oscar Peterson which I had
> very much liked. When I heard that he was in Mont-
> real, I went to see him in a night club near the Windsor
> Station. ... I introduced myself to him during an
> interval. He had never heard of the National Film
> Board. I told him that I wanted to make an abstract
> film to his music. What on earth's that? he retorted.

Come to the Film Board tomorrow and I will show
you some films, I replied. Then you can decide. The
next day he and his two musicians came to the National Film Board and I showed them *Dots, Loops* and
Stars and Stripes. Oscar told me: Oh I understand
perfectly. When I asked him when he wanted to start
to work for me, he replied: Immediately of course.
So we went back to the club, which is empty during
the day time, and laid down the broad lines of his
work. I knew what I wanted, so many seconds for the
title, and three parts of which the first was to be
medium fast, the second very slow and the third very
fast. Since I did not want to use any known theme,
on which there would be royalties to pay, Oscar
improvised a few tunes for me.[374]

He said, "I'll play a few bars" and he played half a
dozen things and said "There, how about that for the
first shooting?" One of them I liked very much so I
said "Let's develop this one", and we started expand-
ing the tune. I started making suggestions because
some of the things he was doing gave me ideas. There
were stretches where it was too hectic for too long a
time. The eye would be tired with a fast movement,
so I said "Calm that down. Make it slow for this part
or that part." And he'd do it. He'd give me half a dozen
slow sections. So we shaped it, building up cre-
scendos here and making the music thin there, cutting out the piano here and just having drums there.
I made many suggestions. He would always pick them
up and provide several examples of what I had suggested. He had a back of an envelope on the piano
and he would occasionally write down the music. We
went through the film in four days. I was very happy
because I felt not only had he given me pictures and
images to create a movement, but he'd left me leeway
to be free to do anything. He'd have a passage where
I could treat it this way or that way or any other way.[375]

... everything was ready. He played the whole piece.
I asked him if we could record it the next day. No,
he protested, I must polish the whole of it. In two
weeks everything will be ready. And indeed, a fort-
night later, Oscar Peterson came to Montreal and we
met at the recording studio. I asked him to play me
back the whole piece as a rehearsal. I recognized

374 Norman McLaren as
quoted in "Interview",
*Norman McLaren,
exhibition and films*
(Edinburgh:Scottish
Arts Council, 1977) 24.

375 Norman McLaren as
quoted in Maynard
Collins, *Norman
McLaren* (Ottawa:
Canadian Film
Institute, 1976) 76.

almost nothing. Oscar Peterson is a born impro-viser.[376]

Every time they rehearsed it, he improvised some-thing new. And the new things get incorporated. And the whole shifts a little bit. Some of the new things he'd done were better than our original thing, but many of the things he had changed were not as good for me. We spent the first hour of the recording session trying to partly get it back to its original shape, while preserving the *good*, new things he had impro-vised.[377]

But I used what was most suitable for the film. So I divided the music into pieces and I painted on the film placed on a big table, using a moviola. After having "painted" four or five "seconds", Evelyn Lam-bart and myself put on the visual film and the sound tape together, to see what the effect would be. If it did not work, we would repaint or move onto differ-ent attempts. It was a very satisfying and very pleasant way of working.[378]

That was a good example of the cooperation, the give and take, between the composer and the person who's doing the picture.[379]

From this account several features of *Begone Dull Care* become apparent. Firstly, McLaren and Lambart, for the most part, worked on four or five-second sections of a film at a time. On viewing the completed film, the result of this working method is manifest. Rather than ascribing to every note, to every sound, a visual equivalence, as had been attempted in his earlier films, and as was impossible to achieve with the scintillating music of the Oscar Peterson Trio, McLaren and Lambart interpreted phrases of the music. By giving the visual-track the same phrase division as the music, not only is the unity between the auditory and visual components of the film enhanced, but so too is the film's visual structure. A comprehension of the totality of vision and sound is, thereby, aided. The structure of visual, temporal pattern is further enhanced by the use of repeats, which parallel repeat passages in the music. The comb-like image used in one sequence of repeats bears a remarkable resemblance to some of the forms, used twenty five years earlier, by Viking Eggeling in his pioneering abstract film *Diagonal Symphony* (1923–24). Although McLaren's combs are scratchily drawn and vertically

376 McLaren as quoted in "Interview", Scottish Arts Council 25.

377 McLaren as quoted in Collins 76–77.

378 McLaren as quoted in "Interview", Scottish Arts Council 25.

379 McLaren as quoted in Collins 77.

Fig. 104. Begone Dull
Care. *One of the
comb-like images that
echoes Eggeling's*
Diagonal Symphony
*and which also prefigure
aspects of McLaren's
later film* Synchromy.
[NFB.]

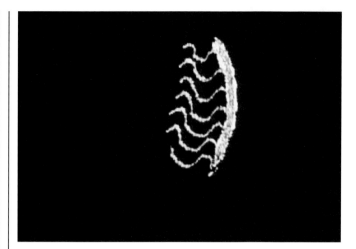

oriented, one senses a debt, albeit an unconscious one, to Eggeling. Curiously, the comb-like forms in *Begone Dull Care*, together with the movement associated with them, are somewhat similar to some of those that McLaren was later to use in *Synchromy*. The use of symmetrically opposed answering repeats in *Begone Dull Care* also pre-figures some of the visual phrasing of *Synchromy*.

As well as indicating the division of his work into phrases, McLaren's account also reveals the overall tripartite structuring of the film. *Begone Dull Care* is comprised of a fast (allegro) first movement, a slow (molto andante) second movement and a very fast (prestissimo) final section.[380] The middle section differs not only in tempo from its adjacent sections. The simplification of the music of this central section allows McLaren to explore a more detailed correlation between the visual and the auditory aspects of the film. He augmented and modified his phrase division with the interpretation of individual sounds. In this section, the temporal spacing of the musical events and his sound-by-sound interpretation allow McLaren to visually display such attributes of the music as attack and decay and resonance. McLaren's use of an overall sonata structure, borrowed from music, was not only a consequence of his seeing music and abstract film as being based on common precepts, but also a consequence of his general attitude to structure or composition:

Many years ago I was confronted with a problem regarding abstract film visuals. It is relatively easy to make a one or two minute abstract film that will hang together and be a unity. But with an eight or ten

380 McLaren used these musical terms to describe the different tempi of the three sections. McLaren letter to Gascard 3.

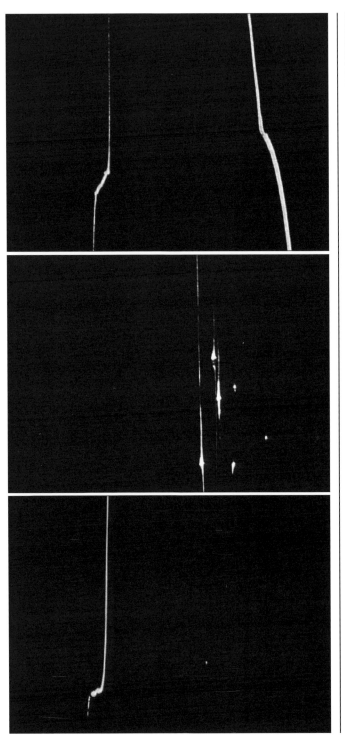

Fig. 105. Three
non-adjacent frames
from the slow, middle
section of Begone Dull
Care.
[NFB.]

Fig. 106. Begone Dull Care. *A frame from the scintillating energetic section which follows the slow middle section.* [NFB.]

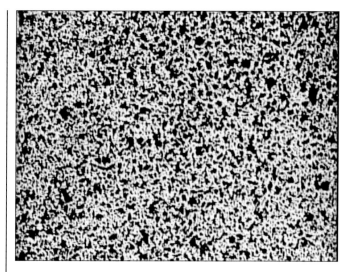

minute abstraction, it is much more difficult. One runs the risk of creating either too much monotony, or too much diversity. Some kind of format or structure seemed necessary to vary the uniformity or to discipline the variety.

I found that some of the forms which music has evolved (to solve the same problem) lent themselves to abstract visuals.

I used the ABA form of European classical music in *Begone Dull Care* and *Spheres*, and a short rondo-like form in *Short and Suite.*[381]

In adopting a familiar musical structure and strongly relating the visual and auditory components of *Begone Dull Care*, McLaren was able to introduce another element he considered desirable in a successful composition – surprise. With such a familiar musical structure, both in the particular and in the general, an observer is able to anticipate. By reinforcing this anticipation, and on occasions, thwarting it, McLaren (and Peterson as well) has a means to create additional emphasis in the film. On occasions, even the anticipation of a change is an insufficient warning of the change's nature. In such cases, when the change exceeds expectation, the surprise can be even more exciting and intense than normal variations from the anticipated. In *Begone Dull Care*, the anticipated change from the slow middle section to the fast concluding section is such a case. The visual eruption into this final section is almost overwhelming.

381 McLaren as quoted in Stadtrucker 5.

The relationship between sound and vision is the essence of such films as *Begone Dull Care*. Throughout *Begone Dull Care* there is a recognizable, if variable, accord between these two elements of the film. The temporal accordance, as well as being expressed in phrases, is on some occasions also expressed note-by-note. Movement also varies. A lateral movement of the image is, at times, used to express melodic intervals, and at other times a general frenzy of movement is used to convey the energy of a musical passage. The complexity of the sound image is also interpreted in different ways on the visual-track. Sometimes the complexity is conveyed by the sustained presentation of an intricate moving pattern (see Fig. 79), and at other times the complexity is conveyed by simpler images presented in very quick succession. The lack of a systematic approach to the visual interpretation of sound has allowed the visual-track to function as an additional musical line. Rather than running parallel, the visual and aural threads of the film are interwoven. The visual and aural lines relate in a contrapuntal way. These elements of the film, therefore, neither conflict nor completely merge, yet they do run together, cross, merge and separate as the streams of a braided river. Such visual interpretation of the sound is a consequence of McLaren interpreting what he called, 'the spirit of the music'.[382] The sound-image relationship was also at the core of the last abstract film McLaren made.

Synchromy: vision and sound

Norman McLaren's whimsical pun in the title of his film *Synchromy* (1971) not only acknowledges the pioneering American group of abstract painters of whom the youthful McLaren read in the Klein book (see Chapter Two), but also, alludes to several aspects of the film. The word 'Synchromy' sounds a little like the word 'symphony'. Thus a musical connection is immediately implied. As well, the component parts of the word 'Synchromy' make more specific allusions. Attention is drawn to the qualities of the film as they occur in its finished form. The film is ostensibly a synchronous event (synchronistic) concerned with colour and light (chromatic). The auditory and visual presentations of the film are indeed very tightly synchronized. The title also may be seen as alluding to the sources McLaren used in making the film since synthetic-sound (syn) provides not only the sound, but also the visual imagery of *Synchromy*.

[382] McLaren in Stadtrucker 4.

*Fig. 107. Norman
McLaren around 1970
when he made*
Synchromy.
*[McLaren
Archive/NFB.]*

383 Lazlo Moholy-Nagy,
Rudolph Pfenninger
and Oskar Fischinger
are notable pioneers of
this approach. For a
fuller account see:
Norman McLaren,
"Notes on Animated
Sound", *The Quarterly
of Film Radio and
Television* (Spring,
1953): 223–229, and
chapter three above,
76–81.

384 Moholy-Nagy also
presented the
sound-track on the
screen in his film,
Sound ABC (1932).
Because
Moholy-Nagy's film
ignores
frame-divisions and,
thereby, also ignores
the correlation
between the visual and
aural manifestations, a
specific influence on
McLaren's work in
Synchromy may be
discounted.

385 *The Eye Hears, The Ear
Sees*, dir. Gavin Millar
National Film Board
of Canada and British
Broadcasting
Corporation, 1970.

A knowledge of the making of *Synchromy* is necessary for a fuller understanding of the film. As it will be recalled McLaren, like others before him, saw that it would be possible to construct, on the sound-track, visual patterns of one's own making, either by drawing directly onto the track or by photographing prepared drawings on to it.[383] McLaren had, in the nineteen-forties, developed a system which enabled him to produce a range of sounds of any particular pitch or volume. Such a system has two advantages over normal sound-production methods: the sound produced has very distinct qualities: and by photographing the sound-track designs frame-by-frame, their relationship to the visual configurations appearing on the screen may be determined precisely. What makes *Synchromy* most fascinating, however, is that McLaren also presented the sound-track on the screen.[384] The pattern that makes the sound is seen on the screen simultaneously with the auditory presentation of the sound.

It would seem that McLaren, at a stroke, had been able to produce a film which was synaesthetically perfect. Moreover, he had a system which would give an exact visual equivalent of sound. Interpreting the 'spirit' of the music would appear to be a redundant concept. As Gavin Millar emphatically put it in his tribute to Norman McLaren: "The Eye Hears, The Ear Sees".[385] However, things are not quite so straightforward. In his finished version of *Synchromy*, McLaren had introduced variations into the visual part of the film. Logically, these variations could be expected to create conflict between the film's visual and auditory presentations. What are these variations? Why did

McLaren introduce them? What effect do they have?

Variations

One of the most noticeable variations is the repeating of the sound-track's appearance up to eleven times across the screen. The sound-track's single presentation on the screen, which in fact is how *Synchromy* begins, occupies only a narrow section of the screen, that is, one-eleventh of the total width (see Fig. 108).

It has been suggested, somewhat cynically, that one of the reasons for the multiplications of the track was an effort on McLaren's part to deal with the awkward areas left over on the screen.[386] There is a less harsh explanation of the filmmaker's intentions. McLaren knew full well that the film's visual component, when restricted to a narrow vertical band within a large rectangular screen, would not be likely to have the same range of impact as its auditory equivalent. An examination of the places in the film where the multiplication of the bands is introduced, or withdrawn, shows that such changes coincide with the beginnings, or endings, of the musical phrases of the sound-track. Furthermore, as the auditory component increases in complexity, so more bands occur on the screen. In short, McLaren has used the multiplication of the bands

Fig. 108. Synchromy. A frame from the film's introduction. The single band on which the striations appear allows an unambiguous demonstration of the direct relationship of the visual and aural imagery. [NFB.]

386 David Curtis, "Where does one put Norman McLaren?" in *Norman McLaren* (Edinburgh: Scottish Arts Council, 1977) 53.

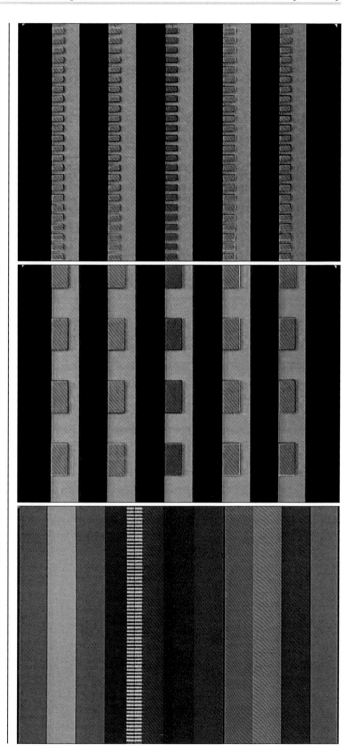

Fig. 109. Synchromy. *A single, high frequency striation (the visual manifestation of a high sound) is repeated a further four times across the screen. Notice also the added colour.* [NFB.]

Fig. 110. Synchromy. *A single, low frequency striation (the visual manifestation of a low sound) is repeated a further four times across the screen. Notice also the added colour.* [NFB.]

Fig. 111. Synchromy. *This frame is part of a sequence which shows the striations moving from right to left across the screen, jumping from one band to the next. As the striations move from one band to the next, successive bands change colour, giving the illusion that the colours are following the lateral movement of the striations.* [NFB.]

to bring the sound and visuals of *Synchromy* more in accord with one another.

There is another obvious variation which has been introduced into the visual imagery of *Synchromy*, and that is colour. The images on the sound-track are black and white (black on clear film). The unmodified visual images derived from these sound-track images would also be monochromatic. However, in the film *Synchromy*, McLaren has introduced colour, and, like the multiplication of the track bands, the introduction of changes in colour coincides with the introduction of musical changes in the sound-track. Also, like the previously discussed modification, the complexity of the colour areas increases in proportion to the musical complexity (contrast Fig. 108, from the film's simple beginning, with the complexity of the frames in Figs. 118 and 119 from the film's climactic section). So, again, the introduced variation supports a closer relationship of the sound and visual tracks.

Two other less noticeable variations also occur and can also be shown to draw the auditory and visual elements of the film closer together. Movements across the screen are introduced by McLaren in the third and climactic section of the film. These occur when the striations that relate to a sound are displayed first in one band and then, when the auditory phrase is continued, in the next band – which changes to the colour of the first band to accommodate the striations – and then the next band, and so on. Needless to say, at this point the film has reached the stage where the screen is filled with eleven bands. The striations and bands, therefore, appear to move across the width of the screen (Fig. 111). As with other modifications of the visual presentation of the sound-track, the occurrence of this type of movement coincides with clearly defined sections of music. This particular modification, however, is used rather sparingly. It is introduced in the complex passages at, or near, the film's climax. The sweeping nature of this lateral movement gives the viewer a relatively rare chance in the film to retain an image. In addition, as it is the bands that are changing colour in this evocation of movement, the viewer's attention shifts from the rapidly changing striations to the more stable bands upon which the striations occur. For both these reasons the introduction of this lateral movement helps to visually unify a particularly complicated part of the film. Furthermore, it does so not by reducing the intricacy of the image, but by

Figs. 112 and 113 (two upper images): Synchromy *(Fig. 112, Voice 1) & (Fig. 113, Voice 2). In this part of the film, McLaren visually separated two of the elements of the music. The striations corresponding to the two musical 'voices' have been placed on bands which initially appear on opposite sides of the screen. Although of different pitch, and therefore represented by different striation sizes, the sounds are rhythmically similar. Note by note, the sounds respond to each other, their visual manifestations appearing in sequence on their respective bands. McLaren has also used colour to visually differentiate the musical elements.* [NFB.]

Fig. 114. Synchromy. *This frame shows the film's gathering complexity. After the film's introduction in which just one band appears (Fig. 108), a second band is introduced. The striations on them simultaneously depict the same sound but one set is the mirror image of the other. McLaren has used the opportunity of the second band's introduction to create a symmetry of the bands and of the striations which appear on them.* [NFB.]

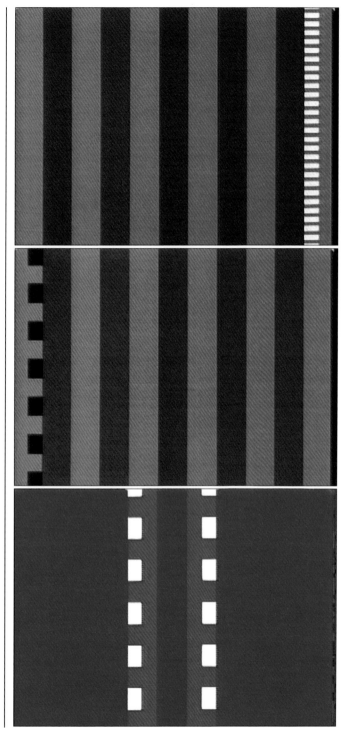

adding a further element to the film.

A similar sort of movement is introduced by McLaren when just the striations, as opposed to the bands with their striations, succeed each other as they appear on one band, and then the next, and so on. This lateral movement, being of the pulsating striations themselves, is not so inherently stable as the movement of the bands. However, McLaren has allied the movement with another feature which visually identifies elements of the music. The music for this section contains two 'voices' which rhythmically imitate each other note by note.

McLaren has visually separated these 'voices' by placing their striations in bands on opposite sides of the screen (Figs. 112 and 113). He further distinguishes the two voices by making one voice white and the other brown. They then appear to move, band by band, in response to each other, and in quickening tempo, towards the centre of the screen. After a brief interplay on the centre band, they then, each on their alternate bands, multiply outwards, towards both sides of the screen. By making these visual aspects of the two musical voices also distinct – in movement, location and colour – McLaren has once again introduced variations which bring the auditory and visual images into greater accord.

Yet another modification to the visual representation of the sound-track is made by McLaren. The striations in the bands are usually narrower than the width of the bands, unless the loudest of the dynamic range is being used.[387] McLaren usually positioned striations that were narrower than the full band-width on the left of their respective bands. This location of the striations has no bearing on the sound produced. It does, however, have a considerable impact on the screen. McLaren was aware of this. The asymmetry of the striations, on the opening single band, is balanced at the first opportunity – when the second band is introduced it is seen to be a mirror of its partner (see Fig. 114). The bands are positioned symmetrically on the screen and the images, within each band, point towards the centre. Thus greater sympathy with the sound-track's calm, opening passages is achieved.

Considering that there are up to eleven bars displayed on the screen at any one time, the number of possible permutations of the left/right positioning of the striations within the bars is extensive. McLaren used a number of permutations and his use achieves ends which accord with

[387] The volume of the sound is varied on the sound-track by changing the width, or area, of the striations.

Fig. 115. Synchromy. Here, the striations not only have mirror equivalents appearing on other bands. The placing of the bands next to each other allows the various striations to merge with their neighbouring striations and thereby make bigger, more emphatic shapes. [NFB.]

musical and visual themes. An instance which may be cited concerns the previously mentioned section where two voices are displayed. Until they reach the centre and occupy the same band, the two configurations are aligned on different sides of their respective bands, and thus the distinction between the two voices is enhanced.

The visual range of the film was extended by McLaren in a particularly noteworthy use of left and right-sided configurations. When two adjacent bands both display the same striations, those striations join and form much larger shapes if the striations are arranged back to back (Figs. 115 and 119).

A use of this increase in visual dynamics occurs following the two 'voices' section. Its introduction marks a fresh section of music, a particularly vigorous and energetic section. The use of the larger shapes not only helps to indicate the section, it also emphasizes the vigour of this part of *Synchromy*. Once again, McLaren's divergence from an unadulterated visual projection of the sound-track brings the auditory and visual components of the film into greater sympathy with each other.

There is one further variation of the auditory and visual configurations that should be mentioned. When McLaren made *Synchromy*, he first composed the music, which he then photographed onto the sound track of the film. There are three musical themes which run through the film and McLaren shot a separate sound-track for each theme. He later mixed these separate themes into the single sound-track of the finished film. In the visual track of the first two sections the themes are not differentiated from each other (see Figs. 116 and 117). However, in the third and final section of the film, he introduced a visual separation of the themes. The visual presentation of each theme has its own band or, if multiplied, bands. This approach allowed him to expand the visual parameters of the climactic section. In this final section, McLaren displays on the screen stunning arrangements of ordered complexity which are made possible by the visual separation of the themes. Thematic identification through colour also achieves this end. The stunningly complex visuals parallel the climactic intricacies of the music being heard. Yet again, the modification to the visual presentation brings the visual and auditory aspects of *Synchromy* closer together.

Synchromy: the paradox

It is now time to approach the paradox which has been assembled.

In *Synchromy* the optical sound-track is visually presented on the screen, simultaneously with its acoustic presentation. The accord between vision and sound would be expected to be absolute. However, McLaren's introduction of modifications to the visual presentation achieves a greater agreement between visuals and sound. This could only be the case if the original accord was not, in the first place, absolute. A closer examination of this original relationship is, therefore, necessary.

Pitch is visually represented in *Synchromy* by horizontal striations, within a vertical band, of differing frequencies. Narrow striations close together equal high sounds, broad striations further apart equal low sounds (see Figs. 109 and 110). Such a system of visually representing (musical) sounds is unusual. One of two predominant, traditional ways of representing sound visually is through colour. Synaesthetic experiments from the sixteenth century to the earlier part of the twentieth century equated certain pitches with certain colours – usually the octave with the spectrum. Unfortunately, many of these experiments were limited by technical factors and narrow conceptual parameters. For example, the important visual

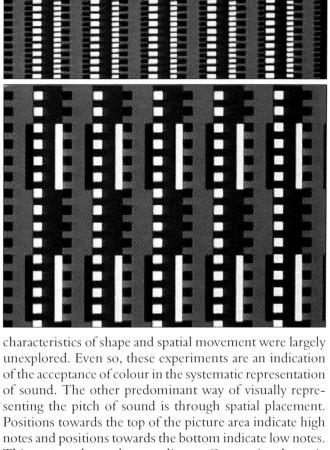

Fig. 116. Synchromy. A total of eleven bands appear across the screen in this frame from the climactic section of the film. There are two types of band alternately repeated. One is red with two sets of black striations, the other is brown with two sets of white, but otherwise similar, striations. [NFB.]

Fig. 117. Synchromy. This frame is similar to Fig. 116. However the larger striations associated with lower sounds clearly shows the relationship between the repeated shapes. [NFB.]

388 See Elaine Dobson, *Graphic Notation: Approaches and Developments*, unpublished thesis, University of Queensland, 1971.

characteristics of shape and spatial movement were largely unexplored. Even so, these experiments are an indication of the acceptance of colour in the systematic representation of sound. The other predominant way of visually representing the pitch of sound is through spatial placement. Positions towards the top of the picture area indicate high notes and positions towards the bottom indicate low notes. This system has a long pedigree. Conventional music notation is constructed in such a way. That graphic musical scores also use the convention shows how deeply ingrained it is.[388] Although, in *Synchromy*, the sound-track's high and low frequency code that is translated by the movie projector's photo- electric eye, may be a logical way of representing pitch, it is, nevertheless, an unconventional one

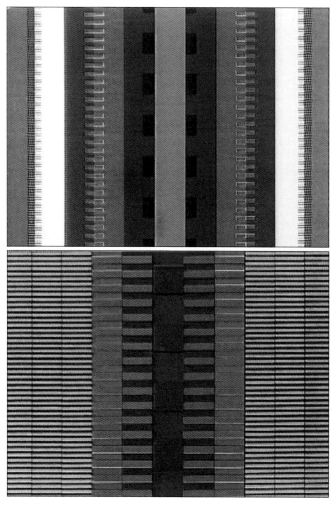

and therefore difficult to grasp during viewing. McLaren realized this. He began *Synchromy* with a demonstration (exposition) of the pitch configurations (Fig. 108). The representation of sound volume is also clearly shown at this stage. The relationship of sound-pitch to the visual frequencies displayed on the bands, therefore, can be recognized in the earlier, simpler part of the film. The strict temporal accordance, note by note, helps the viewer identify an auditory-visual relationship. The perceived strength and extent of such a relationship, however, remain constrained by the unorthodox visual representation and the extreme visual complexity of the latter part of the film.

There is a brief segment of *Synchromy*, specifically the coda between the second and third parts of the film, which shows a spatial interpretation of pitch. The visual presentation of the sound track is presented in triple width, that is, as a very wide band, on a black screen. As in the rest of the film, pitch is indicated by the thickness and frequency of the striations within the bands. In this segment though, pitch is also indicated by the position of the bands. These wide bands occur on the left of the screen if they represent a low sound, and across to the right if a high sound is denoted. Intermediate positioning also occurs. Although this type of pitch presentation is just a small part of *Synchromy*, the coda does nevertheless, fit the film's overall structure. It forms a distinctive division, which, apart from the spatial pitch presentation, is similar to the coda between the first and second parts of the film. The coda is also an effective introduction to the final part of the film, in that the lateral movement of the bands prefigures the sweeping movements of that final section. The coda, then, represents yet another modification to the visual presentation of the sound track. The spatial interpretation of pitch brings greater accord between the visual and auditory aspects of the film. Its structural functions also lend the visual aspect of the film some increased coherence, giving greater accord with its auditory counterpart.

At this point it is appropriate to consider the types of movement used by McLaren in *Synchromy*. Mention has been made of the sweeping movements induced by band multiplication, colour changes from one band to the next, or striation displacement from one band to the next. These sweeps move only in a horizontal direction. They are also used sparingly. When they do occur, however, they do increase the visual perception of phrases. Such visual temporal links are not encouraged by the other type of movement in *Synchromy*.

The dominant type of movement in the film is a mesmeric flicker. This results from the absolute temporal unity between sound and vision. In *Synchromy* the sounds, or notes, are staccato and have very short silences between them. Aurally, the continuity – or overall shape or melody of the sounds – remains paramount. This is not the case with the visual presentation. The pulsating effect, which is perceived as just one feature of the sound presentation, completely dominates visual perception of the film to the extent that the recognition of temporal phrases is seriously impaired. Yet, on the sound track, the temporal organization into patterns or phrases, despite the staccato of the music, is the overwhelming impression. This discrepancy between visual and aural perception could have been reduced had McLaren used legato, or joined, notes. The relationship between a note and its predecessor and successor would have been far easier to see, and the visual perception of temporal groups far more likely. McLaren, however, chose not to adopt this approach. Several reasons may be offered for his decision. In constructing the three sound-tracks, McLaren allowed only one sound to occur at any one time.[389] Such an approach would have had technical advantages. By avoiding chords, which would entail placing more than one striation on a band, McLaren considerably simplified his later task of placing on single bands the multiple thematic sets of striations. The duration of sound in some frequencies was limited by the striations' slight jump, in relation to each other at the horizontal junction between one frame and the next. By using notes of short duration McLaren minimized this potential difficulty. These problems, however, could have been overcome by such a problem-solver as McLaren. The overriding reason for the adoption of staccato sound was simply that the staccato approach, with its dominant visual pulsations, was the effect desired by McLaren. In other words, the flicker effect excited him to the extent that he preferred not to sacrifice it in order to gain greater visual continuity. The pulsating flicker effect conveys an enormous amount of energy. As well, the pulse is remorseless. The viewer is compelled by it, not daring to look away from the screen for an instant. The dominance of the pulse is maintained over the introduction of colour and multiplication of image, giving the film, together with its unvaried vertical format, a visually unified essence.

Be that as it may, the pulsating movements seen on the screen do not accord, in a lyrical sense, with the sounds heard. Visual perception works differently from auditory perception, at least in this case. The micro-silences between staccato notes are heard but do not break the continuity of the melodic line.[390] When the visual equivalent is used on the screen the result is perceived as a flicker. However, the difficulties in recognizing the visual equivalent of pitch in *Synchromy*, are not just caused by perceptual process differences between the senses of sight and hearing. In the movie projector sound is produced by continuously moving the sound track, with its striations, across the photo electric cell. From the point of view of the 'eye' – the photo electric

389 Although this is generally true, it should be acknowledged that there are a couple of brief instances during which chords are used.

390 Ray Jackendoff and Fred Lerdahl, *Generative Theory of Tonal Music*. MIT Press Series on Cognitive Theory of Representation (Cambridge, Mass: MIT Press, 1983). The authors show that musical perception is most commonly based on the recognition of groups of notes in a phrase.

cell – the signals come continuously at a very fast rate. A very fast pulse occurs. Certain striations, when sustained, produce a particular pitch. The visual image, in *Synchromy*, however, is produced by a sequence of static images. If the same note is held for several seconds, the image on the screen will be a static one. Thus the projector decodes the similar images of the visual and sound tracks differently. Even had the the visual and sound tracks' decoding been an identical process, it would not follow that their subsequent manifestations would, when perceived by a human being, induce two identical states in that person. In introducing variations which, as has been shown, bring the auditory and visual experiences closer together, McLaren has acknowledged that the visual and auditory correspondences of the film, in its original form, occurred more in theoretical construct than in actuality. These observations are not intended as an indictment of the film, but of its interpretation as an ultimate synaesthetic event.

McLaren often cited one of Oskar Fischinger's films, *Study No. 7*, as a major influence on his work. He was aware that Fischinger's approach, in interpreting music visually, was to interpret the music as a whole and not elementally, note by note. In his own earlier abstract films, from *Boogie Doodle* through *Fiddle-de-dee*, *Begone Dull Care* to *Short and Suite*, McLaren adopted a similar approach. His film *Synchromy* does not approach the sound-image relationship in the same manner. Despite McLaren's modifications, which were based upon interpretations of the 'spirit' of the soundtrack and aimed at bringing the component parts of the film closer together, the union of visual image and sound experience is not achieved. But a relationship does exist, the confluence and conflicts of which give the film an immense tension. In this regard the film is more successful than an absolutely accurate accord between vision and sound, whatever that may look or sound like. *Synchromy* possesses as much, and if not more, of this tension or conflict between the visual and auditory components as his earlier attempts to interpret music visually on film. The abstract features of McLaren's films – their movement, their pace, their dynamics and their tension – are those that inspired Len Lye, the New Zealand pioneer filmmaker and artist, to comment: "When a film by Norman hits me, I stay hit. Sometimes, he simply rocks my kinetic heart, other times he spins it ... I'm for Norman McLaren. I don't think we can appreciate him enough."[391]

391 Andre Martin, *Norman McLaren* (Annecy: Journees internationales du cinema d'animation; Montreal: Cinémathèque canadienne, 1965) n. pag.

Chapter Eight

Venus and Mars

At first sight, *Hell UnLtd* (1936) is a shocking film. That it is a Norman McLaren film makes it doubly so. McLaren's pursuit of new and diverse techniques in making his films meant that the viewer could not anticipate what each new McLaren film would be like. The discerning viewer, therefore, grew to expect to be shocked on seeing a McLaren film for the first time, and further, this anticipation could be expected to reduce the shock. Why then is *Hell UnLtd* so shocking?

Hell UnLtd contains blatant anti-war, anti-capitalist messages. Even the title, which is read as Hell UnLimited, contains anti-capitalist overtones. It incorporates a pun using the commercial abbreviation of Ltd for the word Limited, thereby associating commerce with the title's hell of war and armaments. The film also urges viewers to take direct civil action. Could this film involve the same film-maker who created such films as *Pas de deux*, *Fiddle-de-dee*, *Begone Dull Care* and *Spheres*?[392]

It is the openness and directness of the anti-war themes of *Hell UnLtd* that surprise. But then, it is a film of McLaren's youth and so exuberance and dogmatic idealism may be expected to overwhelm any aspiration to subtlety. The strength of the message was all-important to the young filmmaker. The concern over conflict however, was a theme which was to return in his later film work. One of McLaren's most celebrated films, *Neighbours*, does not just deplore conflict. McLaren uses conflict and its repercussions to make a telling pacifist statement. Love of beauty, in this case a flower, turns into possessive greed, jealousy and eventually a horribly escalating battle which envelopes

[392] McLaren collaborated with Helen Biggar in making *Hell UnLtd*.

Fig. 120. Norman McLaren not long after completing Hell UnLtd. *[McLaren Archive/NFB.]*

not only the protagonists but also their homes and families. It leads to complete destruction and death which are commemorated, to the pertinent lack of appreciation by the dead and buried combatants, by the flower which adorns each of their graves.

The bulk of McLaren's film work falls within two categories. The first category contains the largest proportion of his films. The films of this category display those qualities most often associated with McLaren: fun, whimsy, gentleness, beauty and excitement. The titles alone evoke the spirit of these films; e.g. *Fiddle-de-dee, Begone Dull Care, Short and Suite, Boogie Doodle*.

Hell UnLtd

Films in the second category contain aggression and conflict as major factors. They therefore may be termed the 'Mars' films of Norman McLaren. Although only a small number of his films belong in this category, they nevertheless have a powerful impact and contain the film which McLaren himself counted as his most important.[393] Those that belong to this category are: *Defence of Madrid* (1936) in which McLaren was cinematographer, *Hell UnLtd* (1936),

393 This film is *Neighbours.* See McLaren as quoted in Maynard Collins, *Norman McLaren* (Ottawa: Canadian Film Institute, 1976) 69.

Neighbours (1952), *Blinkity Blank* (1955) and *A Chairy Tale* (1957). Two further films, *Rythmetic* (1956) and *Opening Speech* (1960), may also be included in the category. The question that begs to be answered is: Why did, or how could, McLaren make these films? That one could equally ask a similar question concerning his more usual lyrical work of the first category suggests that the question that is really being asked is: How could McLaren make two such seemingly disparate groups of films? The dates have been given with the titles of these films to establish part of the context that shaped McLaren and the films – relevant here are the Great Depression (1929–1934), the Spanish Civil War (1936–1939), the rise of Nazism (1932–1939), the Second World War (1939–1945), and the Cold War (1945–1989) with its attendant manifestation of McCarthyism. Also significant in establishing the context is the place – in McLaren's case these are Scotland, London, New York and Canada, as well as China and India. Thirdly the artist, in this instance McLaren, is important. What prior knowledge, perceptions, interpretations and conclusions does he bring to his context of time and place? What artistic knowledge and intent does he apply in producing the artistic statement?

While it is not necessary to detail again all the formative events of McLaren's life, the context of his subsequent social attitudes should be summarized. McLaren's account of an early experience serves this purpose:

> I had already been appalled when I was about 13 or 14, when I was in the Boy Scout movement taking Christmas packages to the poor people in the slums. We got inside where they lived and I was so utterly appalled by the lack of furniture, lack of a carpet, everything dirty and grimy, no running water, except for a tap shared by several houses. These tenements were very old ... and overcrowded. When I got home and found myself in a nice clean home with more rooms to spare – I was just so appalled – why do those people have to live that way and we live this way? I felt very guilty and I thought something's wrong.

> A big impact, therefore was the difference between the way I lived with my family and with others although the way we lived was modest. My friend Billy Finlayson lived in an apartment. It was a shock to me that he had to live there all the time and not

with a garden. We had a car in fact. I remember being embarrassed travelling in the car even especially when we got a new car. I felt guilty. My motivation was honest – it came from within – an immediate reaction.[394]

McLaren's subsequent experiences in the Spanish Civil War as Ivor Montagu's cameraman for *The Defence of Madrid*, confirmed his political beliefs and, as well, aroused an intolerance of violence which remained all his life.

Just before his experiences in Spain, McLaren had with Helen Biggar, completed *Hell UnLtd* at the Glasgow School of Art. His communist beliefs were prevalent at the time of making this film. Biggar also had left-wing credentials.[395] The earlier-mentioned anti-capitalist tone of the film is an expression of these beliefs, as is the film's advocacy of direct action – the film advocates the refusal to pay for armaments. Even so, the film's overriding message is anti-war, which McLaren freely acknowledged and for which he made no apology.[396] As he later recalled, in 1977, he had been terrified by Hitler's growth in power during the thirties and, even though he believed a film could not stop war, he wanted to do his best to make his contribution.[397] Many years after the making of *Hell UnLtd*, McLaren did express some reservations about the film. He felt its form and its structure had been neglected when it was being made. "I was so preoccupied with the content that I did not spend much time thinking of the form, or the structure. I wanted to do something, to make something, and was not worrying about form or structure. What did it matter whether the film was good or bad! At that time I absolutely had to make a film."[398] McLaren classified this film as juvenilia.[399] Indeed, the film's structure and approach do give it dogmatic overtones. McLaren has suggested that the greater acceptance of demonstrators and protests in more recent years would have meant that "[t]oday, obviously, the same message would have to be presented another way".[400] Other McLaren films, however, have not been so drastically affected by the passage of time, for example *Pas de deux*, *Lines Vertical* and *Blinkity Blank*. The problem associated with *Hell UnLtd* lies not only in the crudity with which the ideas have been presented, but also with the specificity of their presentation. Specific events, names, problems and solutions are referred to, and so locate the film firmly in a particular time and place.

394 Norman McLaren as quoted in Donald McWilliams, *Creative Process* proposal, ts. June 1985, NFB Montreal, 36–37.

395 Anna Shepherd, "Helen Biggar and Norman McLaren: Based on a MS 'Helen Unlimited'", *New Edinburgh Review*, 1978, 25.

396 Norman McLaren as quoted in "Interview", *Norman McLaren: exhibition and films*, (Edinburgh: Scottish Arts Council, 1977) 9.

397 McLaren as quoted in "Interview", Scottish Arts Council 9.

398 McLaren as quoted in "Interview'" Scottish Arts Council 11.

399 McLaren as quoted in "Interview'" Scottish Arts Council 11.

400 McLaren as quoted in "Interview'" Scottish Arts Council 10.

Fig. 121. Norman
McLaren checks a shot
during the making of
Neighbours.
[Photo by Evelyn
Lambart, McLaren
Archive/NFB.]

Neighbours

The next film in the 'Mars' category is *Neighbours,* which turned out to be one of McLaren's most acclaimed films and the NFB's most successful film ever in terms of numbers of bookings.[401] It is also the film that gave most satisfaction to McLaren:

> But other things about my work have pleased me more. A few years ago, for example, I found our title department making the title for *Neighbours* in several different African languages. It turned out they wanted to show the film to a number of warring African tribes with the hope of convincing them of the futility of war. That's the kind of recognition I most appreciate.[402]

McLaren also said, on a number of occasions, that *Neighbours* was the film he most wished to be saved for posterity.[403] The film's artistic achievements owe much to what happened to McLaren's career in the years preceding 1952.

As the Second World War approached, McLaren relinquished his position of filmmaker at the GPO Film Unit. He had learned important filmic lessons concerning improvisation and film structure, and had completed a film, *Love on the Wing*, which established enduring McLaren characteristics of fun and whimsy. But he was concerned at being directly involved in a war which "... at the time looked pretty certain in Europe. Because of my Spanish experience with its bombings, people mangled, I could not

401 The NFB figures as of August 1987 list *Neighbours* as the NFB's most popular film with 108,000 bookings at home and abroad. Gary Evans *In the National Interest: A Chronicle of the National Film Board of Canada, 1949–1989,* unpublished manuscript 1990 71.

402 McLaren as quoted in Susan Carson, "Bore People? Fat chance , Norman McLaren", *Toronto Telegram Weekend Magazine* 30 March 1974 20–21.

403 McLaren in Collins 69, and in Donald McWilliams and Susan Huycke, *Creative Process: Norman McLaren,* dir. Donald McWilliams, National Film Board of Canada, 1991, script 28.

stand up to the strain of a major war around me."[404]
McLaren's pacifist beliefs were sufficiently strong as to
determine the pattern of his life. The eventual victory of
the Allies in the Second World War did not bring the
anticipated state of harmony to the world. By 1949,
McLaren could no longer resist his need to be of practical
use to those people less fortunate than himself. As a consequence, the world's division into two antagonistic political groups – the Western and communist blocs – would
come to arouse a conflict of loyalties and sympathies within
McLaren:

> Although I only saw the beginnings of Mao's revolu-
> tion [during his work for UNESCO in China], my
> faith in human nature was reinvigorated by it. Then
> I came back to Quebec and the Korean War began.
> My sympathies were divided at that time. I felt myself
> to be as close to the Chinese people as I felt proud of
> my status as a Canadian. I decided to make a really
> strong film about anti-militarism and against war.[405]

McLaren's decision was not made quite so quickly.
As well, there were other associated events, of which
McLaren was to remain unaware, that give *Neighbours* an
added, if ironic, triumph.

After the war, and Grierson's departure, the National
Film Board of Canada came under pressure. Government
politicians questioned the need for taxpayers to support a
government filmmaking organization and opposition politicians had previously made capital of the insinuated links
from Grierson to his former secretary to a Soviet spy
network. Grierson successfully rebutted the charges and
duly completed his planned term as NFB Commissioner.
However, the post-War communist scare intensified and
the ensuing pressures ended the term of Grierson's immediate successor. The subsequent Film Commissioner, Arthur Irwin, not only had to restore staff morale but also had
to restore NFB credibility with the government.

The government's top-secret Psychological Warfare
Committee had been in existence since the war years and,
with the intensification of the Cold War between the
democracies of the West and the communist bloc, took on
the responsibility of fostering propaganda films which were
to promote the virtues of the democratic system. An ad-
ministrative programme, called *Freedom Speaks*, was set up
with $250,000 ear-marked for making such films. One

[404] McLaren as quoted in
Creative Process
proposal 40.

[405] McLaren, "Interview",
28.

Fig. 122. Norman McLaren (dark suit) and Arthur Irwin (bow-tie) at a 1950s film-screening. [NFB.]

didactic propagandist film was made using part of these funds. Having thus assuaged the government critics with this film, Irwin spent the rest of this money on "... fairly non-political subjects".[406]

Meanwhile, McLaren had returned from China to Canada. Although he felt "very socially aware" and wanted to do a "serious piece" he was diverted.[407] He made two 3D films for the Festival of Britain. On their completion, he got together with Grant Munro to explore the new technique he called pixillation. This film was to be about highway safety. Work on the film proceeded and, keeping in mind the need for economy and speed, McLaren proposed to use every test in the finished film.[408]

The new Commissioner was curious to know what McLaren was doing. Irwin was excited by the new technique and immediately suggested that McLaren consider a new theme, an international one, for which there was some money. (The money to which Irwin was referring was derived from the *Freedom Speaks* programme.) A few days later, on viewing the Highway test rushes, McLaren saw two figures "... exchanging supernaturally violent fisti-

406 Evans 47.

407 Evans 53.

408 Grant Munro, personal interview 23 October 1990.

In the following frames, the theme of Neighbours *is illustrated.* [NFB.]

Fig. 123. To begin, two amiable neighbours mirror each other.

Fig. 124. A flower appears.

Fig. 125. The flower gives the neighbours ecstatic pleasure.

Fig. 126. They cavort and fly in sheer joy.

Fig. 127. Each neighbour claims the flower.

Fig. 128. A scuffle ensues.

Fig. 129. The position of the neighbours' boundary is disputed in the developing conflict over the ownership of the flower.

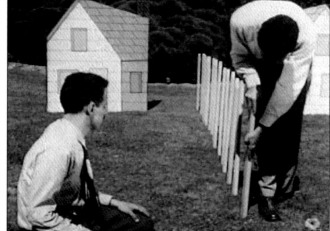

Fig. 130. A hand deemed too near the flower is stomped on.

Fig. 131. There is a retaliatory slap.

Fig. 132. The slap is interpreted as a challenge and a duel, using fence palings as swords, ensues.

Fig. 133. The fight becomes a little more serious when fists are used.

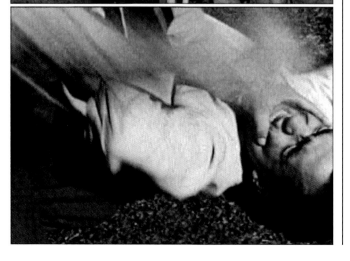

Fig. 134. The violence escalates.

Fig. 135. The distorting make-up on the protagonists' faces shows the mounting horror of the fight.

Fig. 136. Meanwhile the subject of the conflict, the flower, is forgotten. In the fight it is trampled underfoot.

Fig. 137. The innocent become victims. Each neighbour viscously attacks the other's wife and baby.

Fig. 138. The
protagonists have killed
each other.

Fig. 139. And finally, a
flower appears on each
neighbour's grave.

cuffs".[409] McLaren recalled the event: "Immediately, I said
to myself 'I've got it'. And my ideas took shape from there[:]
Two men, friends to begin with, but whose relationship
gets steadily worse until they end up fighting. The idea of
the flower came shortly after that as well."[410]

Like all his films with the sole exception of *Narcissus*,
Neighbours came in under budget. It cost just $14,963 and
was one of the cheapest films made at the NFB in 1952.[411]
Regardless of the amount, the irony remains that this film,
McLaren's statement concerning the futility, horror and
destruction of an incremental antagonism, was funded by
money which was intended to be used to show the supe-
riority of one antagonist (the West) over the other (communism). Had McLaren known of this irony, it would have

409 Evans 54.

410 McLaren as quoted in
"Interview", Scottish
Arts Council 28.

411 Evans 52.

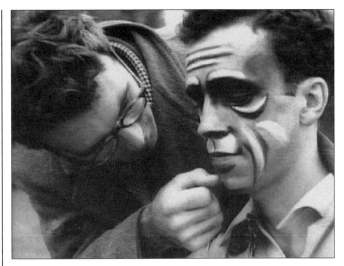

amused him greatly and added to his satisfaction at *Neighbours'* success.

Neighbours shows the artistic lessons learnt by McLaren. The startling new technique which he uses, is always subservient to the overall theme of the film. It also provides humour and grace. These contrast with, and, therefore, also heighten the horror of the latter part of the film. Woody Allen's theory about laughter is applicable to McLaren's film.[412] According to Allen, laughter releases tension when viewers watch, for example, a confrontation – and this situation certainly applies to *Neighbours*. In the film, McLaren's protagonists confront each other, but the humour of their pixillated movement causes the viewers to laugh, and, thereby, release the tension they might feel. But, when the viewers see the escalating horror, particularly the attacks on the women and the babies, the humour evaporates, and the tensions which remain are thereby heightened. Thus, the viewers' sense of horror is intensified.

Stylisation of movement and imagery as well as of the sound-track – McLaren uses his synthetic-sound technique for this film – gives the film a cohesive strength. This stylisation also helps to remove the film from a specific context. Indeed the film is a parable and assumes a universality of application. Such an obvious anti-war, anti-violence statement expressed in *Neighbours* was a brave one to make in the 1950s of McCarthyism and the Korean War. In that context, the film takes on the mantle of a political statement.[413] The film was championed by some – it won

412 As expounded by Woody Allen on *The South Bank Show*, dir. Nigel Waters 1994.

413 Curtis' assertion (David Curtis, "Where does one put Norman McLaren?" Scottish Arts Council 48), that *Neighbours* is a non-political film does not give sufficient weight to the context of the early fifties.

Fig. 141. Neighbours.
The attack on a wife
and child as shown in a
still photograph.
[NFB.]

Fig. 142. Neighbours.
A frame from the
climactic section of the
film.
[NFB.]

Fig. 143. Neighbours.
Another frame from the
violent climax of the film.
[NFB.]

McLaren an Oscar in 1953 – and decried by others. McLaren came to see the Academy Award as a political gesture by Hollywood against the rages of McCarthyism, which was then sweeping the USA. The wide distribution gained through the Oscar award also brought problems. Some distributors wanted the award-winning movie, but without the violent sequences. The footage showing the brutal attacks on the two mothers and their babies was removed after distributors in the USA and Europe (to be precise, Italy) refused to accept the film in its original form.

Several aspects of this censorship are notable. The removal of these most violent and shocking scenes weakens the film's pacifist statement. Further, as the scenes depict the fate of innocents, an important allegorical extension of the moral of the film was deleted. Did the objections to these scenes stem from concern about the depiction of violence, or were they an attempt to mute the message of the film? No doubt, it was the former, as it is hard to imagine pro-war censors being so subtle as to only partially censor the film. It is therefore ironic that the removal of the allegedly over-violent scenes reduced the strength of the film's pacifist statement. McLaren took a pragmatic stand over the issue. He felt it better to distribute the film in its cut form than not at all. He had had reservations about the offending scenes, not because of their violence, but because the women and children do not appear anywhere else in the film and their presence spoilt what McLaren called the classical unity of the piece.[414] So McLaren himself authorized the subsequent distribution of cut versions. Although he did not come to regret the distribution of the cut version to schools, he did subsequently feel, in the much more questioning atmosphere surrounding the Vietnam War, that he had been wrong to remove the scenes depicting innocent victims. He therefore reinstated the scenes. McLaren's attitude to the distribution of his films, and to his potential audience, is also pertinent to the film *Blinkity Blank*.

Optimism

Blinkity Blank (1955), unlike other films being discussed in this category, was not made by photographing people or objects but by scratching and painting directly onto film. In this film, McLaren scratched on clusters of, in the main, two, three or four frames, leaving an intervening number

414 McLaren in Collins 69.

of blank frames, usually ten or twelve. The effect is a series of stroboscopic explosions of energy.

McLaren's original intention was to make an abstract film and he had made two-thirds of it before he abandoned it, fearing that the abstract *Blinkity Blank* would not maintain the spectator's interest.[415] Considerations such as this, and the concern over the distribution of *Neighbours*, confirm that McLaren believed it important that his films be seen, and appreciated, by as large, and as wide, an audience as possible. His obligations to be a useful public servant, and, in a broader context, his desire to perform a function of maximum benefit to others, are consistent with his aspiration for a wide audience, and also with his associated feeling – the fear of boring an audience. Coinciding with the internationalist ramifications of his concept of social duty was McLaren's preference for not using words, spoken or written, in his films. McLaren felt the spoken or written word "... to be far removed from the language of visual motion – almost another substance".[416] The absence of speech suited not only his international audience, but also his multi-language Canadian one. McLaren wished to maximise the inter-cultural acceptability of his work. For example, *Rythmetic* was at one stage envisaged as a film of letters and words. Ultimately he chose the near-universal symbols of Arabic numerals so that the film would be more widely understood.

McLaren's reliance on, and choice of, music in his films also served his internationalist purpose. Although he was aware that music was not an international language, and that cultural musical differences exist, for him music contained fewer and lesser barriers to international communication than verbal language. For example, when making the film *A Chairy Tale*, McLaren felt able to ask the Indian sitar player, Ravi Shankar, to produce a compromise between Indian ragas and western music. As McLaren said "I wanted a kind of international music".[417] In other films, McLaren's use of his own drawn-on synthetic sound allowed his music track to achieve a measure of cultural neutrality, and, therefore, also an international character, since synthetic sound enabled him to avoid using traditional instruments from a specific culture.[418] The technique's percussive sound also placed an emphasis on the rhythmic component of music which, for McLaren, was the most inter-cultural aspect of music. Even though rhythmic concepts vary from culture to culture, they are

415 McLaren, "Interview", Scottish Arts Council 32.

416 McLaren as quoted in Ivan Stadrucker, questionnaire, 7 March 1975 4. NFB Archives.

417 McLaren as quoted in "Interview", Scottish Arts Council 34.

418 That advanced technological sound may be identified with western culture was not as strongly felt in the 1950s when it was optimistically held that technology was the property of all.

more readily grasped than, for example, alien tonal systems, or even timbres.

In *Chairy Tale*, the desire to make an internationally understood film meant that the style and colour of the man's clothes had to be carefully considered. "McLaren had just been in India and China. Maybe [the man should wear] just white trousers and white shoes and white shirt. These were the garments worn by people all over the world. So we had a man in white against a black background."[419] The chair also had to be carefully selected:

> We had dozens of chairs taking screen-tests. We were very aware of the anthropomorphic qualities of the chairs. We were talking about which was the sexiest and how sexy it should be. Should it have curves, straight lines, things like that. We finally decided on the humble, most ordinary looking, functional chair. Anybody who used a chair would recognize it as a chair with nothing special about it stylistically or culturally.[420]

Although it should not be forgotten that artistic and technical considerations were also important to McLaren when he decided, for example, to select a particular chair, to use numbers rather than words, to use drawn synthetic sound and to place particular emphasis on music, the cumulative nature of such decisions lends weight to the notion that an internationalist concern for humanity was a powerful element of McLaren's personality. That McLaren twice spent lengthy sabbaticals, in China and then in India, teaching fundamental visual communication skills in order to improve health and sanitation, underscores this aspect of his work.

McLaren's social beliefs form the themes of *A Chairy Tale*, *Opening Speech* and *Blinkity Blank*. But whereas *Neighbours* marked an artistic change from *Hell UnLtd*, these later films show a marked development of the theme itself from the preceding themes of *Hell UnLtd* and *Neighbours*. Selfish greed and its consequences, death and destruction, are replaced. In *A Chairy Tale* and *Opening Speech*, McLaren shows the rebellion of an inanimate utility against its human user. However, his attitude to possible symbolism in these films' respective depictions is somewhat ambiguous. To the suggestion that *Opening Speech*, with its rebellious microphone, may be compared with *A Chairy Tale*, with its rebellious chair, McLaren responded: "It's especially

419 Claude Jutra as quoted in *Creative Process,* proposal 26.

420 Claude Jutra as quoted in *Creative Process,* proposal 26–27.

Fig. 144. Norman McLaren and Ravi Shankar discuss the music track for A Chairy Tale. [NFB.]

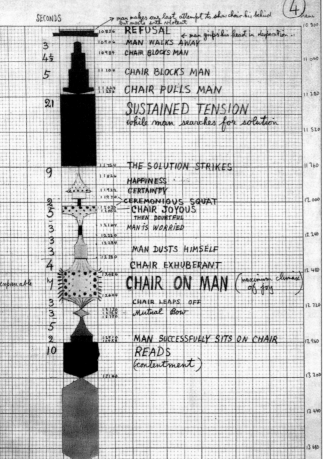

Fig. 145. The final part of the visual outline of A Chairy Tale prepared by McLaren for Ravi Shankar so that the director could more clearly explain the emotional and dynamic structure that would be the basis of the film's music. [McLaren Archive/NFB.]

Fig. 146 (i).
A Chairy Tale. *The chair avoids the man's attempts to sit on it by repeatedly moving away from him.*
[NFB.]

Fig. 146 (ii).
A Chairy Tale. *The man chases the chair, oblivious that the chair calmly watches his blurred rushes.*
[NFB.]

Fig. 146 (iii).
A Chairy Tale. *In an attempt to secure the chair, the man wrestles with the object. He meets resistance.*
[NFB.]

Fig. 146 (iv).
A Chairy Tale. *Still trying to subdue it, the man rides the rebellious chair.*

Fig. 146 (v).
A Chairy Tale. *The man finally understands the chair's point. The man allows the chair sit on him.*
[NFB.]

and they sat
happily
ever
after

Fig. 146 (vi).
A Chairy Tale. *Having made its point, the chair allows the now enlightened man to sit.*
[NFB.]

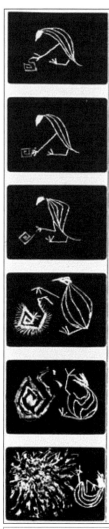

Fig. 147. Six frames from Blinkity Blank *in which the angular bird gives the inquisitive curvilinear bird a shock. [NFB.]*

421 McLaren as quoted in "Interview", Scottish Arts Council 39.

422 McLaren as quoted in "Interview", Scottish Arts Council 35.

423 McLaren as quoted in "Interview", Scottish Arts Council 35.

important not to look for heavy philosophical meditations in these films".[421] This disavowal, which centres on *Opening Speech*, is inconsistent with McLaren's attitude towards other films, like *Neighbours* and *A Chairy Tale* itself, and, therefore, needs closer scrutiny.

The fact that the conception for *Opening Speech* arose from McLaren's own reluctance to give a speech in person, would have caused unease, if not guilt, for switching the impediment in this film from himself to the microphone. More importantly, he would have felt uncomfortable with the symbolism of the film's ending – the conflict is resolved by unplugging the microphone, that is, making one of the film's protagonists lifeless. This resolution is at odds with the more positive conclusions offered, with increasing conviction, in his other 'conflict' films of this era. It was this context of *Opening Speech* which precipitated such a dismissive response to the question of symbolism. This is supported by a declaration given by McLaren earlier in the very same interview when *A Chairy Tale* was being discussed. He was asked: "How does matter come to revolt against man? Why? Does it have a reason?", to which he replied "My first idea was that the chair is a symbol – how shall I put it – of exploitation".[422] The quandary of a chair that refuses to be sat upon is resolved, although not quite in the manner originally envisaged by McLaren. The film was to have ended with the chair sitting on the man; however, it was changed because, "... [it] didn't work visually with the man under the chair".[423] So the chair, after briefly sitting on the man, joins the man. They acknowledge each other with a bow. Having made its point the chair *allows the man* to sit on it. They can thus live happily ever after. This conclusion gives the parable of *A Chairy Tale* some egalitarianism and a degree of optimism that was missing from *Neighbours*. It thus gives the film a greater accord with the theme of *Blinkity Blank*. *A Chairy Tale* is, therefore, more in sympathy with the trend shown by McLaren as the fifties progressed, of resolving conflicts, aggression and exploitation so that a state of unity and egalitarian equilibrium is achieved. This aspect is also apparent in *Rythmetic*. The rebellious numbers of the arithmetical equations have great fun jumping, changing places and changing forms, but, in the end, they contribute dutifully to the enormous sets of equations that fill the screen.

Blinkity Blank has been referred to many times. The theme of the film is as follows: two birds (one angular, the

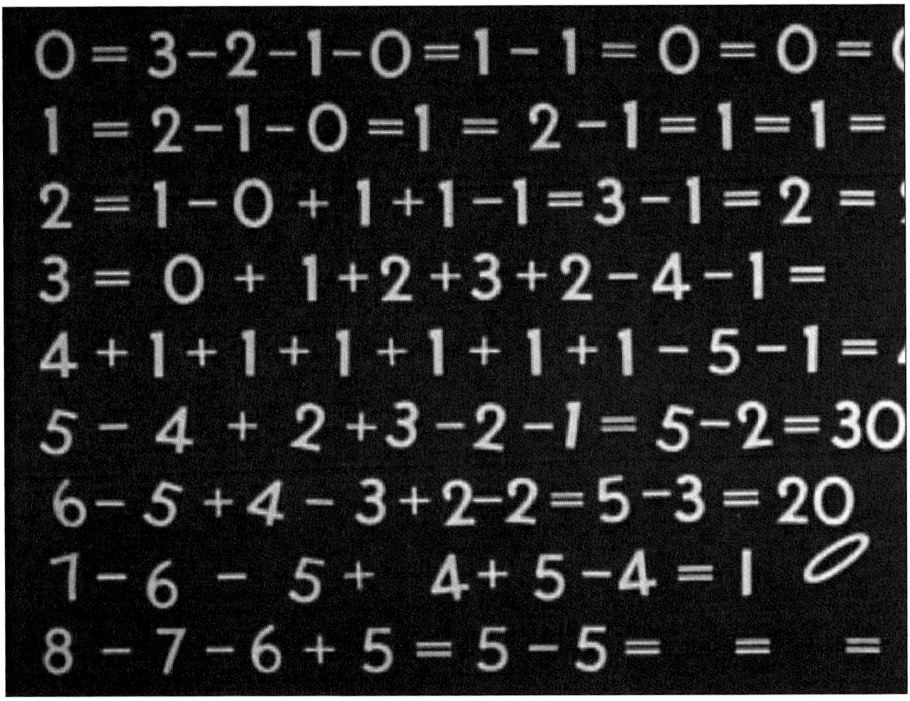

$$0 = 3-2-1-0 = 1-1 = 0 = 0 = ($$
$$1 = 2-1-0 = 1 = 2-1 = 1 = 1 =$$
$$2 = 1-0+1+1-1 = 3-1 = 2 =$$
$$3 = 0+1+2+3+2-4-1 =$$
$$4+1+1+1+1+1+1-5-1 =$$
$$5-4+2+3-2-1 = 5-2 = 30$$
$$6-5+4-3+2-2 = 5-3 = 20$$
$$7-6-5+4+5-4 = 1 \; 0$$
$$8-7-6+5 = 5-5 = \quad = \quad =$$

other curvilinear) initially fight, then fall in love, admiring each other's differences, mate, and produce an egg the result of which is an offspring. The offspring resembles each of its parents. The allegory is clear: Differences are not bad things, they are good – to be absorbed and perpetuated. As well, differences can produce new forms and new consequences.

There are two factors which, on the surface, tend to diminish the importance of the theme of *Blinkity Blank*. Firstly, it will be recalled that the figurative nature of *Blinkity Blank* was only adopted by McLaren when he became convinced that the original abstract work could not sufficiently hold an audience's interest (His work on *Short and Suite* [1959], *Serenal* [1959], the series of Lines films [1960–1965] and *Synchromy* [1971], suggests he subsequently reviewed his estimation of audience capability). Although the figurative nature of *Blinkity Blank* was a second idea, that does not in itself reduce the efficacy, or power, of that second idea. Whether or not the original idea of an abstract approach would have produced a better film is beside the point. What has to be considered is the film as it stands.

McLaren also down-played the importance of

Fig. 148. In Rythmetic, the numbers rebel. [NFB.]

Fig. 149.
Blinkity Blank
(i) The angular bird.
[NFB.]

Fig. 150.
Blinkity Blank
(ii) The curvilinear bird.
[NFB.]

Fig. 151.
Blinkity Blank
*(iii) The angular bird
showing sympathy with
the curvilinear bird.*
[NFB.]

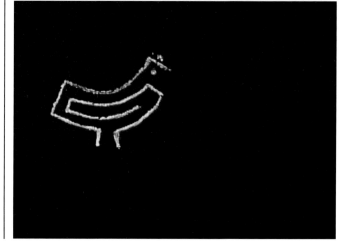

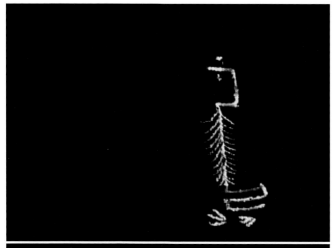

Fig. 152.
Blinkity Blank
(iv) The curvilinear bird
showing sympathy for
the angular bird.
[NFB.]

Fig. 153.
Blinkity Blank
(v) The offspring
emerges from the egg.
[NFB.]

Blinkity Blank's theme when he said of it: "It's what I'm drawing that interests me most, not the story. The form is of more interest to me than the content."[424] It should be noted that McLaren is talking here in relative terms. He is not saying that the story is unimportant, just that it is of less interest to him. It should also be remembered that McLaren was invariably reticent to explain his work other than in terms of the techniques he used.[425] The theme, then, retains its significance.

Seen in the context of McLaren's other allegorical films, the message cannot be mistaken. In that same context, the theme may be seen to have made another step in the direction of resolving conflicts so that an optimistic and harmonious state is reached. In *Blinkity Blank* a cyclical pattern is implied. The resolution of the conflict produces

[424] McLaren as quoted in "Interview", Scottish Arts Council 33.

[425] It will be recalled that McLaren's reluctance to explain his work stems from influences from surrealism.

Fig. 154. Pas de deux. *The dancer at first dances with another image of her own self before taking up with the male partner who, in this shot, has just appeared on the left.* [NFB.]

Fig. 155. Pas de deux. *As the female dancer begins dancing with her new partner, the images gradually increase in size and in complexity.* [NFB.]

Fig. 156. Pas de deux. *At the climax of the film, the images of the two dancers fill the screen. Reflecting the relationship of the dancers, their images overlap, intertwine and merge.* [NFB.]

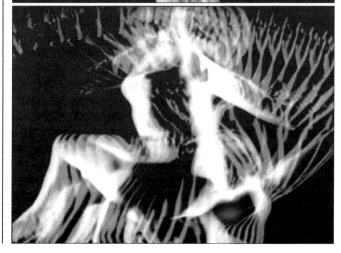

an offspring which is comprised of a combination of its parents' differences. The pattern suggests that future encounters, when they occur, may go through similar productive resolutions.

McLaren's more positive outlook, in his later years, may be attributed to two factors. Firstly, the social climate of the fifties had become progressively less astringently divisive. Secondly, illness curtailed McLaren's travels. After his work in India, where he contracted rheumatic fever – a cause of a continuing heart problem from then on – he was never to return to Asia for UNESCO. His environment, of home, work and close circle of friends, gave his life a measure of insulation and so films of aggression and conflict not only became more optimistic, but gradually diminished and finally disappeared from his output.

Through the sixties and seventies his films fell into the categories of abstraction, dance and didacticism. In this latter category are *Rythmetic* (despite its theme of conflict, this film also has strong didactic qualities), *Pinscreen* (1973, a documentary describing the pinscreen animation method of Alexeieff and Parker) and *Animated Motion Parts 1–5* (1976–78, a series of films demonstrating and classifying aspects of animated motion). *Synchromy* was also originally envisaged as a didactic, visual demonstration of a film sound-track. However, of McLaren's later years, the dance films *Pas de deux* (1967), *Ballet Adagio* (1972), and *Narcissus* (1981) may be seen as allegorical. The necessity of social interaction and of love for another remains, in these films, central to McLaren's concerns. In *Pas de deux* and *Narcissus*, however, McLaren succeeds in portraying an inner conflict. The conflict is between concern for the self and concern for another. In one film, *Pas de deux*, love and union with another are achieved. The principal dancer initially flirts with her own image. However, it is not until the second dancer appears that the screen begins to fill with a series of unfolding, cascading images of the two dancers, thus giving a visual consummation of the film's theme. In the other film, *Narcissus*, love and union are not achieved, but the bleak outlook portrayed for Narcissus at the end of this film leaves the viewer in no doubt as to the moral of the story, that is, that fulfilment and happiness are achieved, not through egocentricity, but through altruism.

McLaren became convinced that narcissism was the major contemporary sin.[426] The film *Narcissus* is not just a generally applicable parable. It is also an autobiographical

426 *Creative Process: Norman McLaren* dir. Donald McWilliams, 1st assembly (film), 1989.

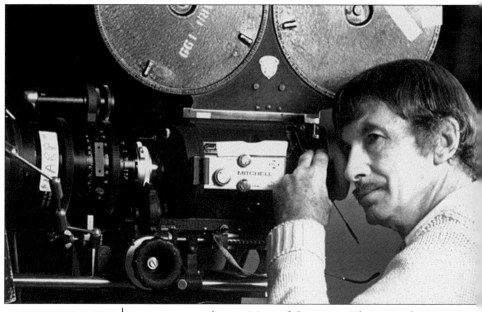

Fig. 157. Norman McLaren lines up a shot during the making of Narcissus. *[Photo by R.S. Diamond, June 1980. NFB.]*

comment on the position of the artist. The artist does not produce work just for his or her own gratification. The work must be for others. It should communicate with others. Such a philosophy is consistent with McLaren's earlier-mentioned concern for the scope, size and capability of his audience. There is an irony, however. In making his anti-narcissistic statement, McLaren has indulged his own narcissism to an uncharacteristic extent. Unlike his other work, the film is introspective and remote. The principal dancer occupies a lonely and circumscribed space on the screen. This prevents the film from establishing a kinesthetic empathy with the viewer, which further qualifies the film as unique in McLaren's filmic output at the NFB. In making *Narcissus*, McLaren almost became a victim of the very fault he was denouncing. It should be said however, that the distinctiveness of the *Narcissus* theme as well as those climactic moments of the film in which McLaren's blurs at last suffuse the screen, prevent the film from falling completely into that trap. Be all that as it may, what is unambiguous is that the film's theme is entirely consistent with McLaren's enduring concern for others. The negative conclusion of the film is a denouncement of narcissism, in himself, and in others.

Consistency has been apparent throughout McLaren's films involving conflict and aggression, from *Hell UnLtd* to *Blinkity Blank*. His message has invariably

been an evocation of peaceful and harmonious resolution of conflict. In place of egocentricity McLaren advocates a sympathy, respect, and even love, for others. This overriding concern goes a long way to answering the question posed earlier: How could McLaren make such disparate films, of joy and exuberance on the one hand, and aggression and conflict on the other? The two categories are not nearly so different or distinct as they first appeared. McLaren's aggressive films have an altruistic purpose. For McLaren, Mars was really Venus all the time.

Fig. 158. Fernand Nault (choreographer), Grant Muro and Norman McLaren during the making of Narcissus. [Photo by R.S. Diamond, July 1980. NFB.]

Conclusion

I t would be strange if there were no discernible changes in Norman McLaren's work, and in his attitudes to his work, throughout a filmmaking career which spanned fifty years. It was in the area of technical innovation and inventiveness that McLaren showed his greatest inclination to introduce change. This inclination was so strong and consistent that the startling changes it induced became an identifying characteristic of his work.

Throughout McLaren's career some general changes in the type of technical innovation may be observed. Beginning with the second Lines film, *Lines Horizontal*, McLaren's technical innovations centre, increasingly, on the laboratory or the optical printer. The manipulation of physical objects such as a pen or brush-drawn image, a paper cut-out, or two people, gives way to the manipulation of a machine.[427] The change, from direct manipulation of the image, to a manipulation through machines, may be attributed to several factors. From the 1960s, McLaren experienced a worsening of his health problems. The result was that his dexterity deteriorated to the extent that he was unable to consistently apply, on the fine scale required, the predominantly manual animation techniques he had been using in the earlier part of his career. The switch to machinery and processing therefore was partly caused by necessity. The change also was induced by the new technical processes which had become more readily available. McLaren felt compelled to explore their potential. The change, when it occurred, while seeming an abrupt and conscious decision on McLaren's part, was the consequence of a gradual change of emphasis which grew from

[427] It should be remembered that from earlier in his career he had recourse to direct the laboratory to process colour for his film.

his circumstances and the series of possibilities – both technical and artistic – that he saw in the first Lines film. After the completion of the hand-scratched *Lines Vertical* (the scratching on which, pertinently, had been done largely by Evelyn Lambart) it occurred to McLaren that the horizontal display of the same lines would produce a different effect. It did, but the change to horizontal orientation was achieved by passing the images of *Lines Vertical* through prisms. The next film, *Mosaic*, was an overlay of *Lines Vertical* and *Lines Horizontal*, again achieved through laboratory work. Thus, one direct-animation film had produced, by laboratory manipulation, two further films. For his next new film, 1967's *Pas de deux*, which, with the exception of *Canon* (1964), was the only new film for the decade up to 1971's *Synchromy* that was not a reprise or a modification of an earlier film, McLaren made extensive and innovatory use of the optical printing process. By this time, McLaren was accustomed to, and locked into the process of making images through laboratory and mechanical means. A further reason for the change to such means of working was that McLaren had simply, to his mind, exhausted the possibilities of the 'low-tech' methods which he had previously been using.

The change to 'high-tech' which was confirmed in the optical printing of *Pas de deux*, was not an unheralded one. For example, McLaren had done tests on the optical printer in the *Leap Frog Tests* of 1961, and these live-action optical-printing tests sprang from even earlier, pre-1955, optical-printing tests with scratch-mark-derived images. McLaren's blur tests also pre-date his Lines films. Further, his film *Synchromy* uses indexed cards, each displaying different patterns and frequencies of lines – a system he had developed well before his abandonment of low-tech animation. Thus even in his later more highly technical work, an overlap with his low-tech work exists. This suggests that the change to high-tech was not an abrupt change in his approach to his materials.

McLaren did, however, have to modify his working methods somewhat as the more complicated processes required more planning. Shots had to be calculated beforehand to ensure that the laboratory had the correct materials to achieve McLaren's desired result. Thus, although there was the added factor of McLaren's health to consider in the equation, the increase in technology increased McLaren's workload and slowed his filmmaking. He also had to rely

Fig. 159. Norman McLaren in 1971. [NFB.]

increasingly on the technicians who operated the optical printers and ran the laboratories. McLaren, therefore, adapted to the requirement for increased planning. Again, however, it is important to note that in some of his earlier films he did use a plan. The method of creating *Begone Dull Care* confirms this point.

McLaren's inclination to use complicated technology in his filmmaking is a plausible extension of his attitude to technology. His working method, of exploring technique and using technique as a springboard for his approach to a new film, did not change with his adoption of more complicated forms of technology. His technically inventive working method, and his reliance on technology as a means of generating a new film, remained constant throughout his career.

McLaren's adoption of more complicated production processes did affect another aspect of his work. His use of surrealist imagery, movement and change, becomes less overt in his mature years. Much of McLaren's surrealism was expressed through his painted and drawn imagery. This

Fig. 160. Norman McLaren around 1970. [NFB.]

method of working gave him direct and frame-by-frame control of the imagery, and so the possibility of image manipulation according to the artist's aim was maximized. As well, the process allowed a spontaneous approach. Both of these factors were reduced as McLaren came to use more complicated technology.

A further factor which inhibited surrealist expression in McLaren's later years was his absorption in making abstract films. Moreover, the nature of his abstract films changed. In earlier years films like *Dots* contained surrealist overtones in their anthropomorphic movement and their images' existence in the illusion of a three-dimensional space. Other earlier abstract films contained occasional glimpses of representational imagery, such as a butterfly or bird which can be explained as surreal interjections. Further, if Absrtact Expressionism can be regarded as an extension of surrealism then the jazz-and-sloshed-paint of earlier abstract films such as *Begone Dull Care*, may reveal the psyche of the filmmaker as in Abstract Expressionism. McLaren's later abstract films, however, contained less anthropomorphic movement, almost no 'extraneous' representational imagery (the exception here is *Mosaic's* ball-in-the-pocket parentheses), and were produced through a technological rather than a gestural process. *Synchromy*, his last abstract film, remains McLaren's most absolute abstract film.

Despite these shifts, McLaren continued to adhere to two fundamental attitudes which stemmed from surrealism. His work continued to evolve from his technical

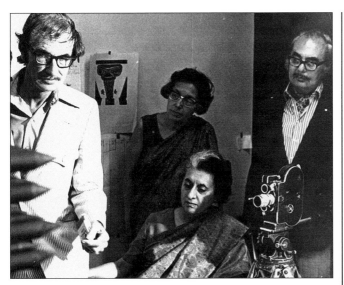

Fig. 161. Norman McLaren with Mrs Indira Gandhi at the NFB's studios in Montreal. During her visit to Canada, the Indian Prime Minister had specially requested to meet the renowned film-maker. [NFB.]

investigations, which were McLaren's way of drawing his work from his subconscious thoughts and desires. Only in his last film, *Narcissus*, did a preconceived theme take artistic precedence over the medium. His other trait derived from surrealism was his reluctance to talk about his work – except in general terms, particularly while it was in generation and progress – and about his overall artistic attitudes. He maintained this stance throughout his film career, often giving evasive and sometimes contradictory answers to interviewers' questions. Two factors mitigate this situation for the reviewer of McLaren's work. Firstly, he had a long career and, so, from the many statements, a pattern, as well as the occasional unintended insight, occurs. Secondly, after his retirement, McLaren relaxed his attitude somewhat, often giving a more insightful account of his work.

The tensions and conflicts McLaren felt throughout his career are encapsulated in his oscillation between abstract and representational imagery. In his mature years these oscillations became more extreme and, generally, more protracted. The reason for this lies in the technical challenges that ensued from the abstract *Lines Vertical* film. These challenges, in turn, produced two further abstract films, *Lines Horizontal* and *Mosaic*. Apart from *Opening Speech* and the collaborative work with René Jodoin and Grant Munro, these three films had continued into the mid-1960s an abstract period that had started years earlier, in 1959, with *Short and Suite*, *Serenal* and *Mail Early for Christmas*. Thus, when the reaction occurred it was more extreme. McLaren swung back to representational film work by animating live-action shots of dancers in *Pas de deux*. After a return to abstraction for his culminative work of that type, *Synchromy*, McLaren resumed his representational work with almost a moral zeal. He said at the time: "I've felt very annoyed with myself for making so many abstract films. My early films were playful and free but they became more rigid, more strict and geometrical. I was fascinated with the geometrical element in art. Now I'm caught up in the human aspect."[428] Through his career, those McLaren films which use representational imagery and the subjects of which were created by McLaren, tend to employ themes of conflict. As has been shown, the bulk of these films are positive in conclusion and thus accord with the exuberance of his abstract films. McLaren himself, however, came to see a clear distinction between his abstract and his representational films:

> For me, moral art is the greatest kind of art. Amoral art, such as abstract painting and decoration, many kinds of music and dance, fine cuisine, etc. is predominately an appeal to our senses, and although a very vital and essential part of human activity, is of a lower order. Moral art appeals not only to our senses, but through our senses to our whole being. The good moral work of art should have formal unity, balance, contrast and a sensitivity to the material out of which it is made. But it has in addition an even more precious quality – a consciousness of the human intelligence, of the human spirit, that man is a social creature.[429]

This emphasis on the importance of his representational work was made during a swing towards that aspect of his work, and is dismissive, by implication, of his own abstract film work. The statement does, however, underscore the importance of social, and political, objectives in his art. It also furthers an understanding of McLaren's guilt at making those abstract films towards which both his technical inclinations and his rapport with the film medium and its effects impelled him.

McLaren's long filmmaking career is one of some change and some oscillation resulting from considerable inner-conflict. But, on the whole, what emerges is a remarkable consistency of approach to filmmaking, and a consistency of concerns about his work. Although his work

428 Norman McLaren as quoted in Susan Carson, "Bore People? Fat Chance, Norman McLaren", *Toronto Telegram:Weekend Magazine* 30 March 1974 21.

429 Norman McLaren as quoted in Donald McWilliams, *Creative Process*, proposal July 1985 35, NFB Archives.

is premised on technical innovation, it is also based on concepts which accord with his social beliefs. McLaren wished his films to have a wide and beneficial impact on people's lives. Accordingly, he consistently displayed a concern for the size and scope of his potential audience. He also structured his films in a traditional way, even borrowing established temporal structures from the art of music. Each film has an obvious beginning, middle and end. The adoption of familiar and usually simple structures also served his social objectives – as well, by structurally circumscribing his work, the adoption suited his method of working within prescribed limits.

Just as McLaren's social and political beliefs can be traced to his early years, so too can other aspects of his work. From Grierson's GPO Film Unit, McLaren was imbued with the value of film as an instrument of social change. Also from that source came McLaren's belief in the importance of a cogent film structure. His exposure to surrealism also occurred during the 1930s. His acknowledged filmic influences – the abstraction and movement of Fischinger's films, the metamorphosis of Cohl's, the poetic imagination

Fig. 162. Norman McLaren late in life. [NFB.]

of Alexeieff and Parker, the technique of Lye and the general inspiration derived from the montage of Pudovkin and Eisenstein – all occurred at that time. McLaren experienced no subsequent artistic influences. From the late 1930s onwards, he was artistically secure. "I feel perpetually grateful to the people who influenced me. They gave me the necessary boost I needed when I was getting started. Now I'm not really influenced by anyone. I just do what I feel is right."[430]

In the years immediately after the war, McLaren's technical innovation, and his use of abstract and also surreal imagery, gave the impression that his work was avant garde. However, within the new and growing film festival circuit, McLaren's work achieved tangible success. His work won scores of awards[431] and his recognition grew to the point where he was even sought out by a world leader such as India's Indira Gandhi (see Fig. 161). In avant-garde circles there was at the same time an increasing sensitivity to the perceived hegemony of the commercial narrative cinema. It is not hard to understand how a filmmaker with McLaren's festival success might be seen by the avant-garde as belonging to the enemy camp. There is some truth in the notion about the film festivals. The big festivals did increasingly become commercial show-cases of the animation industry. Their increasing conservatism is reflected by the fact that even McLaren's *Synchromy* was booed by a section of the audience at the Annecy Animation Festival of 1971.[432]

The negative attitude of each of these groups was not caused by any change of position on the part of McLaren. He remained constant. As his work became accepted by the establishment as that of their acclaimed experimentalist, so he became marginalized by the avant-garde. Meanwhile, the composition of the festival establishment changed and, as a consequence, McLaren's pre-eminent position came to be seen as less than central.

McLaren's dismissal by the avant-garde is more extensive than this foregoing account implies. Even McLaren's early work is seldom included in retrospectives of innovative film. When he has been considered by Modernist critics, his work has been seen as inconsistent and compromised. However, this has arisen partly from a misreading of McLaren's work. His work only appears to be inconsistent if insufficient account is taken of his fascination with surreal imagery and, also, the consistent

430 McLaren as quoted in Carson 21.

431 141 are listed in Maynard Collins *Norman McLaren* (Ottawa : Canadian Film Institute, 1976).

432 Pierre Hébert, personal interview 19 November 1990.

importance to him of technical innovation in his working methods. That McLaren's work is often suffused with humour makes it harder to include in a generally serious category. One of the main concerns of avant-garde critics is the degree to which McLaren's awareness of his potential audience compromised his work. In this respect such critics seem to have a point. McLaren was aware of his potential audience. He did not wish to create films that would not be seen. It is evident that McLaren did not adhere to this aspect of the avant-garde – the notion that the artist's function is to indulge him or herself and not worry about a potential audience since the duty of the avant-garde is to progress the art form. Attempting to put McLaren into the avant-garde box leads to the misjudgment that he 'compromised' his work and thus is a failed modernist. That he did not fit into the box means he simply had different aims.[433]

However, whether or not McLaren's work has been unjustly disregarded by writers on the avant-garde is not the important issue, because it does not reflect what McLaren has achieved. His work does not have to be categorized in order for his achievements to be realized. What McLaren has achieved is measured by the effect his films have had on people. McLaren recognized this in his concern for his audience and in his lack of concern as to whether or not his films were categorized as avant-garde.[434]

McLaren displayed a similarly tolerant attitude to the animators whom he taught through his years at the National Film Board of Canada. Their subsequently diverse careers in different areas of animation, applying different animation techniques in their films, is testimony to his maxim of encouraging experimentation and a freedom of expression. McLaren taught through example, informal discussion and more formal workshops. He reached an even wider student body through his didactic films. In the early 1960s McLaren attempted to set up an NFB school of animation. In spite of the failure to establish such a school, McLaren's achievements in teaching remain impressive.

Of McLaren's achievements the most tangible are the numerous awards he gained. These, however, were only tangentially important to McLaren and his work. They were useful in justifying to officialdom his worth as a public servant. They were of greater importance, however, in increasing the distribution of his films in terms of both frequency and geography.

[433] David Curtis "Where does one put Norman McLaren?", *Norman McLaren, exhibition and films.* (Edinburgh: Scottish Arts Council, 1977) 47–53. Rev. in "Locating McLaren", *Undercut* 13 (1984) 1–7. William Moritz, "Norman McLaren and Jules Engel: Post-modernists", *A Reader in Animation Studies*, Jayne Pilling (ed.). (Sydney: John Libbey, 1997) 104–111. Curtis' evaluation of McLaren as modernist is refuted by Moritz who argued that Curtis' premise – that McLaren was a modernist – was incorrect, and that McLaren in fact displayed what were later to be called post-modernist qualities (his concern for his audience being one of these qualities).

[434] Evelyn Lambart, personal interview 31 October 1990 and Grant Munro, personal interview 23 October 1990.

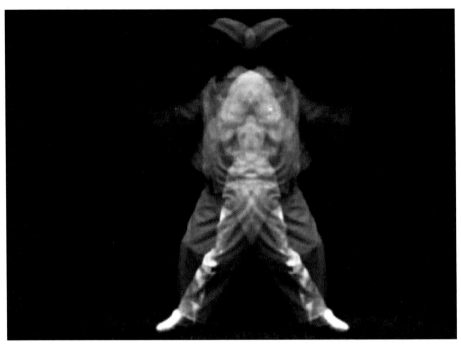

Fig. 163. Norman McLaren performing in Don McWilliams' Creative Process. McWilliams has used McLaren's blur and mirror techniques for what turned out to be McLaren's last film performance. [NFB.]

In the field of animation, McLaren's achievements are extensive in scope and time. Through nearly fifty years of filmmaking, McLaren revealed animation as an exciting medium full of dazzling movement and vibrant imagery.

For his technical achievements alone, he is a figure of considerable consequence. Many of his innovations have been adopted by other animators and also by the commercial sector. However, an even more important legacy left by McLaren is his film work. For McLaren, though, even this was not as important as the effect his films had on people and their lives. Assessment of this effect is elusive, but the fact that his work was, and is, in continual demand, and that it has aroused much reaction, most of it positive, is an indication that McLaren's films approached the objectives he set for them.

McLaren's concern for his audience stemmed from his political convictions. He wished to improve and enrich other people's lives. Although this aspiration created an inner conflict, resulting in an oscillation between the creation of an abstract output and work of a more directly social function, his film work, as a whole, retained a positive vision. What comes through his work and his life is an optimism that, ultimately, things can be made better. His films are testimony to the validity of that outlook.

Norman McLaren's Chronology

1914	Born 11 April, in Stirling, Scotland
1932–36	Attends the Glasgow School of Art and makes his first films
1936–39	Works for the General Post Office Film Unit, London
1936	November, cameraman in Spain during the civil war
1939	September, leaves Britain for New York
1941	September, moves to Canada to join the National Film Board
1949–50	August to April, works for UNESCO in Peh pei, China
1952–53	November to May, works for UNESCO in Delhi and Mysore, India
1984	March, retires from the National Film Board of Canada
1987	Dies 27 January, in Montreal, Canada

Bibliography

BOOKS AND ARTICLES

Aitken, Ian. *Film and Reform: John Grierson and the Documentary Film Movement.* London: Routledge, 1990.

Alaton, Salem. "McLaren tribute will include peek at documentary". *Toronto Globe and Mail.* 20 March 1987.

Alexieff, Alexandre. "McLaren". *Le disque vert* July–August 1953: 101–104.

Anderson, Bert. "An interview with Norman McLaren". *Film Library Quarterly 3* (Spring 1970): 13–17.

Anderson, Celia. "Neighbors and Delinquents". *Educational Film Library Assoc. Bulletin.* Ts. 1962.

Anderson, Jon. "Novel Visions, Dandy Doodles". *Time-Canada.* 13 October 1975: 11.

Andrew, J. Dudley. *The Major Film Theories.* Oxford: OUP, 1976.

"Animated Sound: A Canadian composer's unique contribution to the advance of the cinema". *Canadian Composer* 3 (October 1965).

"Animation at the National Film Board". *Séquences* 23.91 (octobre 1978): complete issue.

"L'animation stéréographique". *Cahiers du Cinéma* 14 (juillet–août 1952): 25–33.

Annear, Judy. Ed. *Len Lye.* Sydney: Art Gallery of NSW, 2000.

Archibald, Lewis. "the editors bless (and blast) Film Animation: why does the U.S. lag so far behind?" *Show* February 1973: 18–19.

Bassan, R. "Fondu au noir". *Revue du Cinéma* I425 (mai 1987): 14–15.

– – –"Norman McLaren ou les discrétions de Promethée". *Revue du Cinema* 383 (mars 1983): 77–91.

Bastiancich, Alfio. *Immagine per immagine: Cinema animazione al National Film Board of Canada.* Milano: Azzurra Editrice, 1989.

– – –*L'opera di Norman McLaren.* Torino: Giappichelli, 1981.

Bazin, André. *What is Cinema?* Berkeley: University of California Press, 1967.

– – –"Rythme éthique ou la preuve par le neuf". *Cahiers du Cinéma* 62 (août-septembre 1956): 32–33.

Beath, Linda. "Ballet Adagio". *Pot Pourri* April 1974: n. pag.

Beaudet, Louise. "An Irreparable Loss". *Anima Film* May 1987: 1.

– – –*L'art du cinéma d'animation/The Art of Animated Films.* Catalogue. Montreal: Montreal Museum of Fine Arts, 1982.

Beaulieu, Janick. "Humour et fantasie". *Séquences* 82 (octobre 1975): 110–117.

Belmans, Jacques. "Norman McLaren, le découvreur des terres vierges". *Media- Animation* 5. (août 1973): 13–15.

Benayoun, Robert. *Dessin animé après Walt Disney.* Paris: Pauvert, 1961: 24–28, 92–108.

Bendazzi, Giannalberto. *Cartoons: One Hundred Years of Cinema Animation.* London: John Libbey, 1994.

– – –.*Le film d'animation: du dessin animé à l'image de synthèse.* Trans. Geneviève Vidal. Vol. I Grenoble: La PenséeSauvage, 1985.

Benson, Harold. "Movies Without a Camera". *The Emergence of Film Art : The evolution and development of the motion picture as an art, from 1900 to the present.*. Ed. Lewis Jacobs. NY: Hopkinson and Blake, 1969, 258–261.

Beveridge, James. *John Grierson: Film Master*. NY: Macmillan, 1978.

Binkley, Alex. "McLaren called gentle genius of film world". *Leader-Post* . Regina, Sask. 27 January 1972.

Biographical notes on Norman McLaren. National Film Board of Canada. 5p.

Blackburn, Marthe and Norman McLaren. "Canon". *Journal Musical Canadien* 6.5 (avr.-mai, 1960): 7.

– – –"Fugue". *Journal Musical Canadien* 6.6 (juin, 1960): 7.

– – –"Le Rondo". *Journal Musical Canadien* 6.1 (novembre 1959): 5.

– – –*Six Formes Musicales: Six dessins de Norman McLaren mis en musique par Maurice Blackburn*. Montreal: Jeunesses Musicales du Canada, 1967.

– – –"Le Sonata". *Journal Musical Canadien* 6.4 (25 mars 1960): 7.

– – –"Theme". *Journal Musical Canadien* 6.2 (27 décembre 1959): 5.

Blackburn, Maurice. "The Music in Narcissus". *Animafilm* 2 (April–June 1984): 3.

– – –"Notes on the music of Blinkity-Blank. Unpublished ts. Montreal: NFB, nd.

– – –"Notes on the music of 'Pas de deux' – 1967". Unpublished ts. Montreal: NFB, 1967.

Blain, Gilles. "La place de McLaren dans l'histoire de l'animation". *Séquences* 82 (octobre 1975): 122–125.

Blumer, Ronald. "Pas de deux". *Take one 1* (June 1968): 28.

Bonneville, Léo. "Les métamorphoses d'un poéte". *Sequences* 82 (octobre1975): 95–98.

– – –"Norman McLaren". *Séquences* 7 (1955–56): 35, 37–39

– – –Interview, "Norman McLaren". *Séquences* 82 (octobre 1975): 1–155. [Eng Trans. in *Norman McLaren, exhibition and films*].

– – –et al. "Norman McLaren". *Séquences*. 129 (avril 1987): 3, 12–21.

Borshell, Alan. "Blinkity Blank". *Film* 6 (January–February 1956): 22.

Bouhours, Jean-Michel and Roger Horrocks. Eds. *Len Lye*. Paris: Centre Pompidou, 2000.

Boussinot, Roger. *Encyclopédie du cinéma*. Paris: Bordas, 1967. 989–991.

Bowness, Alan. *Modern European Art*. London: Thames and Hudson, 1972.

Bradwell, David and Kristin Thompson. *Film Art: An Introduction*. 3rd. Ed. NY: McGraw-Hill, 1990.

Breton, André. *What is Surrealism? Selected Writings* . Ed. Franklin Rosemount London: Pluto Press, 1978.

Briggs, Paul. "A Mathematician Looks at McLaren". *Grasshopper News* [London} January 1961.

[Bromelow, Howard] J.B. "McLaren Makes Whoopee: The 1940's saw the departure from these shores of Norman McLaren, a graduate of the school and one of the greatest artists of the cinema". *GSA friends* 10 (August 1993): n.p.

Brougher, Kerry, Jeremy Strick, Ari Wiseman and Judith Zilczer. Eds. *Visual Music: Synaesthesia in Art and Music Since 1900*. N.Y.: Thames and Hudson, 2005.

Brown, Lorna. "Narcissus: Norman McLaren Returns to Dance". *Dance Canada* 31 (Spring 1982): 6–10.

Brunel, Adrian. *Nice Work: The Story of Thirty Years in British Film Production*. London: Forbes Robertson, 1949.

Burns, Dan. "Pixillation". *Film Quarterly*. Fall 1968: 36–41.

Buruiana, Michel. "La carrière de Norman McLaren. *24 Images*. 33 (Spring 1987): 28–32.

– – –"Grant Munro Parle de McLaren". *24 Images* (Spring 1987): 33–36.

Butler, Patricia. *Norman McLaren: Bibliography/Bibliographie*. Unpublished Ts. Montreal: NFB, 1984.

Callenbach, Ernest. "The craft of Norman McLaren". *Film Quarterly* 16 (Winter 1962–1963): 17–19.

"The Career of Norman McLaren". *Cinema Canada*. 9 (August–September 1973): 42–49.

Carson, Susan. "Bore People? Fat chance Norman McLaren". *Telegram Toronto: Weekend Magazine*. 30 March 1974: 20–21.

Cawkwell, Tim. "Beyond the Camera Barrier". *Undercut* 13 (Winter 1984–85): 32–35.

Chipp, Herschel B. *Theories of Modern Art: A Source Book by Artists and Critics*. Berkeley: University of California Press, 1971.

Cholodenko, Alan. Ed. *The Illusion of Life: Essays on Animation*. Sydney: Power Publishing, 1991.

Chrichton, Mamie. "Cinema Topics, An Expert on Three Dimensional Films". *Glasgow Evening News* 16 May: 51

"Le cinéaste sans caméra". *Perspectives* 43 (23 October 1965): 28–30.

Cinéma d'animation sans caméra: technique mise au point par Norman McLaren. (Réimpression de *l'Art de réaliser des films d'animation sans caméra*).Office national du film du Canada, 1959.

"Un cinéma que vous ne connaissez pas". *L'Ecran et la vie* 20 (juillet 1965): 28–30.

Cinemateca nacional (Portugal). *Retrospectiva Norman McLaren. Exposicao Norman McLaren.* Lisboa: Secretariado nacional da informacao, cultura popular e Turismo, 1966. 13.

Cinémathèque canadienne. *Norman McLaren: Publié à l'occasion des Journées internationales du cinéma d'animation.* Annecy: 1965.

– – –Une exposition George Meliès. Montréal: 1965. 17p.

"Cinquante ans au service de l'expérimentation". *La Revue du Cinéma* 383 (mai 1983): 78–91.

Clark, Ken. "Tribute to McLaren". *Animator* 19 (April–January 1987): 21–23.

Cloutier, Léo. "L'univers des sons". *Séquences* 82 (octobre 1975): 105–109.

Collins, Maynard. *Norman McLaren.* Ottawa: Canadian Film Institute, 1976.

– – –"Norman McLaren: A Retrospective". *Canadian Review* 3.2 (May 1976): 22–24.

Columbo, John Robert, *Translation from the English: found poems.* Drawings by Norman McLaren. Toronto: Peter Martin, 1974.

Côté, Guy L. "[*Blinkity Blank* at] The Cannes Film Festival". Official Government Report ts. 10 June 1955. 16 p.

– – –*Le cinéma image par image à l'Office national du film du Canada.* Montreal: NFB, 1956. 27p.

– – –"Norman McLaren, poète du mouvement". *Ciné-Orientations* 3.2 (novembre–décembre 1956): 27–30.

Culhane, Shamus. *Animation: From Script to Screen.* London: Columbus Books, 1989.

Curnow, Wystan and Roger Horrocks. Eds. *Figures of Motion: Len Lye/Selected Writings.* Auckland: Auckland University Press, 1984.

Curtis, David. *Experimental Cinema, A Fifty-Year Evolution.* NY: Delta, 1971.

– – –"Locating McLaren". *Undercut* 13 (Winter 1984–85): 1–7.

– – –"Norman McLaren: Scratching for a living". *The Movie* 33: 652–654.

Cutler, May-Ebbitt. "The Unique Genius of Norman McLaren". *Canadian Art* 97 (May–June 1965): 8–17.

Daudelin, Robert. "Norman McLaren, premier cinéaste d'animation au monde". *Actualité ma paroisse* (mars 1961): 8.

Davis, Eileen. "Paint a Movie on Film!" *Popular Photography* 56 (May 1965): 120.

Denslow, Phil. "The Art and Language of Animation". *Animatrix* December 1984: 5–9.

Deren, Maya. "The Poetic Film". *Canadian Film News* February 1951: 7–8.

Deschin, Jacob. "Hand-Drawn Movie Film".*New York Times* 26 December 1948, sec. 2.

De Witt, Tom. "Visual Music: Searching for an Aesthetic". *Leonardo* 20.2 (1987): 115–122.

"Dix-sept artisans du cinéma canadien".*Objectif* 1961: 21–22.

Dobson, Elaine. Graphic Notation: Approaches and Developments. Unpublished thesis. University of Queensland, 1971.

Dobson, Terence. "McLaren and Grierson: Intersections". *Screening the Past*. www.latrobe.edu.au/www/screeningthepast June 1999: 1–12.

– – –."Norman McLaren: His UNESCO Work in Asia". *Animation Journal* 8.2 (Spring 2000): 4–17.

– – –."Norman McLaren's Visit to London: An Informative Drawing". *Animation Journal* 4.1 (Fall 1995): 4–20.

– – –.Towards Abstract Film. Unpublished Masters thesis. Griffith University, Queensland, 1984.

D'Yvoire, Jean. "Les démons de McLaren". *Radio-Cinéma-Télévision* 441 (29 juin 1958): 44–45.

Egly, Max. "Klee, Steinberg, McLaren". *Image et son* (mai 1965): 58–62.

Eisenstein, Sergei. *The Film Sense*. Trans. Jay Leyda. London: Faber, 1943.

Ekstrand, G. "Ett porträtt av Norman McLaren". *Chaplin* 14.6 (117)(1972): 208–211.

– – –"Norman McLaren. Animationens grand old man". *Chaplin* 26.1 (1984): 23–25.

Elley, D. "Rhythm 'n' truths". *Films & Filming* 20. 9 (June 1974): 30–36.

Elliott, Lawrence. "Norman McLaren: Gentle Genius of the Screen". *Reader's Digest* (August 1971): Canada.

Epstein, Rudolph Rolf. *Multiple Music Recording Technique For The Film: "Lines Horizontal"*. Unpublished ts. Montreal: NFB, 1960.

Evans, Gary. *In the National Interest: A Chronicle of the National Film Board of Canada, 1949–1989*. Unpublished manuscript. 1990.

– – –*John Grierson and the National Film Board: The Politics of Wartime Propaganda*. Toronto: University of Totonto Press, 1984.

"the eye hears and the ear sees .../l'oeil entend et l'oreille voit ... ". *Canadian Composer/ Compositeur Canadien* 44 (November 1969): 29–30.

Feldman, Seth. Ed.*Take Two*. Toronto: Irwin, 1984.

– – –and Joyce Nelson. Eds. *Canadian Film Reader*. Toronto: Peter Martin, 1977.

Festival Internacional De CineExperimental Y Documental. Schedule for 13–17 August 1964. Ts. Universidad Catolica De Cordoba, Argentina.

Festival of Britain stereoscopic and stereophonic film. London, 4 May 1951.

Fetherling, Douglas. Ed. *Documents in Canadian Film*. Peterborough, Can.: Broadview, 1988.

film as film. formal experiment in film 1910–1975. Catalogue. Hayward Gallery, South bank 3 May–17 June 1979. London: Arts Council of Great Britain, 1979. 152 p.

Findlay, Elsa. *Rhythm and Movement: Applications of Dalcrose Eurhythmics*. Evanston, Illinois: Summy-Birchard, 1971.

Fischinger, Oskar. "My Statements are in My Work". *Art in Cinema: a synopsis on the avant-garde film.* Ed. Frank Stauffacher. 1947 rpt. NY: Arno Press, 1968, 38–40.

"Flight". Cover drawing. *Canadian Forum* 19 (June 1969).

Frame by Frame. Montreal: National Film Board of Canada, 1978.

Frys, M. "Norman McLaren " *Film a Doba.* 32.4 (April 1986): 212–216.

"Fugue". *Arts Canada.* 25 (June 1968): 12.

Furniss, Maureen. *Art in Motion: Animation Aesthetics.* Sydney: John Libbey, 1998.

Gianini, G. "Norman McLaren. L'animatore dell'impossibile". *Bianco & Nero* 48.2 (April–June 1987): 73–76.

Gidal, Peter. *Materialist Film.* London: Routledge, 1989.

Gilmour, Clyde. "Film animator McLaren honoured". *Toronto Star.* 11 August 1977. F6.

Glover, Guy. "Creative Film Making in a Government Organization", text of address to the New York Film Council, NY, 24 April 1962. NFB Archives, McLaren Files,1184 D-112.

– – –"Down Memory Lane". *Perforations* 4.2 (March–April 1984): 14, 20.

– – –"film". *The Arts in Canada: A Stock-Taking at Mid-Century.* Ed. Ross Malcolm. [Montreal]. Macmillan, 1958: 104–113.

– – –*McLaren.* Montreal: NFB, 1980.

– – –"Nine film animators speak". *Arts Canada* 27 (April 1970): 28–34.

– – –"Norman McLaren". *Canadian Forum* 30 (July 1950): 81–82.

– – –"Technical Notes on 'Pinscreen (1973)". Unpublished ts. Montreal: NFB, 1973.

Glover, Guy et al. *Technical Aspects of NFB Animation Chiefly in the 1941–51 Period.* 1981. NFB Archives.

Graham, Gerald. *Canadian Film Technology, 1896–1986.* Newark: University of Delaware, 1989.

Grelier, Robert. "De McLaren à Foldes". *Image et son* 291 (décembre 1974): 80–81.

Guitar, Mary-Anne. "Facts On Film". *Nation* 26 August 1950: 194.

Halas, John. *Masters of Animation.* Topsfield, Mass.: Salem House, 1987.

– – –and Roger Manvell. *Art in Movement – New Directions In Animation.* London: Studio Vista, 1970, 19–21.

– – –*Design in Motion.* NY: Hastings House, 1968.

– – –*Technique of Film Animation.* 4th Ed. London: Focal, 1976.

Hamlyn, Nicky. "Frameless Film". *Undercut* 13 (Winter 1984–85): 26–31.

"The Happy Chance". *Time.* 20 August 1965. The Arts.

Harcourt, Peter. *Movies and Mythologies: towards a national cinema.* Toronto: CBC, 1977.

Hawkins, Gerald. " Liberty Profile: Norman McLaren". *Liberty* 18 (January 1947).

Heckd, James. "McLaren film festival". *American Libraries Journal* December1971: 1195–1197.

"Hommage à Norman McLaren". *Séquences* 3 (janvier 1983): 52–53.

"Hommage à Norman McLaren". *Séquences* 129 (avril 1987): 12–21.

Hommage à Norman McLaren 1914–1987. Programme. Ts. Cinématheque Québeçoise 22 mars 1987. 41 p.

Horrocks, Roger. *Composing Motion: Len Lye and Experimental Film-Making*. Wellington NZ: National Art Gallery, 1991.

– – –"Len Lye". *Alternative Cinema* February 1979: 5–31.

– – –*Len Lye: a biography*. Auckland: Auckland University Press, 2001.

Hunter, Martin. "Animated Magnetism". *Canadian Art*. Winter 1987: 60–63.

The Invisible Cinema 1989: Avant garde filmmaking from North America. Cur. Martin Rumsby. Catalogue. New Plymouth NZ: Govett-Brewster Art Gallery, 1989.

Jackendoff, Ray and Fred Lerdahl. *A Generative Theory of Tonal Music*. MIT Press Series on Cognitive Theory and Mental Representation. Cambridge, Mass.: MIT Press, 1983.

Jacobs, Lewis. *The Emergence of Film Art: The evolution and development of the motion picture as an art, from 1900 to the present*. NY: Hopkinson and Blake, 1969.

Joachin, Robin Jon. "Une entreview avec Norman McLaren. *Cahiers du cinéma* 53 (déc. 1955) 11–12.

Jones, David Barker. *movies and memoranda: An Interpretive History of the National Film Board of Canada*. Ottawa: Canadian Film Institute; Deneau, 1981.

– – –.*The Best Butler in the Business: Tom Daly of the National Film Board of Canada*. Toronto: University of Toronto Press, 1996.

Jordan, William E. "Norman McLaren: His Career and Techniques". *Quarterly of Film, Radio and Television* 8.1 (1953): 1–14. Rpt. Montreal: National Film Board of Canada, [1964]: 1–16.

Jutra, Claude. "PETITE CANTATE POUR McLaren". Ts. extract from *Tours* 23 November 1957.

Kerr, Mary. "Synchromy". *Pot Pourri* April 1972: 19.

Kidd, J.R. "Films". *Canadian Assoc. for Adult Education* 10 (May 1950): 19.

Klein, Adrian Bernard. *Coloured Light: An Art Medium, Being the Third Edition Enlarged of "Colour Music"*. London: Technical Press. 1937.

Koenig, Wolf. "into animation". *Pot Pourri* April 1972: 7–8.

Kostelanetz, Richard. Ed. *Moholy-Nagy*. Documentary Monographs in Modern Art. London: Allen Lane, 1970

"Kudos for McLaren". *Montrealer*. August 1965. Montreal, 21.

Lambart, Evelyn. *McLaren's Techniques as developed at the National Film Board of Canada 1940–1962*. Montreal: National Film Board of Canada, 1962. 8p.

Langer, Mark. "The Disney-Fleischer dilemmas product differentiation and technological innovatiom". *Screen* 33.4 (Winter, 1992): 343–359.

Larkin, T. "Art Films". *School Arts* 57 (October 1957): 48.

La Rochelle, Réal. "Entretien avec Norman McLaren et Maurice Blackburn". *Séquences* 42 (octobre 1965):52–55.

Lasalle Le Messager. Quebec 9 November 1971. National Film Archives, Montreal. McLaren File.

Lawder, Standish D. *The Cubist Cinema.* NY: NY University Press, 1975.

Laybourne, Kit.*The Animation Book: a complete guide to animated film-making from flip-books to sound cartoons.* NY: Crown, 1979.

Le Grice, Malcolm. *Abstract film and beyond.* London: Studio Vista, 1977.

Lees, Gene. *Oscar Peterson: The Will To Swing.* London: Macmillan, 1988.

Leroux, André. "Une oeuvre ouverte". *Séquences* 82 (octobre 1975): 118–121.

Levering, Philip. "Pas de deux". *Film Library Quarterly* 3 (Winter 1969–1970): 38–39.

Levin, Gail. *Synchromism and American Colour Abstraction 1910–1925.* NY: George Braziller, 1978.

Levin, G. Roy. *Documentary Explorations: 15 Interviews with Film-makers.* NY: Anchor,1971.

Levitan, Ell L. *Handbook of Animation Techniques.* NY: Van Nostrand Reinhold, 1979.

Lindgren, Ernest. *The Art of the Film*, 2nd Ed. London: Allen & Unwin, 1963.

Littler, William. "McLaren's finale both sad shock and movie magic". *Toronto Star*, 10 September 1983.

Lukach, Joan M. *Hilla Rebay: In Search of the Spirit in Art.* NY: George Braziller, 1983.

Lutz, Bernard. "NFB Pioneer Producer Dies Near Montreal". NFB News Release, 19 May 1987. NFB Archives.

MacDermot, Anne. "Etchcraft On Celluloid". *UNESCO Courier* January 1964: 20–23.

– – –"Norman McLaren O della purezza nel cinema". *Bianco & Nero* 1–2 (January–February 1955): 31–49.

McKay, Marjorie. "History of the National Film Board of Canada". Unpublished ts. 1965 28–29.

McLaren, Norman. "Animated Films". *Documentary Film News* May 1948: 52–53.

– – –"Animated Sound on Film". Unpublished ts. Montreal: NFB, 1953, 1957, 1961.

– – –"Animation of Furniture". Unpublished ts. Montreal: NFB, 1957.

– – –"L'animation stéréographique". *Cahiers du cinéma* 14 (juillet-août 1952): 25–33.

– – –"L'art de réaliser des films d'animation sans caméra". *Education de base et éducation des adultes* 1.4 (octobre 1949).

– – –"Black and White Cut-outs, with Coloured Background". Unpublished ts. Montreal: NFB, n.d.

– – –*"Blinkity Blank": Technical Notes On The Visuals.* Ottawa: National Film Board of Canada, 1955.

– – –"A Brief Summary of the Early Hstory of Animated Sound on Film (From Available Information)". Unpublished ts. Montreal: NFB, 1952. No. 23.

– – –"Cameraless animation: a technique developed at the National Film Board of Canada " *Unesco Fundamental Education* October 1949: n.d. Rpt. "Cameraless Animation". Montreal: National Film Board of Canada, 1958.

– – –Christmas Card. n.d. Grierson Archives, University of Stirling, Stirling, Scotland. GAA: 31: 100.

– – –"Combining Animated Sound and Picture". Unpublished ts. 1971.

– – –"Comments on the International Experimental Film Competition", 1958. Unpublished ts. Grierson Archives, University of Stirling, Stirling, Scotland. 7: 36: 1.

– – –"Direct Hand-Drawn Animation of Film". Unpublished ts. Montreal: NFB, 1947.

– – –"Drawing on Film: Cinematic Picture and Sound Without a Camera", 30 January 1971. Don McWilliams Collection.

– – –*The Drawings of Norman McLaren*. Ed. Michael White. Montreal: Tundra Books, 1975.

– – –"Further Notes on the shooting of 'Neighbours'". Unpublished ts. Montreal: NFB, 1973.

– – –"Fugue". *Arts Canada* 25 (June 1968) 12.

– – –"Hand-Drawn Sound Track". Unpublished ts. Montreal: NFB, 1952.

– – –"Hand-engraving". Unpublished ts. Montreal: NFB, 1961: 1962.

– – –"Handmade Sound Track". Unpublished ts. Montreal: NFB, 1955.

– – –"Hommages à Georges Méliès". *ASIFA* 15.1 (Avril 1987): 3–5.

– – –"How to Make Animated Movies Without a Camera". *Fundamental Education* 1.4 (October 1949): 32–40.

– – –"I Saw The Chinese Reds Take Over". *McLean's Magazine* 15 October 1950: 10–11, 73–76.

– – –*INTERPLAY, album of 8 serigraphs by McLaren*. Montreal: Graphic Guild, 1971.

– – –Interview. *Film Library Quarterly* (Spring 1969).

– – –Interview. By [Claude] Jutra. Ts. n.d. National Film Board Archives, Montreal. McLaren File

– – –Interview. "A Dictionary of Movement". By Melanie Magisos. *Wide Angle* 3.4 (1980): 60–69.

– – –Interview. *Dots and Loops: the story of a Scottish film cartoonist: Norman McLaren*, by Forsyth Hardy. Ts. Edinburgh: BBC, 22 November 1951. 12 p.

– – –Interview for *The Grierson Project*, by Tom Daly. Montreal: McGill Archives, n.d. Container 13 File 197.

– – –Interview. *Norman McLaren Scottish Feature Programme*, by F.H. [Forsyth Hardy]. Grierson Archives, University of Stirling, Stirling, Scotland, n.d. [22 November 1951].

– – –Interview. *Radio interview with Norman McLaren in August 1949*. Ts. August 1949, CBC. 3 p.

– – –Interview. *talking to a great film artist*, by Don McWilliams *McGill reporter* 1.35 (28 April 1969): 3–5.

– – –Interview *The work and aims of a famous film artist*, by Leslie McFarlane. Ts. Canadian Broadcasting Corporation, March 1960.

– – –*The Low Budget And Experimental Film*. Unpublished ts. Montreal: NFB, September 1955.

– – –"Mahatma Gandhi". *The School On The Rock* [The Magazine of the High School of Stirling], 8 (June 1931): 8.

– – –"Making Films On Small Budgets". *Film* 6 (December 1955): 15–17.

– – –Message, delivered on his behalf, in his absence, Academy of Motion Picture Arts and Science's Tribute, 17 June 1985. [Los Angeles]. Unpublished ts. Montreal: NFB,

– – –Message to his colleagues. April 1984. Unpublished ts. Montreal: NFB.

– – –"Mix and Match Techniques". Unpublished ts. Montreal: NFB, 1971.

– – –"Multiple Image Technique". Unpublished ts. Montreal: NFB, 1967.

– – –"Neighbours". Unpublished ts. Montreal: NFB, 3 June 1952.

– – –"Nine animators speak". *Arts Canada* 27 (April 1970): 30.

– – –*Notes for Aspen*. Ts. 1956. Grierson Archives, University of Stirling, Stirling, Scotland. GAA: 31:55.

– – –"Notes on Animated Sound". *Quarterly Of Film, Radio And Television* 7.3 (Spring 1953): 223–229.

– – –"Notes on the Film Workshop Experiments in Animated Sound". NY: NFB, 22 December 1948.

– – –"Notes on the Release Printing of 'Rythmetic': Unpublished ts. Montreal: NFB, Prod. # 53–234, 1 February 1956.

– – –"Notes on Visual Demonstration of Canonic Devices in Music". Unpublished ts. Montreal: NFB, 1964.

– – –"Observations on the Screening of 'Vertical Lines' & 'Horizontal Lines'. Unpublished ts. Montreal: NFB, 14 October 1960.

– – –"Où va l'animation?" *Ecran* 73. 11 (janvier 1973): 4.

– – –"Pastels and Cut-Outs". Unpublished ts. Montreal: NFB, 1953.

– – –"Pastels and Metamorphosis of Images". Unpublished ts. Montreal: NFB, 1947.

– – –"Pixillation". *Canadian Film News*. (October 1953): 2–4, 6.

– – –"Producing Sound Track by Engraving". Unpublished ts. Montreal: NFB, 1955.

– – –*Radio Interview With Norman McLaren In August, 1949*. Grierson Archives, University of Stirling, Stirling, Scotland. GAA: 31: 177.

– – –"Rigid and Articulated Cardboard Cut-outs". Unpublished ts. Montreal: NFB, 1956.

– – –"sch(me)ool: a picture poem". *The School on the Rock* [The Magazine of the High School of Stirling], 8 (June1931): 21.

– – –"some notes on animated sound: abridged from a paper by Norman McLaren". *Canadian Composer* 44 (November 1969): 31–33.

– – –"Some Notes on Animated Sound As Developed at the National Film Board of Canada 1952 and as used in the films 'Love Your Neighbour', *'Now is the Time'*, 'Two Bagatelles' 'Twirling' and 'Phantasy'". Unpublished ts. Montreal: NFB, 15 August 1952. Rev copy. 1961.

– – –"Some Notes on Stop-Motion Live-Actor Technique as used in the visuals of 'NEIGHBOURS' (1952) and 'TWO BAGA-TELLES" (1952)". Unpublished ts. Montreal: NFB, 1952.

– – –"Statistical Breakdown on McLaren Films". Unpublished ts. Montreal: NFB, March 1984.

– – –*Synchromy* Dope Sheets. Unpublished ts. Montreal: NFB, nd.

– – –"Technical Notes for Sound on 'Dots' and 'Loops' (1940)". Unpublished ts. Montreal: NFB, 1940.

– – –"Technical Notes on 'Alouette' (1944) from the sing-along series 'Let's All Sing Together. No. 1". Unpublished ts. Montreal: NFB, 1984.

– – –"Technical Notes on 'Ballet Adagio' (1972)". Unpublished ts. Montreal: NFB, 1973.

– – –"Technical Notes on 'Begone Dull Care' (1949)". Unpublished ts. Montreal: NFB, 1949.

– – –"Technical Notes on 'Blinkity Blank' (1955)". Unpublished ts. Montreal: NFB, 1955.

– – –"Technical Notes on 'Canon' (1964)". Unpublished ts. Montreal: NFB, 7 March 1973.

– – –"Technical Notes on The Card Method of Optical Animated Sound: as developed at the NFB of Canada by Evelyn Lambart and Norman McLaren (1952)". Unpublished ts. Montreal: NFB, 1985.

– – –"Technical Notes for "'C'est l'aviron' (1944) in the folksong series 'Chants Populaires, No. 5'". Unpublished ts. Montreal: NFB, 1944, rev. 1983.

– – –"Technical Notes on 'A Chairy Tale' – (1957)". Unpublished ts. Montreal: NFB, 1957 rev. 1984.

– – –"Technical Notes on Earliest Films (1933–1939)". Unpublished ts. Montreal: NFB, 1984.

– – –"Technical Notes on 'Fiddle-De-Dee' – (1947)". Unpublished ts. Montreal: NFB, 1947 rev. 1983.

– – –"Technical Notes on La-Haut Sur Ces Montagnes (1945) in the folksong series 'Chants Populaires, No. 6". Unpublished ts. Montreal: NFB, 1945.

– – –"Technical Notes on 'Keep Your Mouth Shut' 1944". Unpublished ts. Montreal: NFB, 1984.

– – –"Technical Notes on the visuals of 'Lines Horizontal' (1961–62)". Unpublished ts. Montreal: NFB, 1962.

– – –"Technical Notes on 'A Little Phantasy' (1946)". Unpublished ts. Montreal: NFB, 1946 rev. 1983.

– – –"Technical Notes on 'Le Merle' (1958)". Unpublished ts. Montreal: NFB, 1958.

– – –"Technical Notes on Visuals of 'Mosaic' (1965)". Unpublished ts. Montreal: NFB, 1965.

– – –"Technical Notes on the Multiple Image Technique of 'Pas De Deux' (Titled 'Duo' for 35mm. Theatrical release in the USA.)". Unpublished ts. Montreal: NFB, 1967.

– – –"Technical Notes on 'Narcissus' (1983)". Unpublished ts. Montreal: NFB, 1984.

– – –"Technical Notes on 'New York Lightboard' (1961)". Unpublished ts. Montreal: NFB, 1961.

– – –"Technical Notes on 'Opening Speech' (1960)". Unpublished ts. Montreal: NFB, 1984.

– – –"Technical Notes on 'La Poulette Grise' (1947)" Unpublished ts. Montreal: NFB, 1947 rev. 1984.

– – –"Technical Notes on 'A Phantasy' (1948)". Unpublished ts. Montreal: NFB, 1984.

– – –"Technical Notes on 'Rythmetic' (1956)". Unpublished ts. Montreal: NFB, 1956 rev. 1984.

– – –"Technical Notes on 'Serenal' (1959) and 'Mail Early for Christmas' (1959)". Unpublished ts. Montreal: NFB, 1959.

– – –"Technical Notes on 'Short and Suite' (1959)". Unpublished ts. Montreal: NFB, 1959.

– – –"Technical Notes on 'Spheres' (Visuals shot in 1948) (Music added & film released in 1969)". Unpublished ts. Montreal: NFB, 1984.

– – –"Technical Notes on: Stars and Stripes (1939) Dots (1940) Loops (1940) Boogie Doodle (1940) Mail Early for Christmas (1941) V for Victory (1941) Hen Hop (1942)". Unpublished ts. Montreal: NFB, nd.

– – –"Technical Notes on 'Synchromy' (1971)". Unpublished ts. Montreal: NFB, 1984.

– – –and Evelyn Lambart. "Technical Notes on 'Lines-Vertical' (1960)" Unpublished ts. Montreal: NFB, 1960.

– – –"Three Dimensional Animation". *JSMPTE* 57 (December 1951)

– – –"Use of Variable-sized Discs to Convey Zoom". Unpublished ts. Montreal: NFB, 1969.

– – –"Variation of Hand-engraved Animation". Unpublished ts. Montreal: NFB, 1959.

– – –"Wither Animation?" *Ecran* 11 (janvier 1973): 4. (Letter).

– – –"Zoom Technique". Unpublished ts. 1944.

McLaren, Norman and Chester Beachell. "Stereographic Animation – The Synthesis of Stereoscopic Depth From Flat Drawings and Art Work", *JSMPTE* 57 (December 1951): 513–520.

McLaren, Norman and Guy Glover. "The synthesis of artificial movements in motion picture projection". *Film Culture* 7 (April–May 1973): 12.

"McLaren Honored in Philadelphia". *Cinema Canada* 7 (April–May 1973): 12.

McLaughlin, Dan. "Animation and Modernism", *Animatrix* December 1984: 10–12.

McWilliams, Donald. "An Evening With Norman McLaren's Works". *ASIFA* 12.3 (décembre 1984): 3.

– – –*Biography – Norman McLaren*. Unpublished ts. 1986.

– – –*Creative Process*. Proposal. July, 1985. Unpublished ts. National Film Board of Canada Archives. 50 p. Programming letters 4 p.

– – –"Narcissus". *Animafilm* 2 (April–June 1984): 37–41.

– – –"Norman McLaren: 1914–1987". *ASIFA* 15.1 (avril 1987):1.

– – –"Norman McLaren and Synthetic Sound". *ASIFA* 14. 3 (décembre 1986): 4–6.

– – –*On Making The Creative Process: Norman McLaren*. Ts. Montreal: Cinémathèque Québecoise, 1989.

– – –"Working with McLaren". *Animafilm* 2 (April–June 1984): 42.

– – –and Susan Huycke. *Creative Process: Norman McLaren*. Dir. Don McWilliams. Script. National Film Board of Canada. 31 p.

Madsen, Roy. "Unusual Animation Techniques" *Animated Film-Concepts, Methods, Uses*. NY: Interland, 1969. 181–189.

Magisos, M. and G[rant] Munro. "A dictionary of movement: and interview with Norman McLaren". *Wide Angle* 3 4 80: 60–69.

Magny, J. "De Norman McLaren à Peter Foldes. *Télécine* 191–192 (septembre–octobre 1974): 36.

Mahaffy, R.U. "McLaren: A Canadian Disney". *Saturday Night* 5 December 1950: 14.

Malina, Martin and Henry Lehmann. "Norman McLaren at play: 'Film is my work'. 'Drawing is my play'". *Montreal Star*. 27 September 1975. D1, D4.

Manceau, J - L. "McLaren disparait". *Cinema (Par)*. 386 (4 February 1987): 16.

Manvell, Roger. Ed. *The International Encyclopedia of Film*. NY: Crown, 1972, 349–350.

– – –Ed. *Experiment in the Film*. The Literature of Cinema. NY: Arno & New York Times, 1970.

– – –and John Huntley. *The Technique of Film Music*. London: Focal Press, 1975.

Marcotte, Gilles. "Norman McLaren et le langage du mouvement". *Presse* 31 Juillet 1965. Montreal.

Martin, André. "Cinéma d'animation millésime 54 and 55". *Cahiers du Cinéma* (juillet 1955) 16–26.

– – –"i x i ... ou le cinéma de deux mains". *Cahiers du Cinéma* 79 (janvier 1958): 5–19.

– – –"i x i ... ou le cinéma de deux mains. Portrait d'un aventurier". *Cahiers du Cinéma* 80 (février 1958): 27–35.

– – –"i x i ... mystère d'un cinéma instrumental. II. Secrets de fabrication". *Cahiers du Cinéma* 8 (mars 1958): 27–35.

– – –"i x i ... mystère d'un cinéma instrumental. III. On a touché au cinéma. *Cahiers du Cinéma* 82 (avril 1958): 34–47.

– – –"McLaren franchit le cap des tempêtes". *Cahiers du Cinéma* 62 (août–septembre 1956): 33–34.

– – –*Norman McLaren*. Annecy: Journees internationales du cinema d'animation Montreal: Cinemathèque Canadienne, 1965.

– – –"Le petit journal du cinéma. *Cahiers du Cinéma* 57 (mars 1956): 42.

Martin, Gordon and L. Martin. "Norman McLaren. Reflections on a life. Narcissus". *Cinéma Canada* 99 (September 1983): 21–23.

Martin, J. L., Ben Nicholson and N. Gabo. *Circle: International Survey of Constructive Art.* NY: Praeger, 1971.

Martin, Lyn. "Norman McLaren's Narcissus". *Cinema Canada* September 1983: 23.

Metz, Albert. "The Scotchman With The Pan Pipes". *Polition* 19 October 1947. Copenhagen. Trans. Albert Metz. Ts. 2 p. National Film board Archives, Montreal. McLaren File.

Moholy-Nagy, Lazlo. *Painting Photography Film.* Trans. Janet Seligman. London: Lund Humphries,1969.

Montagu, Ivor. *With Eisenstein in Hollywood.* Berlin: Seven Seas, 1968.

Moritz, William. "Abstract Film and Colour Music". *The Spiritual in Art: Abstract Painting 1890- 1985.* NY: LA County Museum of Art and Abbeville, 1986, 296–311.

– – –"The Films of Oscar Fischinger". *Film Culture* 58–60 (1974): 37–188.

– – –."Norman McLaren and Jules Engel: Post-modernists". *A Reader in Animation Studies.* Jayne Pilling ed. Sydney: John Libbey, 1997.

– – –.*Optical Poetry: The Life and Work of Oskar Fischinger.* Eastleigh, UK: John Libbey, 2004.

– – –"Towards an Aesthetics of Visual Music".*ASIFA* 14. 3 (December 1986): 1–3.

– – –"Towards a Visual Music". *Cantrills' Film Notes* August 1985: 35–42.

Morriss, Frank. "McLaren's Magic Fails With Distributors". *Toronto Globe and Mail* 20 March 1965.

"Movies Without A Camera, Music Without Instruments". *Theatre Arts* 36 (October 1952): 16–17.

"multi-mclaren". *Take One* 1.1 (September–October 1966): 18–22.

Munro, Grant. "Interview for film *Has Anyone Seen Canada? Dreamland II.*" Dir. John Kramer. Montreal McGill Archives. Ts. 16 December 1977.

Newman, Ernest. "Blinkity Blank". *The Sunday Times* 9 October 1955.

"NFB Screens Animation Unit Films" *Canadian Composer* 48 (March 1970): 46.

Nelson, Joyce. *The Colonized Eye: Rethinking the Grierson Legend.* Toronto: Between the Lines, 1988.

Noguez, Dominique. *Essais sur le cinéma québécois.* [Montreal]: Editions du Jour, 1970. 141–151.

– – –"McLaren, ou la schizophrénie créatrice". *Vie des Arts* 56 (Autumn 1969): 54–57. English text, Guy Glover, 86–87.

Norman McLaren, exhibition and films. Edinburgh: Scottish Arts Council, 1977.

"Norman McLaren: A Gentle Genius of Movies". *Montreal Star, Weekend Magazine* 43 (1965): 2–6.

"Norman McLaren". Catalogue. Montreal: Cinémathèque canadienne, 1965.

"Norman McLaren: A Survey". *International Film Guide*. NY: Barnes, 1964, 160–162.

"Norman McLaren: An Inspired Doodler". *Sunday Statesman* 2 August 1959. Delhi.

"Norman McLaren au fil de ses films". *Séquences* 82 (octobre 1975). 8–93.

"Norman McLaren or the New Cinema". *Le Mercure de France* 1 August 1951. Trans. Ts. National Film Board Archives, Montreal. McLaren File.

"Norman McLaren, pioneer animator, dies in Montreal". *Variety*. 326. 2 (4 February 1987): 4, 34.

"Norman McLaren Wins Film Grand Prix". *Stirling Journal* 8 September 1965.

"Norman McLaren Wins High Canadian Award". *Box Office* Canadian Edition. 13 December 1971. Toronto.

Notes On Films By McLaren. NY: National Film Board of Canada.

Notes On McLaren's Linear Technique Of Animation. Montreal: National Film Board of Canada, 1960.

Notes On The Music Of The FIlm "Lines Horizontal". Montreal: National Film Board of Canada, 1960.

"Notes sur l'animation sonore, abrégé d'un essai". *Canadian Composer* 44 (November 1969): 30–33.

"L'Oeil entend et l'oréille voit". *Canadian Composer* 44 (November 1969): 28–31.

O'Konor, Louise. *Viking Eggeling 1880–1925: artist and film-maker life and work*. Stockholm: Almqvist & Wiksell, 1971.

"One-Man Film Unit". *Commonwealth Today* 24, 18–19.

A Perspective on English Avant-Garde Film. Catalogue, n pl.: Arts Council of Great Britain and The British Council, 1978.

Phillips, A. "Inspired Doodles Of Norman McLaren". *Maclean's Magazine* 15 December 1952, 22–23, 45–48.

Pierre, José. *Surrealism*. Trans. Paul Eve. Geneva: Edito-Service SA, 1970.

Pilling, Jayne. *Animation: 2D and beyond*. Crans-Pres-Celigney: RotoVision, 2001.

Poncet, Marie-Thérèse. *Dessin animé, art mondial*. Paris: Cercle du Livre, 1956, 301–307.

Pontaut, A. "Salut à McLaren". *Magazine Maclean* 2 (February 1971): 42.

"Portrait". *Canadian Composer* 61 (June 1971): 44.

Portrait d'un studio d'animation: l'art et le cinéma image par image. Montreal: National Film Board of Canada, 1983.

"Portrait". *Food For Thought* 10 (May 1950): 19.

Pratley, Gerald. "The Latest 3-Dimensional Films: Prove That the Movies Still Have An Ace Up Their Sleeve". *Films In Review* 3 (April 1952): 171–174.

Prédal, René. *Jeune cinéma canadien*. Paris: Serdoc, 1967. 85–93.

– – –"Norman McLaren, l'expression par le mouvement". *Jeune Cinéma* 97 (septembre–octobre 1976): 26–31.

"Le Prix Du Quebec". *Le devoir*. Saturday, 27 November 1982. Handscript copy by McLaren. Grierson Archives, University of Stirling, Stirling, Scotland. GAA: 31: 136.

Quéval, Jean. "Norman McLaren, l'inventeur du néo-cinéma". *Radio-Cinéma- Télévision* 73 (10 juin 1951): 4–5.

– – –"Norman McLaren ou le cinéma au XXIe siècle". *Cahiers du Cinéma* 6 (octobre–novembre 1951): 22–29.

– – –"Où va le cinéma anglais? *Cahiers du Cinéma* 3 13 (juin 1952): 33–52.

Richard, Valliere T, *Norman McLaren, Manipulator of Movement: The National Film Board Years*. Newark: University Delaware Press, 1982.

Rimington, A. Wallace. *Colour-Music: The Art of Mobile Colour*. London: Hutchinson, 1912.

Rondolino, Gianni. "Norman McLaren – 15 cortometaggi", *Centrofilm* 1 (September 1959): complete issue.

– – –"Several Considerations on Narcissus".*Animafilm* 2 (April–June 1984): 45–47.

Ropchan. "The career of Norman McLaren". *Cinema Canada* 9 (August–September 1973): 42–49.

Rosenthal, Alan. *The New Documentary in Action*. Berkeley, LA: University of California Press, 1971, 267–279.

– – –"Norman McLaren On *Pas De Deux*". *Journal* 22.1 (1970): 8–15.

Roud, Richard. *Cinema: A Critical Dictionary, The Major Film-makers*. NY: Viking Press, 1980, 2 Vols. 100, 654–655.

Russett, R. and Cecile Starr. *Experimental Animation. Origins of a New Art*. Rev. ed. NY: Da Capo Press, 1976.

Ryan, Terry. "Six filmmakers in search of an alternative".*Arts Canada* (April 1970): 25–27.

Schobert, Walter. *The German Avant-Garde Film of the 1920's*. Eds. Angelika Leitner and Uwe Nitschke. Trans Jeremy Roth. München: Goethe-Institut, 1989.

"Schools face anger of parents over films meant to teach love". *Toronto Globe and Mail* 19 February 1971.

Schupp, Patrick. "Du rythme et des coleurs. *Séquences* 82 (octobre 1975): 99–104.

Schwarz, Angelo. "Norman McLaren un cineasta senza cinepresa". *L' Osservatore Romano Quotidien du Vatican* 17 fevrier 1971.

Seeger, Pete. "Technical Notes for the Music of 'Lines Horizontal' (1961–1962)". Unpublished ts. Montreal: NFB, nd.

Shepherd, Anna. "*Helen Biggar* and *Norman McLaren*: Based on a MS 'Helen Unlimited'". *New Edinburgh Review,* 1978, 25–26.

Sitney, P. Adams. Ed. *Film Culture Reader*. NY: Praeger, 1970.

– – –*Visionary Film: The American Avant-Garde*. NY: Oxford University Press, 1974.

"Sound And Picture Animation Illustrated". *ArtsCanada* 27 (April 1970): 30.

Spottiswoode, Raymond. "Progress in Three-Dimensional Films at the Festival of Britain". *JSMPTE* 58 (January–June 1952): 291–303.

Stadtrucker, Ivan. Questionnaire 7 March 1975. NFB Archives. McLaren File.

Starr, Cecile. "Animation: Abstract And Concrete", *Saturday Review* 35 13 December 1952. 46–48.

– – –*Discovering the Movies*. NY: Van Nostrand Reinhold, 1972, 110–123.

– – –"Ideas on Film: Eyewitnessing the World of the 16mm Motion Picture". *Saturday Revue*. 8 March 1952, 65–67.

Stephenson, Ralph. *The Animated Film*. London: Tantivy, 1973.

– – –"Canadian And British Schools". *Animation in the Cinema*. London: Swemmer, 1967.

"Stirling man showing two Festival films". *Stirling Sentinel* 26 August 1952.

Surnane, Alexandrian. *Surrealist Art*. Trans. Gordon Clough. London: Thames and Hudson, 1970.

Szelei, Julius. "Norman McLaren: Gentle Genius of Movies". *Telegram, Weekend Magazine* 15.43 (23 October 1965): 2–6.

Taaffe, G. "Secrets of Home-Grown Film Genius". *Maclean's Magazine* 78 (4 September 1965): 7.

Tallenay, Jean-Louis. "En couronnant Blinkity Blank, le Jury de Cannes a récompensé vingt ans recherche". *Radio-Cinéma-Télévision* 283 (19 juin 1955): 2.

"Teach Health to Chinese by Pictures". *Ottawa Evening Citizen*. 6 July 1949. Ontario.

"1040 Norman McLaren". *Film Dope* 38 (December 1987):1–4.

Thomas, François. "McLaren ou la musique des sphères". *Positif* 36 (June 1987): 63–65.

Thorpe, Bridget M. "Dance in Animation". *Animatrix* Fall 1986: 41–48.

"3 Canadians win $15,000 art prizes". *Toronto Daily Star* 29 December 1971.

"Triptyque: Serigraph". *ArtsCanada* 26 (August 1969): 28.

Ulushak. Cartoon *Edmonton Journal* 19 February 1971.

Un cineaste canadien d'avant-garde. Ts. Office National du Film, 1960. Rpt Bureau de district, 1 March 1964, Trois-Rivières. 5 p.

"Un cinéma que vous ne connaissez pas. *L'écran et la vie* 20 (juillet 1965): 28–31.

UNESCO. Monographs on Fundamental Education No. 5. *The Healthy Village*. Art Dept. Report by Norman McLaren. Paris, 1951. 41–111.

– – –Monographies sur l'éducation de base, no. 5. *La santé au village*. Rapport par Norman McLaren sur l'oeuvre de la section artistique. Paris, 1951, 49–103, 121–129.

Veronneau, Pierre and Piers Handling. Eds. *Self Portrait: Essays on the Canadian and Quebec Cinema*. Ottawa: Canadian Film Institute, 1980.

Verrall, Bob [Robert] and René Jodoin. "animation: the wider picture". *Pot Pourri* April 1972. 2–6.

Vinet, Pierre. "Multi McLaren". *Take One* 1.1 (September–October 1967): 18–22.

Visser, Maartin. "Norman McLaren ". *Skrien* 131 (October–November 1983):16–17. Abridged Trans. from *Holland Animation Bulletin* October 1983.

– – –"Norman McLaren as Musician". *Holland Animation Bulletin* International Issue 1983: 36–41.

Warkentin, Germaine. "Norman McLaren". *Tamarack Review* (Autumn 1957): 42–54.

Wees, William C. *Light Moving in Time: Studies in the Visual Aesthetics of Avant-Garde Film*. Berkeley: University of California Press, 1992.

Weinberg, Gretchen. "Mc et moi: a spiritual portrait of Norman McLaren" *Film Culture* (Summer 1962): 46–47.

Wells, Paul. Ed. *Art & Design: Art & Animation*. London: Academy, 1997.

White, Michael. "The Graphic side of Norman McLaren". *Montreal Gazette* 4 March 1972.

Whitney, John. *Digital harmony: On the Complementarity of Music and Visual Art* Peterborough, New Hampshire: McGraw-Hill, 1980.

Wintonick, Peter et al. "Tribute". *Cinema Canada* 140 (April 1987): 27–29.

Youngblood, Gene. *Expanded Cinema*. London: Studio Vista, 1970.

LETTERS

Brandt, George. Letter to *The Times*, London, 29 January 1987. [Further appreciation of McLaren's work].

Bishop, Lucile. Memorandum to Robert Montieth. 27 October1977. Govt. of Canada [McLaren Retrospective].

Bromelow, Howard. Letter to Terence Dobson, 11 January 1994. [Helen Biggar].

Chatwin, Len. Memorandum to W. S. Jobbins, 22 March 1954. [Australian censorship of *Neighbours*].

Elton, Arthur. Letter, "Mixed Images and Mr. McLaren" to *The Sunday Times* 23 October 1955. [Response to Newman's article on *Blinkity Blank*].

Grierson, John. Letter to John Devine. American Film Film Center, 2 July 1941. NFB Archives.

– – –Letter to L. K. Elmhirst, 12 February 1934. Dartington Hall Archives, Devon, UK.

– – –Letter to McLaren. 15 December 1939. Grierson Archives, University of Stirling, Stirling, Scotland. G4 23: 56.

– – –NFB Memo. 2 July 1941. NFB Archives.

Johnston, Tom. Memorandum to Paul La Rose. 13 May 1966. [McMaster Univ. LL.D.].

McLaren, Jean. Letter to W. Forsyth Hardy. 23 November 1951 Grierson Archives, University of Stirling, Stirling, Scotland. GAA: 31: 174. [Appreciation of broadcast].

McLaren, Norman. Letter to Lou [Applebaum]. 28 December 1948. Don McWilliams collection, Montreal. [Programme material for workshop on animated sound].

– – –Card to Maurice Blackburn. *ASIFA* 5.1 (April 1987): 81.

– – –Diary. 24 October 1949. Grierson Archives, University of Stirling, Stirling, Scotland. GAA: 31: 63.

– – –Letter to Maurice and Marthe Blackburn, 23 May 1982. *ASIFA* 15.1 (Avril 1987): 8–21. [Encouraging Maurice to write music for *Narcissus*, drawings from letter to mother. GAA: 31: 143].

– – –Letter to Elfriede Fischinger, 22 May 1975. [Oskar Fischinger influence].

– – –Letter to Lorettan Devlin Gascard, 15 April 1981. National Film Board of Canada Archives, Montreal. [Static and temporal motion].

– – –Letter to Theo Goldberg. 27 February 1973. National Film Board of Canada Archives, Montreal. [Visual and sound correlation, *Synchromy*].

– – –Letter to John Grierson. 22 October 1939. Grierson Archives, University of Stirling, Stirling, Scotland.

– – –Letter to John Grierson. 6 December 1939. Grierson Archives, University of Stirling, Stirling, Scotland. GAA 4:23:51.

– – –Letter to John Grierson. 12 December 1939. Grierson Archives, University of Stirling, Stirling, Scotland. GAA: 4: 23:54.

– – –Letter to Jack [John McLaren]. December 1966. Grierson Archives, University of Stirling, Stirling, Scotland. GAA:31:97. [Tehran].

– – –Letter to Jack [John McLaren]. 7 March 1971. Grierson Archives, University of Stirling, Stirling, Scotland. GAA:31:98. [Japan].

– – –Letter to Jack [John McLaren]. 3 March 1979. Grierson Archives, University of Stirling, Stirling, Scotland. GAA: 31:154. [Glasgow and Stirling Universities honorary degrees and health].

– – –Letter to Jack [John McLaren]. 1 May 1983. Grierson Archives, University of Stirling, Stirling, Scotland. GAA:31:157. [Retirement and Don McWilliams].

– – –Letter to Jack and Joan [McLaren] 18 December 1952. Grierson Archives, University of Stirling, Stirling, Scotland. GAA:31:86.

– – –Letter to Jack and Joan [McLaren]. 18 May 1984. Grierson Archives, University of Stirling, Stirling, Scotland. GAA:31:155. [NFB Farewell].

– – –Letter to his mother. 1 May 1949. Grierson Archives, University of Stirling, Stirling, Scotland. GAA.

– – –Letter to his mother. 22 August 1949. Grierson Archives, University of Stirling, Stirling, Scotland. GAA:31:66. [Honolulu, Tokyo, Hong Kong].

– – –Letter to his mother. 24 April 1950. Grierson Archives, University of Stirling, Stirling, Scotland. GAA:31:93. [Peking].

– – –Letter to his mother. n.d. [1963] Grierson Archives, U of Stirling, Stirling, Scotland. GAA:31:153:1–2. [Removal of violent scene in *Neighbours*].

– – –Letter to his mother. 3 October 1964. Grierson Archives, University of Stirling, Stirling, Scotland. GAA:31:93. [South America].

– – –Letter and drawings to his mother n.d. [1963]. Grierson Archives, University of Stirling, Stirling, Scotland. [*Christmas Crackers, Canon, Mosaic* and Eve Lambart].

– – –Letter to his parents. November 1936. Grierson Archives, University of Stirling, Stirling, Scotland. GAA.

– – –Letter to his parents. 2 December 1936. Grierson Archives, University of Stirling, Stirling, Scotland. [Spain].

– – –Letter to his parents. 4 September 1949. Grierson Archives, University of Stirling, Stirling, Scotland. GAA:31:65. [China, accommodation and food].

– – –Letter to his parents. 11 January 1950. Grierson Archives, University of Stirling, Stirling, Scotland. GAA:31:69. [China, Peoples' Army].

– – –Letter to his parents. 29 January 1950. Grierson Archives, University of Stirling, Stirling, Scotland. GAA:31:90. [China].

– – –Letter to his parents 22 March 1950. Grierson Archives, University of Stirling, Stirling, Scotland. GAA:31:71. [China, trip plan from Szechuan to Hong Kong].

– – –Letter to his parents. 1 April 1950. Grierson Archives, University of Stirling, Stirling, Scotland. GAA:31:72. [to Chungking, China].

– – –Letter to his parents. 13 May 1950 Grierson Archives, University of Stirling, Stirling, Scotland. [Death of 'Auntie', religion and life].

– – –Letter to his parents. 17 November 1952. Grierson Archives, University of Stirling, Stirling, Scotland. GAA:31:76. [India].

– – –Memorandum to NFB animators c. 1942. ASIFA 15.1 (avr. 1987): 25. [Conserving materials and equipment].

McLean, Ross. Letter to H. Clegg. 12 July 1941. NFB Archives.

– – –Letter to Masscé- Barnett Co. 21 August 1941. NFB Archives.

McWilliams, Donald. Letter to Charles Solomon. 2 May 1984. National Film Board of Canada Archives, Montreal. McLaren File.[Decline of tribute due to ill health].

– – –NFB Memos to David Verrall. 5 and 6 January 1984. NFB Archives.

– – –NFB Memo to David Verrall. *Lining the Blues.* 5 January 1984. NFB Archives.

Mansur, D. B. War Savings Committee letter to John Grierson, 15 July 1941. NFB Archives.

Masscé-Barnett. Letter to NFB, 19 August 1941. NFB Archives.

Newman, Ernest. Letter, "Mixed Images", to *The Sunday Times* 30 October 1955.[Response to Elton's letter].

Peterson, Oscar. Letter to National Film Board, 28 February 1949. [Permission to use music from *Hues and Blues (Begone Dull Care)*].

Spottiswoode, Raymond. Estimate for War Savings Trailer (*Five for Four*), 12 September 1941. NFB Archives.

Swanson, P. Letter to The [theatre] Manager, 9 April 1953.

Trowles, Peter. Letter to Terence Dobson, 23 November 1993. [Glasgow School of Art, McLaren's studies].

– – –Letter to Terence Dobson, 15 December 1993. [Glasgow School of Art, McLaren's studies].

Truffaut, François. Letter to Norman McLaren, 18 October 1973. *ASIFA* 15.1 (avril 1987): 6–7. ["Nice Letter"].

Verrall, David. NFB Memo to Doug McDonald, 9 January 1984. NFB Archives.

Interviews, Films and Recordings

INTERVIEWS CONDUCTED BY THE AUTHOR

Beaudet, Louise. Personal interview. 14 November 1990. Montreal

Blackburn, Marthe. Personal interview, audio-cassette. 6 November 1990. Montreal

Budner, Gerald. Personal interview 29 October 1990. Montreal

Cloutier, Louise. Personal interview. 12 December 1990. Montreal

Daly, Tom. Personal interview, audio-cassette. 7 November 1990. Montreal

Evans, Gary. Personal interview 20 November 1990. Montreal

Hawes, Stanley. Personal interview. 26 November 1978. Sydney

Hébert, Pierre. Personal interview. 19 November 1990. Montreal

Jodoin, Réné. Personal interview. 5 November 1990. Montreal

Lambart, Evelyn. Telephone interview, audio-cassette. 10 November 1989. Montreal

– – –. Personal interview. 31 October 1990. Sutton, Quebec

Low, Colin. Personal interview. 9 November 1990. Montreal.

McLaren, John. Personal interview, audio-cassette. 5 September 1991. Kettering, UK.

McWilliams, Donald. Personal interview. 24 October 1990. Montreal.

– – –. Personal interviews. October 2001. Montreal.

Munro, Grant. Personal interview, audio-cassette. 23 October 1990. Montreal

Rathburn, Eldon. Telephone interview, audio-cassette. November 1989. Montreal

Verrall, David. Personal interview. 21 November 1990. Montreal

Verrall, Robert. Personal interview. 14 November 1990. Montreal

FILMS

The list of each director's work is arranged in chronological order so that it accords with the structure of this book. The film-gauges listed indicate the films' original format. All films by McLaren are distributed by the NFB Canada.

Brockway, Merrill, director

Norman McLaren: Film Artist, with William Sloan 1970
c. 25 minutes colour sound
NFB/Colombia

Bute, Mary Ellen, director

Spook Sport 1940
9 minutes colour sound 35mm
Animation assistant: Norman McLaren
Music: Camille Saint-Saëns *Danse macabre*.
NFB.

Fischinger, Oscar, director

Study No. 7 (1931)
2 minutes 30 seconds b&w sound
Music: Johannes Brahms *Hungarian Dance No. 5*.
Museum of Modern Art, NY.

Glover, Guy, director

Window on Canada No 29 1954
28 minutes 30 seconds b&w sound 16mm
NFB.

Marching the Colours 1941
2 minutes 58 seconds colour sound 16mm.
NFB.

Glover, Rupert and Michel Patenaud, directors

The Light Fantastick 1974
57 minutes 53 seconds colour sound
NFB.

Kim In Tae, director

Korean Alphabet 1967
7 minutes 14 seconds colour sound 16mm
Sound: Norman McLaren
NFB.

Lye, Len, director

Colour Box 1935
4 minutes colour sound 35mm
Music: *La belle creole* synchronized by Jack Ellitt
GPO Film Unit.

Rainbow Dance 1936
5 minutes colour sound 35mm
Music: *Tony's Wife* (Rico's Creole Band)
GPO Film Unit.

Kaleidoscope 1935
4 minutes 35 seconds colour sound 35mm
Music: 'Biguine d'amour' Don Baretto and Cuban
Orchestra synchronized by Jack Ellitt
GPO Film Unit.

McLaren, Norman, director

(Untitled) 1933
3 minutes colour silent 35mm
Associate director: Stewart McAlistair.

Seven Till Five 1933
10 minutes b&w silent 16mm.

Camera Makes Whoopee 1935
15 minutes b&w silent 16mm.

Polychrome Phantasy 1935
2 minutes colour silent 16mm.

Five Untitled Shorts 1935
5 minutes each colour silent 16mm.

Colour Cocktail 1935
5 minutes colour silent 16mm.

Hell UnLtd 1936
15 minutes b&w silent 16mm
Associate director: Helen Biggar

Book Bargain 1937
10 minutes b&w sound 35mm.

News for the Navy 1937–38
10 minutes b&w sound 35mm.

"Mony a Pickle" 1937–38
10 minutes b&w sound 35mm.

Love on the Wing 1938
5 minutes 30 seconds colour sound 35mm
Music: Jacques Ibert *Divertissiment*.

The Obedient Flame 1939
20 minutes b&w sound 16mm.

NBC Greeting 1939
30 seconds b&w sound 35mm.

Allegro 1939
2 minutes colour sound 35mm.

Stars and Stripes 1940
2 minutes 53 seconds colour sound 35mm
Music: excerpt from a march by J.P. Sousa.

Dots 1940
2 minutes 23 seconds colour sound 35mm
Music: animated sound, Norman McLaren.

Loops 1940
2 minutes 43 seconds colour sound 35mm
Music: animated sound, Norman McLaren.

Boogie Doodle 1940
3 minutes colour sound 35mm
Music: Albert Ammons jazz.

Mail Early 1941
2 minutes colour sound 35mm
Music: Benny Goodman *Jingle Bells*.

V for Victory 1941
2 minutes colour sound 35mm
Music: Sousa *The Thunderer*.

Five for Four 1942
4 minutes colour sound 35 mm
Music: Albert Ammons *Pinetop Boogie*.

Hen Hop 1942
3 minutes 17 seconds colour sound 35mm
Music: Canadian barn dance.

Dollar Dance 1943
5 minutes 30 seconds colour sound
Music: Louis Applebaum.

Alouette 1944
3 minutes b&w sound 35mm
Associate director: René Jodoin
Music: French-Canadian folk song.

Keep Your Mouth Shut 1944
3 minutes b&w sound 35mm
Title animation: George Dunning.

C'est l'aviron 1944
3 minutes b&w sound 35mm
Music: French-Canadian folk song.

Là haut sur ces montagnes 1945
3 minutes b&w sound
Music: French-Canadian folk song.

A Little Phantasy on a 19th-Century Painting 1946
3 minutes 30 seconds colour sound 35mm
Music ed.: Benton Jackson.

Hoppity Pop 1946
2 minutes 28 seconds colour sound
Music: circus calliope.

Fiddle-de-dee 1947
3 minutes 22 seconds colour sound 35mm
Music: Eugène Desormaux, folk-fiddle.

La Poulette grise 1947
5 minutes 32 seconds colour sound 16mm
Music: French lullaby.

A Phantasy 1948, 1953
7 minutes 15 seconds colour sound 16mm
Music: Maurice Blackburn, live and animated.

Begone Dull Care 1949
7 minutes 48 seconds colour sound 35mm
Music: Oscar Peterson.

Now is the Time 1950–51
3 minutes colour stereoscopic vision and sound 35mm
Assistant: Evelyn Lambart
Music: Norman McLaren.

Around is Around 1950–51
10 minutes colour stereoscopic vision and sound 35mm
Assistant: Evelyn Lambart
Music: Louis Applebaum.

Neighbours 1952
8 minutes 10 seconds colour sound 16mm.
Music: animated sound, Norman McLaren
Actors: Grant Munro, Jean-Paul Ladouceur.

Two Bagatelles 1952
2 minutes 22 seconds colour sound 16mm
Associate director: Grant Munro
Music: Norman McLaren, animated sound and calliope.

Blinkity Blank 1955
5 minutes 15 seconds colour sound
Music: Maurice Blackburn.

Rythmetic 1956
8 minutes 35 seconds colour sound
Assistant: Evelyn Lambart
Music: Norman McLaren animated sound.

A Chairy Tale 1957
9 minutes 50 seconds b&w sound 35mm
Associate director: Claude Jutra
Assistant: Evelyn Lambart
Music: Ravi Shankar, Chatur Lal, Modu Mullick
Music assistant: Maurice Blackburn.

Le Merle 1958
4 minutes 7 seconds colour sound
Assistant: Evelyn Lambart
Music: French-Canadian 'nonsense' song, arr.: Maurice
Blackburn.

Short and Suite 1959
4 minutes 47 seconds colour sound
Assistant: Evelyn Lambart
Music: Eldon Rathburn.

Serenal 1959
4 minutes colour sound 16mm
Music: Grand Curucaya Orchestra of Trinidad (steel band).

Mail Early for Christmas 1959
40 seconds colour sound
Music: Eldon Rathburn.

Jack Paar Credit Titles 1959
30 seconds b&w sound
Music: Norman McLaren animated sound.

Lines Vertical 1960
5 minutes 50 seconds colour sound
Associate director: Evelyn Lambart
Music: Maurice Blackburn.

Opening Speech 1960
6 minutes 33 seconds b&w sound
Assistant director: Arthur Lipsett.

New York Lightboard 1961
8 minutes b&w silent 16 mm
Assistants: Kaj Pindal, Ron Tunis, René Jodoin

New York Lightboard Record 1961
8 minutes b&w silent.

Lines Horizontal 1961
5 minutes 58 seconds colour sound
Associate director: Evelyn Lambart
Music: Pete Seeger.

Canon 1964
9 minutes 13 seconds colour sound
Associate director: Grant Munro
Music: Eldon Rathburn.

Mosaic 1965
5 minutes 27 seconds colour sound
Associate director: Evelyn Lambart
Music: animated sound, Norman McLaren.

Pas de deux 1967
13 minutes 22 seconds b&w sound
Music: Dobre Constantin, panpipes and United Folk Orchestra of Romania
Music ed.: Maurice Blackburn
Dancers: Margaret Mecier, Vincent Warren.

Spheres 1969
7 minutes 28 seconds colour sound 16mm
Assistant: René Jodoin
Music: J. S. Bach Fugue 22, Prelude 20, Fugue 14, from *The Well Tempered Clavichord*, Glenn Gould - piano.

Synchromy 1971
7 minutes 27 seconds colour sound
Music: animated sound, Norman McLaren.

Ballet Adagio 1972
9 minutes 59 seconds colour sound
Music: Albinoni *Adagio for Strings*
Dancers: David and Anna Marie Holmes.

Pinscreen 1973
38 minutes 44 seconds colour sound 16mm
Associate directors: Alexander Alexeieff and Claire
Parker.

Animated Motion (Parts 1–5) 1976–78
Part 1: 9 minutes 8 seconds colour sound 16mm
Part 2: 8 minutes 29 seconds colour sound 16mm
Part 3: 9 minutes 53 seconds colour sound 16mm
Part 4: 7 minutes colour sound 16mm
Part 5: 7 minutes 6 seconds 16mm
Acssociate director: Grant Munro.

Narcissus 1981
22 minutes colour sound 35mm
Associate director: Donald McWilliams
Music: Maurice Blackburn
Principal dancer: Jean-Louis Morin
Choreorapher: Fernand Nault.

McWilliams, Donald, director

The Creative Process: Norman McLaren 1st Assembly 1989
c. 3 hours 45 minutes colour sound.

The Creative Process: Norman McLaren 1990
2 hours colour sound.
NFB

The Creative Process 1991
46 minutes colour sound TV version
NFB and Channel 4 UK.

Millar, Gavin, director

The Eye Hears, the Ear Sees 1970
58 minutes 38 seconds colour sound 16mm
NFB.

Montagu, Ivor, director

Defence of Madrid 1936
20 minutes b&w silent 35 mm
Camera: Norman McLaren.
GPO Film Unit, NFB.

Munro, Grant, director

Christmas Cracker 1963
8 minutes 58 seconds colour sound 35mm
NFB.

Holland Animation 1983
8 minutes 59 seconds colour sound 35mm
NFB.

Peters, Don, director
Pen Point Percussion 1951
5 minutes 38 seconds b&w sound 16mm
NFB.

RECORDINGS

Blackburn, Marthe and Maurice Blackburn. *Six Formes Musicales*. Jeunesses Musicales of Canada, 1967. Record Club Disc. CD JMC-7.

Fischinger, Oskar. *The World of Oskar Fischinger: Pioneer of Abstract and Advertising Animation*. Dir. Toshifumi Kawahara. Visual Pathfinder Laser disc 1986.

"Les McLaughlin talks with filmmaker Norman McLaren about the Capital's fireworks-display he designed." *Canada 105*. Part C. 1 July 1972. CBC Radio Archives, Toronto.

"McLaren." *Two Profiles of Canadian Artists*. Part 2. 13 June 1986 and 14 July 1982. CBC Radio Archives, Toronto.

McLaren, Norman. *The World of Norman McLaren: Pioneer of Innovative Animation*. Dir. Toshifumi Kawahara. Visual Pathfinder Laser disc. 1990.

"McLaren: Besson, Clarke and McWilliams talk about the influence of McLaren." *Morningside*. 29 July 1991. CBC Radio Archives, Toronto.

"The NFB and McLaren." *Distinguished Canadians*. 7 August 1972. CBC Television. CBC Radio Archives, Toronto.

"The NFB: The Mirror of a Nation." *Project 68*. Parts (a) John Grierson, (b) Sydney Newman, (f) André Belleau, (J) Robin Spry — McLaren, (l) André Belleau. 10 December 1967. CBC Radio Archives.

"Norman McLaren: A Tribute by Peter Raymont." *Sunday Morning*. 1 February 1987. CBC Radio Archives, Toronto.

"Rick Butler: Interview with McLaren." *The Entertainment Section*. Part 3. 17 August 1976 CBC Radio Archives, Toronto.

"Take Fifteen." *The Art of Glen Gould*. 24 August 1969. CBC Radio Archives, Toronto. [Glen Gould recordings and interviews with McLaren.]

Index